Generals and Scholars

Generals and Scholars

Military Rule in Medieval Korea

Edward J. Shultz

University of Hawai'i Press
Honolulu

Library of Congress Cataloging-in-Publication Data

Shultz, Edward J.
Generals and scholars : military rule in medieval Korea /
Edward J. Shultz.
p. cm.
Includes bibliographical references and index.
ISBN 0–8248–2188–2 (cloth : alk. paper) —
ISBN 0–8248–2324–9 (pbk. : alk. paper)
1. Korea—Politics and government—935–1392. 2. Military
government—Korea—History—To 1500. 3. Korea—History,
Military. I. Title.
DS912.35 .S54 2000
952.9'01—dc21   00–021878

Designed by Kenneth Miyamoto
Printed by The Maple-Vail Book Manufacturing Group

CONTENTS

PREFACE

In the autumn of 1170 a small group of military officers rose in revolt, detained King Ŭijong (r. 1146–1170), and murdered a number of civilian officials. Over the next two decades the kingdom imploded as military officers conspired against each other at the top and unrest among peasants, slaves, and monks rocked the people below. A degree of stability returned with the rise of General Ch'oe Ch'unghŏn (1149–1219) in 1196. General Ch'oe and his descendants ruled the kingdom as military dictators until 1258, when civilian officers negotiated a peace with the Mongols and restored authority to the king. In the twelve years from 1258 until 1270, when the court finally fell under complete Mongol domination, power shifted among several aspiring dictators.

This military phase in the middle of the Koryŏ dynasty has attracted little attention among scholars. In fact, the entire Koryŏ period (918–1392), sequestered between the dramatic founding kingdoms of Koguryŏ, Paekche, and Silla and the five-hundred-year-long Chosŏn dynasty, has received only passing scholarly attention. The military era in particular is nearly forgotten because it was deemed an anomaly: compared with a millennium of civil rule, the century of military domination was considered an exception to the norm and thus unworthy of serious study. Apart from studies on a few military leaders who were dynastic founders or who subdued invading marauders, Korean scholars have focused on the civil elites.

The *Koryŏsa* (History of Koryŏ) and the *Koryŏsa chŏryo* (Essentials of Koryŏ history) are the two key primary sources for Koryŏ in general and the military period in particular. Both histories were written during the first century of the Chosŏn kingdom based on records passed down from Koryŏ. Chosŏn scholars, anxious to substantiate the legitimacy of their dynasty, presented Koryŏ history in a highly critical light and especially singled out the military period as a time of failure: to study the military era, they argued, was to investigate a society that had collapsed. Corruption and degeneration marked the age as murderous generals took over the kingdom illegally. Civilians ceded all power to military officers who ruled through might and fear. The king was a dolt who surrounded himself with sycophants and men of base origin. The compilers of these histories were Confucian scholars who, in their esteem for the legitimacy of dynastic authority, depicted the military era as a dark age. Military figures were dismissed as "rebellious subjects" and their biographies were relegated to the end of the dynastic histories.[1]

This negative interpretation of the military period persisted well into the twentieth century. When the first Western historians of Korea wrote their initial monographs on Korea's past, they relied on Chosŏn sources and merely reiterated the views cited here. Homer Hulbert in recording his eight-hundred-page *History of Korea* (1905) relied heavily on the fifteenth-century *Tongguk T'onggam* (Comprehensive mirror of the Eastern Kingdom), a history that embodied the Confucian historiographic tradition. Hulbert devoted a scant twenty pages to the military period—and much of that focused on the Mongol invasions of the peninsula. When he addressed military rule, he recounted little more than a litany of murder, arson, rebellion, and seduction. Begrudgingly he called Ch'oe Ch'unghŏn a reformer on one page but then quickly noted that he was seduced by "ambition and power." Ch'oe U (d. 1249), Ch'oe Ch'unghŏn's son and successor, fared no better. Hulbert described him as "stealing houses and lands from wherewith to build himself a princely mansion, two hundred paces long." James Scarth Gale, writing at the start of the twentieth century and using similar sources, provided just a few pages on the military and his descriptions were no different. He depicted the Ch'oe family as a "giant vampire" battening on Korea. He added: "To recite all their crimes would fill a volume. There were two brothers and a son, all equally bad." Gale concluded that Ch'oe and his followers turned Korea into a "den of thieves."[2]

During the 1950s, the first winds of change appeared. In 1951, at the height of the Korean War, Hatada Takashi, a Japanese scholar, attempted to give an overview of Korean history: *Chōsen-shi* (History of Korea) was a general survey that allocated fewer than ten pages to the military period. Like earlier historians, Hatada recounted the massacre of civilians during the initial coup and the continuing slaughter that accompanied Ch'oe Ch'unghŏn's rise to power. But along with this now-hackneyed tale Hatada discussed the new institutions and analyzed the changes then occurring. He concluded: "Thus we see that the Ch'oe family, martial though they were, were bureaucrats of the old order, not medieval warriors."[3] In this way Hatada cautiously moved beyond the negative description of the early histories and examined the military leaders in a new light. In his brief presentation of this period he advanced both analysis and interpretation and offered a slightly altered view of the generals.

The 1960s saw several treatments in Korean historical surveys that provided a basis for understanding the dynamics of the military era —Kim Sanggi's *Koryŏ sidaesa* (History of the Koryŏ period), for example, and Yi Pyŏngdo's *Chungsep'yŏn* in the seven-volume *Han-guksa* (Korean history: Middle ages). Yi Pyŏngdo devoted more than seventy-five pages to the military period and detailed the institutional innovations of the military. In 1961 Yi Kibaek published the college history *Kuksa sillon* (New history of Korea), which became the basis for his subsequently republished popular college texts. In these histories he committed an entire chapter to military rule. Not satisfied with just recalling the events of the period, he put the key issues within a historical context in an effort to understand the generals' actions and the conditions that drove them to revolt both in 1170 and in 1196.[4]

Since the early 1970s a number of articles and monographs have further illuminated various aspects of the era. In 1971, Pyŏn T'aesŏp laid the foundations for future scholarship with his definitive study of Koryŏ institutional history. In this work, drawing on his earlier articles, Pyŏn closely examined the social and political status of military and civil officials. A decade and a half later Kim Tangt'aek, first in a doctoral dissertation and then in a book, investigated the military period as a coherent whole, applying more analysis to individuals and institutions than had been presented heretofore in Korean. In 1990 Min Pyŏngha, building on his earlier work, essentially republished his research in a volume titled *Koryŏ musin chŏnggwŏn yŏngu* (A study of Koryŏ military officers' rule). At the same time, Kim Kwang-sik looked at the military period in terms of changes in Buddhism. Hong Sŭnggi shed light on the changes in a number of ways. In his social history *Koryŏ kwijok sahoe wa nobi* (Aristocratic society of Koryŏ and slavery), he focused in several chapters on the social issues that affected slaves during the military period. In 1995 Hong edited a collection of articles by his students and colleagues devoted to key issues of military rule titled *Koryŏ muin chŏnggwŏn yŏngu* (A study of Koryŏ military rule).[5] This volume, like Kim Tangt'aek's earlier work, moved beyond a description of institutions and analyzed the key events of the era as they related to overall themes in Koryŏ history.

To date there has been no single work in English focusing exclusively on the military era. The aim of this study, therefore, is to produce such a work that not only reconsiders the primary sources but builds on the best contemporary scholarship. The *Koryŏsa* and *Koryŏsa chŏryo* are the principal sources for Koryŏ. The *Koryŏsa,* in adherence to Chinese historiographic tradition, comprises four sections: annals, treatises, tables, and biographies. The annals tersely present, in chronological order, the key events of each royal reign. Supplementing this presentation are the treatises, which provide slightly more detail on basic institutions such as recruitment, the land system, and the military order. Tables present a chronological outline of the dynasty according to the sexagenary cycle with reference to events in China. The biography section highlights the lives of significant dynastic personalities, placing them into general categories of royal family, loyal subjects, treacherous officials, and rebellious subjects. The *Koryŏsa chŏryo* is shorter in length than the *Koryŏsa* but provides similar or identical material in the form of chronological annals.

Other Koryŏ sources such as tomb inscriptions and miscellaneous literary writings, though few in number, offer another window into this period. From the twelfth century on, a growing number of tomb monuments detail the lives of famous Koryŏ people. Although, like the official histories, these inscriptions are largely descriptive, they offer added insights into the lives and institutions of the age. Moreover, a number of literary men of the late twelfth and early thirteenth centuries left writings that sometimes afford a detailed account of the period. When these materials are combined with the official dynastic histories, the contours of the military period begin to emerge.

   This book has relevance beyond Korean history, as well, for knowledge of Koryŏ history is important in delineating the outlines of East Asian history. Students of both Japan and China can find here pertinent developments in Korea's past, and the military era is an excellent focus for comparative work. Prior to the twelfth century, Korea modeled many of its political and social institutions on Chinese governance patterns—then, suddenly, with the rise of the military after 1170, new departures appear that bear little resemblance to Chinese models but are surprisingly similar to institutional innovations found in Japan. That the rise of the warrior class in Japan dovetails with the rise of the military in Korea highlights the need to study these two cultures in concert. In the military period, Koryŏ experimented with a number of diverse models for governing: some were found in both Chinese and Japanese traditions; others were novel to Korea. In testing traditions distinct from the Chinese model, Japan ultimately continued to refine certain of its institutional innovations while Korea in the end returned to many of the Chinese patterns. To comprehend these three East Asian histories, a deeper understanding of the separate traditions—and especially the military period, an era that challenged accepted notions of governance—is necessary. This book, I hope, will further that inquiry. *Generals and Scholars* weaves new interpretations that contribute to both Western and non-Western understanding of military rule in medieval Korea. Not only does it describe salient events and personalities, but it seeks to give a new appreciation of this dynamic epoch in Korea's past.

   When I first studied the period of military rule as a dissertation topic, I was guided foremost by my teacher, colleague, and friend, Hugh H. W. Kang of the University of Hawai'i–Manoa. Through his able direction he guided me in the early 1970s to Sogang University and its distinguished history department exemplified by Professors Yi Kibaek (Ki-baik Lee) and Yi Kwangrin. Like Hugh Kang, these scholars gave me time, encouragement, and support in my studies. Their students in turn became colleagues for life. Professors Hong Sŭnggi, Chŏng Tuhŭi, Yi Chonguk, and Kim Hangyu, in particular, have provided a wealth of ideas and years of friendship. Also in Korea, exchanges with Professors Kim Tangt'aek, Pak Chonggi, and Min Hyŏngu have sharpened my understanding of Koryŏ. Many other authors whose works are cited here also deserve thanks. And in Korea I must thank several good friends who would listen sympathetically, send me books and other materials when I needed them, and even offer a place to sleep: Professor Shin Sangch'ŏl, Professor Kim Seonggyung, Yi Kŏn, Professor Hŏ Minho, and Yi Hŭimun.

Professor John B. Duncan of UCLA has been a close friend and colleague who has always willingly shared ideas and offered sound criticism of my work. Professor James Palais of the University of Washington has helped me find a stronger voice and clearer understanding of Koryŏ institutions. At the University of Hawai'i, Professor Yongho Ch'oe has been a rich source on questions of Chosŏn history and Korean history. Professor Kazuhiko Kasaya of the International Research Center for Japanese Studies in Kyoto and Professor George Hlawatsch of Kansai Gaidai University helpfully compared medieval Japanese and Korean institutions. Joel Bradshaw of University of Hawai'i Press, Michael Macmillan of the Center for Korean Studies, and Professor Daniel B. Boylan of University of Hawai'i–West O'ahu have assisted me in making a tighter manuscript. To all of these people I offer my sincere thanks and gratitude. But no words can express my aloha to my immediate family— Kamaile, Keoni, and Kanekoa—and my *ohana* who has been steadfast with words and actions of support.

Introduction

The military era was a transitional period in Koryŏ: civil rule gave way to military domination and then Mongol control starting in 1270. Rebellion and invasion tested Koryŏ's traditions under mounting social, institutional, and intellectual pressures. Yet the importance of civil norms and civil officials, the primacy of the monarchic ideal, the prominence of social elites and kinship ties, and the centrality of Buddhist expression—all standards of Koryŏ—remained fundamental in the military era as well. These traditions, coupled with new developments during military rule, influenced events and institutions in the following Mongol era and then the kingdom of Chosŏn. The generals of this age confronted essential issues of governance: questions of how to deal with demands for social liberation and how to share power.

The coup of 1170 was the culmination of decades of antimilitary discrimination and military entanglement in the divisions among the civil elite (Chapter 1). When the military revolted, Ŭijong abdicated the throne in favor of his brother Myŏngjong (r. 1170–1197). (For a list of the Koryŏ kings, see Figure 1.) Myŏngjong reigned rather than ruled as a succession of generals, starting with the coup leader Chŏng Chungbu (d. 1178), dominated the kingdom. Internal strife, rebellion, and administrative chaos marked the subsequent twenty-six years as coups and assassinations saw authority pass from General Chŏng to General Kyŏng Taesŭng (d. 1184) and then to a man of slave origins, Yi Ŭimin (d. 1196). During this turbulent period, some military leaders continued to work with civilian elites while others arrogantly abused their newfound authority.

1

Figure 1. Koryŏ Kings: 1123–1259

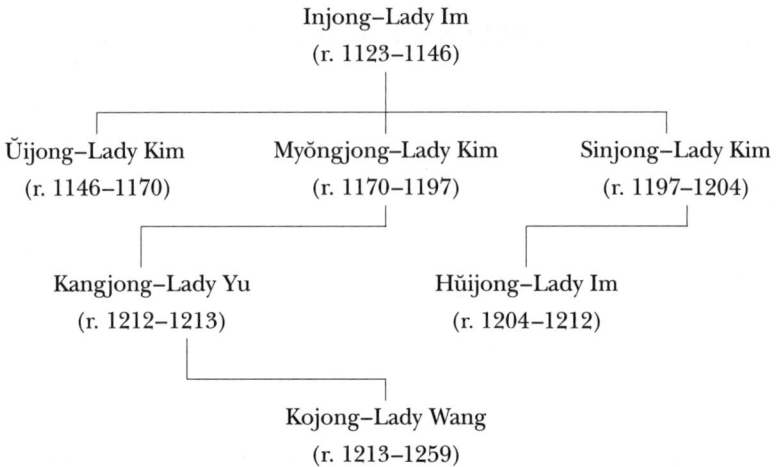

Injong–Lady Im
(r. 1123–1146)

Ŭijong–Lady Kim   Myŏngjong–Lady Kim   Sinjong–Lady Kim
(r. 1146–1170)   (r. 1170–1197)   (r. 1197–1204)

Kangjong–Lady Yu   Hŭijong–Lady Im
(r. 1212–1213)   (r. 1204–1212)

Kojong–Lady Wang
(r. 1213–1259)

Each of the ladies served as queen and in that capacity had a formal reign name. Their family lineage is significant and accordingly their surnames are used here. Most of these kings had only one spouse.

These years of conflict and rebellion spawned the conditions that led to General Ch'oe Ch'unghŏn's coup in 1196 (Chapter 2). Ch'oe finally halted the kingdom's slide into anarchy when he assassinated Yi Ŭimin in 1196 and then forced King Myŏngjong to abdicate to his brother Sinjong (r. 1197–1204) in 1197. Ch'oe Ch'unghŏn, his son U (also known as I), grandson Hang (d. 1257), and great-grandson Ŭi (d. 1258) became the de facto rulers of the kingdom. To preserve a semblance of legitimacy, Ch'oe Ch'unghŏn rapidly enthroned and dethroned a succession of kings during his initial years of consolidation. When Sinjong died after seven years on the throne, his son Hŭijong (r. 1204–1211) became the new king. Hŭijong, after enduring seven years of Ch'oe domination, tried to rebel. When he failed, Ch'oe Ch'unghŏn replaced him in favor of Myŏngjong's son, who became King Kangjong (r. 1211–1213). Kangjong lived for two years. His son became King Kojong (r. 1213–1259) and reigned for forty-six years, dying one year after the last Ch'oe dictator had been assassinated. Through all of this, Ch'oe Ch'unghŏn stabilized the social order and created new private agencies to facilitate his control. Some of these institutions continued long after the Ch'oe House collapsed. In his search for stability, however, he discovered that he could rule most effectively by relying on civil elites to administer Koryŏ.

Chapters 3, 4, and 5 examine the institutions of Ch'oe rule, both military and civilian, as well as the personalities of the era. The legacies of the past helped Ch'oe Ch'unghŏn maintain control. A conservative figure, Ch'oe sought to restore civil elites to administration. And by patronizing Confucian ideology he assured the ongoing acceptance of the monarchy. Politically he continued to rely on consensus-formulating institutions and sought to freeze the social order to limit social emancipation. But Ch'oe Ch'unghŏn was not manacled to the past. Indeed, he developed an innovative dual organization that relied on both dynastic and private institutions. In the years that the Ch'oe House ruled Koryŏ, there were a number of departures from tradition. Private troops that remained loyal to a military lord soon replaced the dynastic forces as the leading arbiters of power. Ch'oe Ch'unghŏn and his family dominated this new order. The men who swore loyalty to the Ch'oe heads became known as retainers (mungaek), and similar ties of fidelity developed between other soldiers and leaders.

Despite Ch'oe Ch'unghŏn's desire to prevent slaves from improving their status, intriguing changes occurred in social conditions (Chapter 6), intellectual and Buddhist institutions (Chapter 7), and economic conditions (Chapter 8). Men of humble social origins who pledged themselves to the Ch'oe heads advanced to positions of significance, surmounting social barriers that had existed from early in the dynasty. Economic change accompanied social change. Gradually the dynasty lost control over the land to private individuals who acquired and distributed wealth without government intervention. Change visited the spiritual realm, too, as Meditation (Sŏn) Buddhism emerged as the key form of religious expression.

In the end the Ch'oe House collapsed for numerous reasons but primarily because of the institutional contradictions that evolved out of its dual administration (Chapter 9). During the Ch'oe rule foreign attacks launched first by the Khitan and then by the far more devastating Mongols despoiled the kingdom and weakened Ch'oe governance. The last Ch'oe leader, a mere youth, could govern neither his house nor the country. At its peak, however, both Ch'oe Ch'unghŏn and Ch'oe U dominated the kingdom as few kings had, emerging as the leading patrons of the arts and religion.

Understanding three Koryŏ institutions—the land system, the military order, and civil recruitment—helps us make sense of the changes occurring during this century of military rule. Although Koryŏ's land system was extremely complex and even today is not adequately understood, certain features are clear. Scholars traditionally believed that Koryŏ had adapted attributes of the Tang equal-field system—whereby peasants were guaranteed a plot of land—but closer scrutiny reveals that even though the terminology used in the two land systems was similar, the operations were quite distinct. When Koryŏ was founded in the tenth century, regional strongmen controlled much of the land. Over the next century, the state sought to increase its control over the land and thereby curtail some of the economic power that elites had come to enjoy. Throughout the first two centuries of Koryŏ, there was a constant struggle between the Koryŏ aristocrats and the state over control of the land.

In 976 King Kyŏngjong (r. 975–981), attempting to assert state authority over land relations, introduced the land stipend *(chŏnsikwa)* system whereby the state granted prebendal rights from paddy land and woodland to officials, military officers, and other government agents. In gaining prebendal rights, the designee was granted the right to collect land rents from a specified amount of land. The collection of this revenue was carried out by the agents of the *chŏnsikwa* holder instead of government clerks. It is believed that prebendal payments may have amounted to 50 percent of the yield of the land. Approximately 20 percent of all arable land in the kingdom fell into this category. Cultivators of this land were both large landowners and peasants. Prebendal rights appear to have been inherited in many cases.

The *chŏnsikwa* did not cover the totality of land tenure relations in Koryŏ. There was land that supplied food for the king and also land to provide revenues for government offices called public land *(kongjŏn)*. People's land, or *minjŏn*, another category of landholding in Koryŏ, was also considered public land. The state collected a tax yield of approximately 25 percent of the produce from this type of public land. Although this money went to the state treasury, *minjŏn* was characterized by its essentially "private" quality in that it could be bought, sold, or transferred. Another category generally referred to as private land was *sajŏn*. Although scholars are far from united in determining an accepted definition, this private land appears to have carried a tax-exempt status enabling the "owner" to pay only minimal levies on the land instead of an onerous levy to the state. Many of the large estates that began to predominate in the countryside in the twelfth century fell into this category, but the large holdings of the local elite from the tenth century on were considered private land as well. The implications for the state were significant, of course, since the expansion of land under this category would immediately curtail the kingdom's tax base and reduce the amount of revenue the state would have going into its granaries to pay for salaries and other expenses.[1]

Apart from the land system, a second controversy needs to be addressed: the nature of the Koryŏ military order. The status of the military had been in decline ever since the founding of the kingdom. By Sŏngjong's reign (981–997) at the end of the tenth century, the dynastic military structure had been placed under the control of the Ministry of Military Affairs (Pyŏngbu) and the Security Council (Ch'umirwŏn). Civil officials staffed both these agencies—which oversaw personnel matters as well as logistics—and accordingly determined most military policy. The military itself was divided into two units called royal armies *(kun)* and six guards *(wi):*

Two Armies

Ŭngyanggun (1,000 men)

Yonghogun (2,000 men)

Six Guards

Chau-wi (13,000 men; standing division)

Sinho-wi (7,000 men; standing division)

Hŭngwi-wi (13,000 men; standing division)

Kŭmo-wi (7,000 men; auxiliary division)

Ch'ŏnu-wi (2,000 men; special division)

Kammun-wi (1,000 men; special division)

Each of these units, regardless of size, had a commander (*sangchan-gun* or supreme general) and deputy commander (*taechanggun* or grand general) who formed a consultative organ known as the Council of Generals (Chungbang).[2] Although the functions of the Council of Generals during early Koryŏ are unclear, it was the assembly of the highest military officers, directly under the top civil agencies, and therefore possessed a unique potential for power.

The two royal armies, perhaps the best equipped and trained units, were responsible for guarding the king. In terms of status they ranked above the six guard divisions. Among these eight units (the two armies and six guards) the commander of the Yonghogun acted as spokesman for the members of the Council of Generals and accordingly garnered great prestige. The three standing divisions were the most important military companies among the six guards: composed of both infantry and cavalry, they were trained for war and indispensable in defending the capital region. The auxiliary division, which performed police functions, maintained both a standing force of about six thousand soldiers and an additional thousand men in a labor battalion. The two special divisions performed several functions: the Ch'ŏnu-wi forces were ceremonial honor guards; the Kammun-wi guarded the palace grounds and capital gates.[3]

There were other units, as well, with military functions. In wartime, special mobilizations, supplementing the capital armies and guards, formed into five emergency armies that were usually placed under the command of a special commander (*wŏnsu*) appointed for the occasion. These armies recruited men from commoner as well as aristocratic backgrounds. The troops served for the duration of the crisis; but once peace was reached, defense responsibilities were relegated to local residents. The two northern frontier districts were divided into various administrative sections called *chu* and *chin*. As each resident was responsible for defense, all taxes remained in the area to meet military requirements. In the southern areas a cavalry (Chŏngyong) evolved for policing and an infantry (Posŭng) for combat duty. A third unit, the P'umgun, performed labor functions. Peasants undoubtedly formed these last three units.[4]

Even though commoners generally entered the provincial forces, the soldiers that formed the capital units seem to have come from a professional military class and the commander—the supreme general and grand general—from a still more prestigious group. The leadership, the men who participated in the Council of Generals, while rarely of the elite aristocratic clans that controlled the civil administration, often came from families that had achieved considerable recognition for their role in the military service. These military officers, called *muban,* were the upper stratum of military-class families *(kunbanssijok),* a special class responsible for supplying soldiers in the Koryŏ dynasty. When a professional soldier grew old or sick, someone in his family inherited his position. In the event that a *kunbanssijok* family died out, a replacement could be selected from among the children of officials of the sixth government grade or lower within Koryŏ's nine-grade scale or from qualified peasants. As men from the *kunbanssijok* could advance into officers' positions, there was potential for men of ordinary background to enter the upper ranks of the military service.[5]

The third Koryŏ institution of interest here is the system of civil recruitment. Just as hereditary privilege was fundamental to the Koryŏ military officer system, lineage influenced selection and promotion within the civil structure. The Koryŏ elite had established a number of institutions to assure that their progeny would influence political decisions. The protective appointment *(ŭm),* which originated within China's political traditions, guaranteed that any man who reached the fifth grade would be able to name an heir to an official post.[6] A more difficult and yet more accessible route to a greater number of people was through the state civil service examination *(kwagŏ).* The examination, modeled on Tang China's example, began in 958. From that time on it was held regularly every two or three years. The average number of men who passed the examination per year went from 7.6 in Sŏngjong's reign (981–997) to 22.5 in Yejong's reign (1105–1122).[7] This examination, which tested men on their knowledge of the Confucian classics, required a high level of scholastic ability and theoretically offered commoners a way to advance into offices of prestige based on individual talent. But to sit for the examination, a candidate had to present an unblemished social history tracing ancestors back four generations and showing no scandal or humble birth in his ancestry. The Ministry of Civil Personnel (Ibu), the Ministry of Rites (Yebu), and the Academy of Letters (Hallimwŏn) oversaw different aspects of the recruitment and advancement process. In addition the policy critics *(kanŭi taebu)* in the Royal Secretariat–Chancellery had the authority to ratify the appointment of civil and military officials.

Each of these institutions was refined in the eleventh century only to confront serious challenges in the twelfth century. It was institutional dysfunctions in the land system, military order, and civil recruitment that raised competition and tension within Koryŏ society, thereby directly contributing to the events of the late twelfth and thirteenth centuries. These institutions, modeled on Chinese systems, had to be reworked to fit Korean norms, and Ch'oe Ch'ung-hŏn in securing his authority paid close attention to them. The land system and military order in particular changed significantly in the thirteenth century to suit Koryŏ societal needs. Of the three, civil recruitment remained largely intact and continued to be an important avenue through which powerful families placed sons in government offices during the military era and in subsequent decades. We will return to all three institutions in the following chapters.

1

The Military Coup

In the eighth lunar month of 1170, as Koryŏ's monarch Ŭijong was visiting several Buddhist temples, General Chŏng Chungbu, head of the palace guards, together with his aides, Executive Captains Yi Ŭibang and Yi Ko, launched a coup that toppled Ŭijong from power and left a number of powerful officials dead. This revolt was not a random act but the result of many forces that exploded in the calm of an autumn excursion.

To understand this coup in all its complexity, a search into its origins is imperative. The coup was much more complicated than a simple armed revolt caused by incensed military officers. Its roots go back to the early days of the dynasty as military officers found themselves forced to yield their authority to civilian leaders. In the early twelfth century, when military officers discovered they were becoming the arbiters of civil disputes, they became less willing to accept rebuke from civilians. As Ŭijong's court became seriously split over royal prerogatives and as the king became less and less attentive to state matters, the military officers launched their coup.

Role of the Military

The status of the military had been in decline ever since the founding of the kingdom. Koryŏ's founder, Wang Kŏn, established his kingdom through military force, sharing his power with his key generals. But to stabilize the dynasty and rule through a strong central government, the Koryŏ court soon pursued a policy of civil supremacy. Koryŏ's military leaders, slow to accept this system, staged a

9

coup in 1014 in a last-ditch attempt to reassert their deteriorating positions. Although the effects of this coup lasted less than half a year, it manifested both the military's discontent over the policy of civil supremacy and its revived political consciousness. Rather than soothe military egos, civilian leaders continued to assert the ideal of civil supremacy. When the dynasty confronted invasions along its northern frontier, it was civil officials who led the dynastic armies: Kang Kamch'an (948–1031) checked the Khitan and Yun Kwan (d. 1111) fought the Jurchen. Similarly, when Sŏgyŏng (the Western Capital, present-day P'yŏngyang) rose in revolt in 1135, it was the renowned scholar Kim Pusik (1075–1151) who charted strategy. As civil officials continued to assume the authority of military commanders, they relegated military officials to supporting roles.

Military and civil officials were separated by tension. And although the civil arm dominated, the military's needs and demands could not be dismissed. At the end of the eleventh century, when one of the dynasty's most prominent officials, Yi Chaŭi, sought to arrogate his authority in 1095, his key opponent, So T'aebo, managed to stay one step ahead of him by winning the support of several generals. Without the crucial backing of these military officials, such as Wang Kungmo, So T'aebo would not have been successful in defeating Yi.[1]

Events in Injong's reign (r. 1122–1146) reveal the ambiguity of the military official in Koryŏ. Two major rebellions, the Yi Chagyŏm and Myoch'ŏng revolts, seriously taxed the dynasty and forced the civilian officials to rely on military support to secure their control over dynastic institutions. Both rebellions exposed the myth of civil supremacy.[2] Despite this charade, the dynasty effectively isolated military officials from major civil positions and decision making. As Hugh Kang has observed:

> The area of duty saved for the military officials was strictly confined to the field military units where they served as the commanders of the six Wi [guards] and two Kun [armies], and where the technical skills of the professional soldiers were presumably best utilized for the most effective result. It is evident that the military officials were completely barred from positions of political responsibility in the early Koryŏ government.[3]

Military officials had harbored a long list of grievances for generations. Certainly their economic position had deteriorated.[4] From

the tenth century, to the detriment of military officers, the dynasty
had favored civil officials in its prebendal allotments. In 1076 a final
revision of the land stipend law *(chŏnsikwa)* appeared. Although the
net impact was to reduce the prebends across the board for all services, those at the lower end suffered greater reductions than those
at the top. In other words: the civil officials who monopolized the
highest offices fared better than the other officials. The military officials did benefit from certain aspects of the new scale. The supreme
general advanced from the fifth rank to the third rank, and lower-
grade military officers enjoyed a similar elevation in scale. But in
real terms the supreme general, for example, who had received a
total prebend of 130 *kyŏl* of land under the old system, received 5
kyŏl less in Munjong's reign (r. 1064–1083). Not only prebends but
salaries too favored the civil officials, who monopolized the top of
these scales. Although it is difficult to assess the quality of the land
used as prebends for the various officials, it appears the military officials may have been victimized here too.[5]

The military official suffered socially and politically as well. Koryŏ
divided its civil and military offices into nine grades with a junior
and senior level in each grade. The highest-ranking military officer
—the supreme general *(sang changgun)*—was placed at senior third
grade. To advance beyond this level, the military officer would have
to assume a civil title—a rare event in the eleventh and twelfth centuries. Not only were military officials denied the right to assume the
top military commands in times of national emergency, but they
were seldom allowed to enter the highest civil offices—and did so
only by assuming civil titles. Rarely did military officials gain prestigious posts in either the Royal Secretariat–Chancellery or the Security Council (collectively called the Chaech'u, or State Council).
During Ŭijong's reign, for example, the dynasty did not admit one
military officer into this group.

The social status of the military officer was equally ambiguous. By
dynastic decree, all officials, both military and civil, who had reached
the fifth rank or above were allowed through the protective *(ŭm)*
appointment to name heirs to dynastic positions, and they also
enjoyed other privileges such as access to government schools for
their children. Moreover, military men start to appear in the biography section of the *Koryŏsa* beginning in the 1040s—another measure of respectability.[6] Equally significant, a number of men with mil-

itary standing held positions in the civil structure. Kigye No kinsmen and Ch'ungju Yang kinsmen are just two examples.[7] These families represented the elite of the military officer corps and presumably there was not an unbridgeable social gap between them and the leading civil elites.

Although they enjoyed a modicum of social acceptance, military officials were made aware of their unequal status. In 1110 the dynasty instituted a military examination that established certain levels of competence for each rank. This examination, which enabled soldiers to be appointed on the basis of their skills, increased the professional standard and the social prestige of the military service. Twenty-three years later, however, civil officials, jealous over the advances of the military officials, forced these examinations to be abandoned.[8] The functions performed by common soldiers changed too. No longer handling only military matters, soldiers increasingly worked on such demeaning tasks as digging ditches and on other public works projects.[9]

By the middle of the twelfth century, Koryŏ's officers and soldiers found themselves locked in a system stacked against them. Yet they were aware of their signal importance: they had checked the Khitan invasions of the tenth and eleventh centuries and then held back the Jurchen at the start of the twelfth century. Indeed, it is quite possible that the military preparation of Koryŏ's armies prevented the Jurchen Chin from conquering Koryŏ as they had overcome China in 1126. Not only was the military effective in defending Koryŏ's northern borders, but it also suppressed the Yi Chaŭi revolt in 1095, the Yi Chagyŏm revolt in 1126, and the Myoch'ŏng revolt in 1135. Despite these invaluable contributions, the Koryŏ soldier was trapped by the social, political, and economic institutions of the dynasty. The situation is even more ironic in that the Koryŏ civilian elite modeled much of its dynastic governance on a Chinese Sung system that at that moment was failing to withstand the onslaught of the Jurchen.[10] Furthermore, the events may well have affected the standing of the military in still another manner. As Koryŏ's northern frontier became stabilized in the 1140s, Koryŏ felt less pressure to defend its borders. According to Michael Rogers, this situation might well have "facilitated the downgrading of Koryŏ's military establishment to the advantage of the civil officialdom."[11] For all these reasons the military chafed under civilian dominance.

Ŭijong's Reign: Royal Family and Court

In addition to military discontent, strife within the royal family stirred the passions of the age. When Ŭijong was still crown prince, both his father Injong and his mother Lady Im questioned his right to succeed to the throne. Injong harbored serious misgivings about Ŭijong's talent and ability to govern; his mother openly favored her second son, Ŭijong's brother Prince Kyŏng. Ŭijong won the throne only because of the staunch support of the royal tutor, Chŏng Sŭp-myŏng, who assured the royal parents that he would personally guide and instruct Ŭijong once he became king.[12] Inheriting the throne under this cloud of opposition, Ŭijong found his effectiveness as a monarch curbed and his ability to exercise royal prerogatives curtailed. Desiring to assert his independence, he allied with any willing group and thereby embroiled himself in an internal power struggle with his family and central aristocrats.[13]

From the start of his reign, Ŭijong remained suspicious of his brother and his mother's family, the Chŏngan Im lineage. One brother quickly abandoned all political designs, choosing to become a Buddhist monk at the prestigious Hŭngwang temple.[14] Another brother, Prince Kyŏng, suffered a more serious setback when Ŭijong stripped him of a number of titles in 1151 and purged a number of his associates. Kyŏng was on good terms with his mother's family, especially Im Kŭkchŏng, and through the Im clan was indirectly related to three purged officials, Chŏng Sŏ, Ch'oe Yuch'ŏng, and Yi Chaksŭng.[15] Ŭijong suspected a plot when the eunuch Chŏng Ham and another civilian, Kim Chonjung, an ally to the king, concocted rumors that Kyŏng and a number of officials associated with the Chŏngan Im clan planned treason.[16] Although the charges were not substantiated, Chŏng Ham and Kim Chonjung reiterated the story, building a case against Kyŏng and his relatives. Kim Chonjung's motives were far from pure. The *Koryŏsa* claims: "Chonjung was on unfriendly terms with the queen's sister's husband, Office Chief of Palace Attendants *(naesi nangjung)* Chŏng Sŏ, and the queen's brother Im Kŭkchŏng."[17] Kim and the eunuch Chŏng Ham had been friends for many years. Now, because of petty grudges, they charged the atmosphere by playing on the king's own fears, culminating in the dismissal of these "anti-Ŭijong " officials.

The men demoted in 1151 shared common bonds through marriage ties, links with the Censorate, and regional origins. Chŏng Sŏ, for example, was from Tongnae near modern Pusan and entered the dynastic service through the *ŭm* privilege of inherited rank, being appointed a palace attendant.[18] The Chŏng family had long been prominent in local politics, and many of its members had acted as county headmen *(hojang)*. While serving as palace attendant, Chŏng Sŏ probably first challenged the eunuchs and Kim Chonjung, contributing to the 1151 incident. But the incident exposes a much deeper schism. Not only was Ŭijong suspicious of his mother's family, he also centered his attack on individuals associated with Han Anin, who had emerged in Yejong's reign (1107–1122) and then was purged by Yi Chagyŏm at the start of Injong's reign.[19] Although Han Anin died in 1122, his associates continued to influence politics in both Injong's and Ŭijong's reigns and emerged as the targets of this purge. These men, some of them censors, quite possibly were guilty of using remonstrance to attack Ŭijong and undermine his authority. The forces at the court, however, were strong. Within one month of Chŏng Sŏ's removal, the dynasty recorded his alleged crimes in the government register along with those of Ch'oe Yuch'ŏng and Yi Chaksŭng.

For the next six years, little was heard from Chŏng Sŏ. Then, in 1157, another schism erupted when Ŭijong exiled his brother Kyŏng to Ch'ŏnanbu and demoted many of the same people he had demoted in 1151—Chŏng Sŏ, Ch'oe Yuch'ŏng, Yi Chaksŭng—as well as Kim Iyŏng and Im Kŭkchŏng. Fearful that his mother Lady Im would attempt to block these actions, Ŭijong first removed her to Poje temple and tried to show he had no power over the ensuing events.[20] One historian commented:

> Prince Kyŏng's treason is not clear. His mother is still alive and suffers because of her son's exile. Ŭijong is ungrateful. [Ch'oe] Yuch'ŏng is upright and a renowned censor of his age. [Yi] Chaksŭng, pure, principled, and in every way a good censor, is disliked by Chŏng Ham and is unable to escape exile. Alas![21]

The men purged at this time generally disappear from court politics until the military coup of 1170. In the 1150s and 1160s, however, these men were developing tenuous and somewhat indirect ties with the military. Kim Iyŏng, for example, was Chŏng Sŏ's brother-in-law and related by marriage to Chŏng Chungbu, the acknowledged leader of the 1170 coup.[22] Ch'oe Yuch'ŏng's sons In and Tang, as registrars in the capital armies, witnessed military grievances and perhaps communicated their own disillusionment with court politics.[23]

Ŭijong was determined to free himself from powerful officials, especially those tied to the Chŏngan Im clan. Ŭijong's own marriage ties reveal this attempt to escape in-law politics—his mother's powerful family in particular. While he was still crown prince, he married a member of his own clan, the daughter of Sado On, who was the great-granddaughter of King Munjong.[24] Kings in the past had turned to their own lineage for spouses in order to curtail outside influences. Ŭijong's second marriage occurred in 1148, when he married the daughter of Ch'oe Tan. Ch'oe Tan's family must have been somewhat of a compromise selection. Tan's father had been purged earlier by a number of new elites under the leadership of Han Anin, yet Tan had married the daughter of the Chongan Im clansman Wŏnae. By allying himself by marriage to a family with no strong political leanings, Ŭijong might have hoped to break free of entanglements.[25]

Traditionally, Koryŏ's kings had had to confront a fractured civil structure. Ŭijong was no exception. Historians of the dynasty are nearly unanimous in concluding that Koryŏ kingship was relatively weak compared to the vast power of the central aristocratic clans. The Chaech'u (State Council) became the locus of political power where many aristocrats held positions. Through group decisions, these men effectively ruled the country; and in their united efforts, even singly at times, they impeded royal action. Although members of this group held divided opinions on Ŭijong, another institution, the censorial offices (Taegan), became increasingly vocal at this time.[26] Dynastic codes mandated that the censorial offices criticize improper royal behavior and mismanagement of state affairs. These offices also ratified the appointment of civil and military officials and became an important institutional constraint on royal authority.

Institutional Remonstrance

During Ŭijong's reign there was a vociferous barrage of criticism leveled against the king and his activities. The censorial agencies had reached their maturity as an institution and were exercising all the power they could muster to enforce their will. The Censorate criticized Ŭijong in countless statements attacking his poor administration, his reckless appointments, and his general deportment. No monarch was a paragon of virtue, least of all Ŭijong, but the censors of this age were exercising remonstrance in the extreme and much of their criticism risked losing its effectiveness.[27] The Censorate not only criticized the general state of affairs. It also attacked repeatedly the king's enjoyment of polo *(kyŏkku)*, making it a cause célèbre, until Ŭijong finally abandoned the game in 1152.[28] The men Ŭijong had recruited were equally suspect and unacceptable to the censors. Policy critics condemned the behavior of high-ranking officials who supported Ŭijong, as well as eunuchs and palace attendants. Chŏng Ham, the eunuch who had helped cashier Prince Kyŏng, was a special target of attacks.[29]

Ŭijong resisted these attacks in a variety of ways. One tactic was simply to ignore the protest.[30] When determined, Ŭijong would pit his will against the censors and force them to accept his decisions.[31] On one occasion Ŭijong was so incensed over the effrontery of a memorial that he burned it before the censor's eyes.[32] But this was extreme action, and Ŭijong preferred to employ diplomatic techniques. He made repeated overtures to leading officials and censors, inviting them to royal banquets and garden parties, and through the tested technique of wining and dining was able to achieve many victories.[33] Ŭijong demonstrated considerable ingenuity in staving off censorial criticism. In 1160, when all other measures seem to have failed, he devised a unique way to silence his critics. The histories relate:

> The king went to Inji Pavilion, also known as Kyŏngyong Pavilion. He presented a poem that read, "In a dream I heard of a truly happy place—the hermitage under Puso mountain." Accordingly the king had pavilions constructed there and decorated them. With palace attendants he got drunk daily and enjoyed himself, having no concern for state affairs. The Censorate requested that he desist, but the king, using his poem, would immediately explain his dream to refute them. After this the censors were silent.[34]

Ŭijong sought to manipulate the Censorate to achieve his own goals. No incident demonstrates this better than when he used the Censorate to remove from power his brother Prince Kyŏng and other potential antagonists in 1151 and then in 1157. On both occasions the king, confident of victory, called upon the Censorate to investigate charges and managed to win verdicts against his opponents.

Ŭijong's Supporters

Ŭijong was not without his defenders. A number of the dynasty's elite allied themselves with the king in his struggles against his mother's family and the censorial organs. As king he not only possessed symbolic power and embodied legitimacy but had great skill in executing affairs. Many aristocrats found their lives easier, and perhaps their personal economics improved, by supporting the status quo and the king. Others allied with Ŭijong because they disliked the people opposing him. Chŏng Sŭpmyŏng, who supported Ŭijong's bid to be king, remained a faithful adviser. Kim Chonjung, earlier introduced as an opponent of the Chŏngan Im lineage, likewise stayed close to Ŭijong. Kim Chonjung passed the state examination, as did many other officials who worked with Ŭijong.[35] Thus the king had a cadre of talent that must have been of great use to him in ruling.

In a search for allies, Ŭijong also found willing accomplices in eunuchs and palace attendants. Eunuchs had always been regarded with skepticism by Confucian writers. Because eunuchs could not produce heirs, some by choice, others by accident, Confucians deemed them to be unfilial. Moreover, eunuchs and Confucian officials frequently competed for royal favor, making them political antagonists. To the compilers of Koryŏ's dynastic histories, they became Ŭijong's nemesis. To Ŭijong himself, however, they were willing and helpful assistants who unfailingly supported his endeavors. Chŏng Ham epitomized the evil perpetrated by this group, but there were others involved in politics who facilitated the advance and demotion of many officials. By accompanying the king on his travels and supervising royal expenses, eunuchs found numerous ways to enrich themselves under Ŭijong's rule.[36]

Palace attendants, too, abetted the royal will. Originally aristocratic youths who acted as pages apprenticed in government offices through royal patronage, these attendants worked daily with the king learning the details of court politics and the intricacies of governing. During Ŭijong's reign, there is a dramatic shift in the social status of the palace attendants as fewer men from prestigious families occupied these positions. Of some thirty-six men known to have been palace attendants during Ŭijong's reign, only five were known to have been successful examination candidates. Six came from distinctly humble or functionary backgrounds; some were eunuchs. Ŭijong needed men to champion his position. By selecting palace attendants of modest backgrounds and bringing them into his court, he found men who were willing to pledge complete support to his cause. They colluded with the king to check his opposition, joined in the endless rounds of entertainment, and generally contributed to a prevailing climate of mismanagement and debauchery.[37]

The palace attendants, instead of acting as a deterrent to less enlightened royal activities, supported the king in his neglect of state affairs. Accompanying Ŭijong on his innumerable journeys, the palace attendants promoted an atmosphere of intoxication. They also incurred fiscal irresponsibility by competing in offering precious gifts to the monarch. Demonstrating the decadence of this group, one history recorded:

> The left and right units of the palace attendants competed in presenting precious gifts to the king. The right unit then had many aristocratic youth in it. Invoking the royal prerogative through the eunuchs, they sought out precious objects as well as calligraphy and paintings from public and private holdings. They also made ladders of satin and put various toys on them. Acting like foreigners offering tribute, they presented two blue and red parasols and two choice horses. The left unit, composed entirely of Confucian scholars, was unfamiliar with such games and therefore presented items not worth one-hundredth of those given by the right. Ashamed at being unable to equal them, they borrowed five fine horses and presented them to the king. The king received all these gifts and gave to the left unit 10 *kŭn* of white silver and 65 *kŭn* of Khitan silk thread, and to the right unit 10 *kŭn* of white silver and 95 *kŭn* of Khitan silk thread. Later the left unit, unable to repay the debt, was daily pressed for it. Contemporaries laughed at them.[38]

The Censorate attacked many of these actions and called for the dismissal of certain palace attendants.[39]

Ŭijong the Man

Ŭijong, at the center of much of the controversy, emerges as a complex figure. Inheriting the throne at a youthful nineteen, his character reveals him to have been more an aesthete than a politician. He enjoyed poetry and frequently wrote about the marvels of nature. He surrounded himself with gardens and artificial ponds. If he heard of a region that was especially scenic, he would visit it or try to embellish it further by planting rare trees. On one such instance he built a waterside pavilion but, finding the water too shallow for boats, he constructed a dam to form a lake.[40] On another occasion a flickering light was spotted moving through the forest at night behind the royal palace. Neighboring residents were alarmed until they discovered that the light was caused by Ŭijong strolling through the trees after dark.[41] He traveled on countless excursions through rural Koryŏ's wooded mountains, being as much at home in the countryside as in his capital, Kaegyŏng.[42]

Buddhism became his spiritual guide. Many of his trips to the countryside were pilgrimages to temples where he prayed, meditated, and observed religious ceremonies. When at home in the palace, Ŭijong found solace in studying sutras and attending Buddhist masses. Outwardly, to demonstrate his faith, he actively repaired and constructed temples and hosted feasts for as many as thirty thousand monks.[43] Once, while on the road to Hŭngwang temple, Ŭijong saw an old woman and gave her cloth and wine. On another trip to Pohyŏn hall, he gave a beggar cloth and cotton and then presented other travelers with enough rice and soup to last two days.[44]

Ŭijong did not, however, neglect Confucian practices.[45] From his youth he had been instructed on the Confucian classics and was expected to rely on Confucian doctrine as a guide. In ruling he often exhorted his officials and subjects to heed Confucian ideals and tried to submit himself to Confucian principles. He expressed personal anxiety over high taxes, full prisons, and unpaid officials. He agonized when Koryŏ experienced natural disasters and evinced genuine concern for his subjects living in poverty.[46] Through such acts, Ŭijong was performing symbolic gestures demonstrating his inherent ability as a Confucian monarch.

To shore up his authority, Ŭijong employed a number of other techniques. He patronized the royal guards, paying special attention to the Kyŏllyong army. To express a sense of royal revival, he even built a temple in the Western Capital (Sŏgyŏng) and to forward that idea named it Chunghŭng (Revival) temple. Furthermore, through the publication of the *Sangjŏng kogŭm yemun* (Detailed arrangement of ancient and current rites), he tried to establish a stronger sense of propriety and thereby elevate royal authority over the officialdom.[47] Ŭijong's reign also witnessed the publication of the *P'yŏnnyŏn t'ongnok* (Comprehensive record arranged by years), written by Kim Kwanŭi, which proclaimed the royal family's divine origins and thereby enhanced Ŭijong's legitimacy.[48]

The Military's Grievances

The internal opposition Ŭijong faced—first from his family and then from a number of aristocrats as voiced by the Censorate—must have taken a toll on the king. As his reign progressed, Ŭijong increasingly shunned political decisions, preferring to indulge himself in travel and aesthetic pursuits. Aristocrats, eunuchs, and palace attendants, ignoring the grievances of military officials and the demands of disgruntled civilian elites, willingly joined the king in these escapes into pleasure. Differences between the military and civil services became more acute. As the civil officials traveled with Ŭijong on trip after trip, military attendants were forced to stand guard weary and cold. Civilian officials, becoming more arrogant, ridiculed even high-ranking military officers. On one occasion, according to the dynastic record, General Chŏng Chungbu, a stately man of over six feet and later a leader of the 1170 revolt, had his long gray beard burned as a practical joke by a civilian from an elite aristocratic family.[49]

Eunuchs joined in the humiliation. Although military officers could rarely match their family status with ranking civilians, they were certainly on a higher social level than eunuchs. Nevertheless eunuchs, emboldened by the permissiveness of Ŭijong, focused many of their character assassinations or jokes on unsuspecting military officers. In 1156, a junior colonel *(nangjang)*, Ch'oe Sukch'ŏng, angered at the churlish behavior of the eunuch Chŏng Ham and the civilian Yi Wŏnŭng, announced his intention to kill them both. On discovering this plot, the court banished Ch'oe.[50] U Hagyu, another military officer, revealed a brewing discontent among the military when he recounted: "My father once warned, 'The military officials have seen injustice for too long. Is it possible for them not to be indignant?'"[51]

The Kyŏllyong army, a detachment of the royal guards, became a locus of discontent. Ŭijong depended on this unit—which first appeared in the late eleventh century to enhance royal power—to bolster his prestige and contain the aspirations of his mother's family.[52] Ŭijong encouraged men of obscure social backgrounds to join this group, hoping they would find in him a benefactor and accordingly pledge their support to him and his causes. Initially Ŭijong showered attention on these men and developed a special rapport through their mutual enjoyment of polo. As his reign progressed, however, he sought favor from powerful civil officials and gradually distanced himself from the Kyŏllyong army, adding to this unit's resentment and the military's disillusionment.[53]

As early as 1164, military officials began considering drastic measures to rectify their grievances. On an excursion to the countryside during the spring of that year, the king was appreciating the scenery with civilian scholars by singing and drinking. The military escorts, generals and soldiers alike, fatigued by countless such jaunts, burned with indignation. It was at this time that Chŏng Chungbu, the commanding general of the royal guards, and other military officers first contemplated a military coup.[54] Although they established no concrete plans, as the years passed they became increasingly desperate and determined to act. To them it appeared that the king and his close aides, eunuchs, palace attendants, and civil aristocrats were neglecting state affairs and devoting their energies to pleasure. Once the beneficiaries of Ŭijong's special attention, the soldiers felt abandoned by this monarch who catered to civilian whims. Not only were military concerns ignored, but the court frequently punished military officers for deeds perpetrated by civilians. On one royal excursion, a civilian official's horse lost its footing, causing a stray arrow to fall near the royal coach. Rather than accept responsibility for the mishap, the man remained silent and allowed the king to believe that his military escort had made an attempt on his life. The guiltless officers in question were banished.[55] After another such episode, two military officers, Yi Ŭibang and Yi Ko, voiced the indignation their fellow officers had suppressed for so long: "Now the civilian officials are haughty, drunk, and full, but the military men are hungry and troubled. How long can this be tolerated?" Chŏng

Chungbu, still resenting that his beard had been burned, seized the opportunity to complete plans for a revolt.[56]

Chŏng Chungbu, the leader of the 1170 coup d'état, was a member of the Haeju Chŏng lineage, which several decades earlier had produced a famous general: Chŏng Chŏngsuk not only helped suppress the Myoch'ŏng revolt but advanced into honorary civilian posts.[57] Chŏng Chungbu undoubtedly recalled that, in the past, military men like his kinsman Chŏngsuk had been called to serve the dynasty when aristocratic civilian leaders were unable to resolve a crisis, be it domestic or international. Chŏng Chungbu was also aware firsthand of the unsettled conditions prevailing at the court. He watched his son's father-in-law's banishment. He witnessed the power of the Censorate erode as eunuchs and place attendants interfered with the management of state affairs. He experienced the growing arrogance of civil officials who flocked to the king.

The other two leaders, Yi Ŭibang and Yi Ko, like Chŏng Chungbu, were also in the Kyŏllyong army and daily witnessed the abuses heaped on military men. As captains they were lower in rank than Chŏng Chungbu, and their social backgrounds were less defined, but they too were incensed at the bad treatment they endured and were vocal in their objections. It was their resentments that impelled Chŏng Chungbu to assume leadership. And in the first months after the coup, they were much more aggressive in their attacks on civilians.[58] Like Chŏng Chungbu, Yi Ŭibang had indirect links with civilian families as his brother was related through marriage to the censor Mun Kŭkkyŏm.[59]

The schism within the civil structure became daily more visible. Ŭijong surrounded himself with sycophants: state councillors, eunuchs, palace attendants. Others, perhaps spurned by these people or disillusioned with state affairs, began to turn away—and some looked to the military as a last resort to bring an end to the rapidly deteriorating state of affairs. The tenuous ties between Prince Kyŏng, the Chŏngan Im lineage, and the military have already been suggested. If there had not been divisions among civilian officials—and if there had not been a core of ranking officials equally disenchanted with court activities—chances for the success of a military coup would have been greatly diminished. By the summer of 1170, these were the prime forces moving the kingdom toward unavoidable conflict. Then, in the eighth lunar month, on a signal from

General Chŏng Chungbu, the military struck, killing or banishing more than fifty civil officials, eunuchs, and palace attendants and forcing Ŭijong to abdicate. The *Koryŏsa* relates:

> As soon as the king entered the gate and his high officials were about to retire, Yi Ko and others killed Im Chŏngsik and Yi Pokki at the gate with their own hands. Han Noe, relying on his close relationship to the eunuchs, hid inside the royal quarters under the king's bed. The king, greatly alarmed, sent his eunuch Wang Kwangch'wi to stop him. . . . Shortly afterward Transmitter Yi Set'ong . . . and others, along with the accompanying civil officials, functionaries, and eunuchs, all met tragedy. Their corpses were piled as high as a mountain.[60]

Aftermath of the Coup

To assure the success of their revolt, the military officers elicited the cooperation of civilian officials. Indeed, many civilian officials who had been critical of Ŭijong and his associates advanced to prominent positions in the new government. These men played supplementary roles, however, for it was military officers who commanded the revolt. The prime instigators were Chŏng Chungbu, Yi Ŭibang and Yi Ko, all members of the royal guard. Although the military leaders did initially murder officers who refused to join their cause, their prime targets were the men who had clustered around Ŭijong and contributed to the mismanagement of the state and the humiliation of the military. The military leaders removed at least twenty-three palace attendants from the power structure.[61] The attendants, by far the largest single group to be ousted, had continually interfered in court affairs during Ŭijong's reign. Always in attendance, they were clearly associated with Ŭijong as his closest advisers and thus had earned the enmity of not only the military but many civilians as well. In addition to the palace attendants, thirteen other men who had attained their positions through devious means or contributed to misgovernment during Ŭijong's reign were dismissed. Many were eunuchs and high-ranking civilians who, like the palace attendants, had harassed the soldiers and officers for years.

The coup also led to the purge of men who had helped chart military policy in Ŭijong's reign. Six members of the Security Council, three members of the Ministry of Military Affairs, and four former military commissioners fell victims of the coup.[62] For the military leaders it was essential to remove these people and other civil officials in military agencies, not only to secure absolute control over the dynastic military structure, but to prevent civilian countercoups. It is noteworthy that the modest goals of the first major military coup of 1014 had been obstructed by just such a countercoup.

Finally, the military also purged men in the State Council as well as officials in the Censorate who had been co-opted into joining Ŭijong in his escapades. The military removed three of the eleven state councillors: Ch'oe Yuch'ing, Ch'oe On, and Hŏ Hungjae, all close associates of Ŭijong. Also dismissed were nine men in the lower ranks of the Security Council and Royal Secretariat–Chancellery. The Security Council discussed matters of national defense and oversaw the transmission of royal documents.[63] In the latter function they could determine issues to be presented to the king and could act as spokesmen for the court. The Royal Secretariat–Chancellery played an important role in daily remonstrances and the drafting of policy. The Censorate, which had been co-opted by Ŭijong during the final years of his reign, was affected, too, with four of its nine ranking members demoted or killed. The Institute of Astronomical Observation (Sach'ŏndae), which was in charge of reporting celestial occurrences and remonstrances through the observation of natural events, similarly had three of its members dismissed. Men in all of these offices had thwarted the aspirations of both military and civil officials and had used Ŭijong to promote their personal interests.

The military leadership did not, as is often charged, ruthlessly slaughter all the civilian officials in the 1170 revolt. They were quite selective in whom they purged. Yun Inch'ŏm, for example, survived the coup and advanced to a position of prestige in the next reign, but his brother Tonsin and his son Chongak were both killed. The military leadership most frequently attacked lax officials who were guilty of mismanagement or extreme ostentation during Ŭijong's reign. Officials who were dedicated servants and honest in their administration were generally spared. Coupled with these indications of reformist tendencies was the military leadership's desire, once in power, to exercise full control over the military establishment as well as the formulation of military policy.

The military leaders were not uniformly in favor of the coup. The prime impetus for the revolt, as noted earlier, came from men in the

Kyŏllyong army, and these are the men who subsequently advanced to positions of importance in the new government.[64] Others, like General U Hakyu, had voiced concern over the consequences of a coup and chose not to join the ringleaders. Later regretting his stand, U Hakyu protected himself by establishing marriage ties with Yi Ŭibang's family.[65] Military officers in the two armies and six guards continued to operate on the fringes of military policy during the first years after the coup.

Although the Council of Generals (Chungbang) became the major center for decision making once the military leaders had firmly established themselves during the reign of Myŏngjong (r. 1170–1197), Ŭijong's brother and successor, the civil structure was still instrumental in effecting policy. The new leaders determined that Koryŏ, long governed through a civil bureaucracy, could best be controlled by retaining civilians. This policy assured that their rule would enjoy both able administration and a sense of legitimacy. An examination of the key personnel in the dynastic civil structure illustrates the novel aspects of the 1170 revolt.

Forty-four men are among those who might have dominated the government in the first five years of Myŏngjong's reign.[66] Only nine (20 percent) were recorded as possessing military ranks, while thirty-four (77 percent) were active in the civilian branch. Of the civilian officials noted, twenty-two (65 percent) had passed the civil service examination—half of the entire group. The lineages of many of these men are unknown but at least twenty-one (48 percent) had fathers who held the fifth rank or higher in the dynastic structure prior to 1170. This figure would probably be higher still if there were complete records. Twelve of the men (27 percent) were found to have had grandfathers in the fifth rank or higher. A number of individuals whose immediate ancestry lay in powerful regional families, such as Ch'oe Yuch'ŏng, also continued to hold positions. Strong provincial elite clans—first seen in Yejong's reign associated with Han Anin and then during Injong's and Ŭijong's reigns as a locus of unity—still carried potential in Myŏngjong's reign.[67] Not a single person of humble origins appeared in these dynastic ranks. In assessing these figures, it becomes apparent that despite the potential for men of common origins to enter the dynastic bureaucracy, if one's father had already had some dynastic service, one's chances of success were decidedly improved. And if one had successfully completed the state examination, one was given even more assurance of a ranking appointment.

These trends are underscored by the composition of the elite State Council. Among the thirteen state councillors listed at this time, four were products of the military service and the remaining nine were civilians. Although military officers had not previously served as state councillors, these men were from well-known families. Three of the four came from clans that had produced distinguished generals in earlier reigns. Yang Suk, for example, had even held a civil position during Ŭijong's reign. Of the nine civilians, at least five had passed the state examination and eight were from families with previous dynastic service. Such men as Im Kŭkch'ung, Ch'oe Yuch'ŏng, and Yun Inch'ŏm became state councillors soon after the coup. The Kyŏngju Kim, Kyŏngwŏn Yi, and Ich'ŏn Sŏ lineages were also represented. Clearly the elite character of the state councillors had not been radically altered by the coup.

The military leaders do not seem to have tried to capture any particular area in the bureaucracy. As in the State Council, the important lower posts of the Security Council were almost equally divided between civilian and military families. Posted in the Ministry of Military Affairs was only one military officer: Yi Ŭibang. Yi was one of the ringleaders of the coup and undoubtedly through this position was able to dictate the work of the ministry, including promotions for many.

For a variety of reasons, then, civilians participated in the new regime. Even though the new leaders forced Ŭijong to abdicate and replaced him with Myŏngjong, the court was still influential in choosing men. Several of Myŏngjong's friends, such as Min Yŏngmo and Ch'oe Yŏhae, as well as royal relatives, received their positions because of their ties to the king.[68] And, as mentioned earlier, civilians lent a sense of legitimacy and ran the administration.

The revolt was a product of political and social tensions that had begun earlier in the dynasty and intensified during Ŭijong's reign. Ŭijong's search for independence ironically destroyed him. He tormented powerful antagonists. His permissiveness, which tolerated debauchery and arrogance among his court officials, eunuchs, and palace attendants, inflamed the passions of civilian and military officials. Cleavages within the court that set the king against his brothers and his own mother further distorted the politics of the age. Nor were the dynastic political institutions able to provide a check: the remonstrances of the censorial agencies—perhaps inspired by political intrigue and certainly overstressed—passed unheeded. Under mounting tension, the grievances of the military leadership and the disillusionment of the civilian scholars coalesced into the 1170 military coup d'état.

With the revolt over and Myŏngjong enthroned, military rule became increasingly problematic and confusing. To some, the start of Myŏngjong's reign offered an opportunity to rectify the grievances of the past. To others, like Yi Ŭibang and then Yi Ŭimin, it presented a chance to grab power and tap the wealth of the kingdom.

2

Myŏngjong's Reign

When the military leaders enthroned Myŏngjong in 1170, they relegated this new king to a subservient position where he became a pawn in the ensuing power struggles. Myŏngjong's reign, one of the most troubled periods in Koryŏ history, witnessed the near collapse of the Koryŏ state. Generals rose in rapid succession through coups and countercoups, and this plunge into anarchy was not arrested until General Ch'oe Ch'unghŏn launched his own coup in 1196 and forced Myŏngjong to abdicate in 1197. This chapter explores the social and political turmoil that besieged Myŏngjong's period of rule. Although the new military leaders sought to redraw the lines of authority between military and civilian officials, they failed in arriving at a new balance. This period vividly shows what happens to any society that loses restraint and gives way to personal whim and cupidity. A product of this age of treachery, General Ch'oe Ch'unghŏn struggled to quell the unrest and find mechanisms to return the kingdom to its former days of glory under his personal authority.

Military in Control

In 1170 the military leaders quickly became the arbiters of power. Although they enthroned Myŏngjong to serve as king and relied on the dynastic institutions to assist in governing, the new regime depended on the military structure and military personnel to lead. In attempting to shape policy, Chŏng Chungbu, together with Yi Ko and Yi Ŭibang, turned to the Council of Generals for assistance. The council had played a significant role during the coup by deciding which civil officials should be spared from prosecution.[1] Now that the

28

revolt was over, Chŏng Chungbu and the other ringleaders worked through the Council of Generals to determine policy. As a supreme consultative body, the Council of Generals deliberated on proper punishments, judicial matters, and even the administration of the civil dynastic structure.[2] In many respects, the Council of Generals assumed the key tasks that the State Council had performed previously. The council also constructed policy to curtail civilian power. It called for a reduction in the number of civil positions. It recommended that palace attendant positions be made concurrent with other offices.[3] It oversaw the civil appointment process, as well, and managed military policy, ordering the dispatch of patrols and enforcing its own form of military justice.[4]

In operation the Council of Generals, like the State Council, depended on consensus in determining policy. Thus the essential oligarchic decision-making process that had been so basic to Koryŏ life before 1170 was carried into the Council of Generals. But now, in place of the ranking civil ministers, generals took over responsibility for many programs. During the first half of Myŏngjong's reign, leaders in the Council of Generals oversaw much of the dynastic authority. In times of peace, this mechanism afforded a degree of stability. But within a few years it had immobilized the regime. With no single person, not even Chŏng Chungbu, able to dominate the state, ambitious officials resorted to power plays, assassinations, and counterassassinations to bolster their positions and control the state.

Chŏng Chungbu was, at best, the first among equals. For Yi Ko and Yi Ŭibang were also contenders for power. Each of these men was in the Kyŏllyong army and, as noted earlier, played a key role in developing the 1170 coup. Through the Council of Generals they established the major contours of state policy. The ruling military leaders also incorporated many civilians into the governing process. The role of certain civilian leaders and their affiliation with military officers in the months before and after the 1170 coup is transparent. Civilian leaders helped stabilize the new military regime and through their efforts brought a degree of legitimacy to the period.

Dynastic Structure

An examination of the civil dynastic structure from 1175 to 1196, when Ch'oe Ch'unghŏn took control, illuminates the subtle changes that were occurring in this period. Among the striking developments were leadership changes—especially the new prominence of military officers—and institutional and social changes as seen in the weakening of class distinctions as a barrier to high office.

Civilians continued to hold a majority of the offices in the dynastic administration at this time (1175–1196).[5] Of the seventy-six men found to have held civil rank during this period, forty-six (61 percent) entered the government through civilian posts and were classified as civilians. Twenty-six men—some 34 percent of the people who held office in the civil ranks—were originally military officers. The service backgrounds of four men are unclear. Compared to the first five years after the coup, as described in Chapter 1, the changes during this period are much more dramatic. Participation of military personnel swelled from 20 percent to 34 percent. Coupled with this change was a decline in the number of men who had passed the state examination. Only thirty-four men (45 percent) were successful candidates, 5 percent less than the earlier period. Nevertheless, given that 74 percent of the civilians had successfully completed it, the examination clearly remained an important step for civilian entrance into dynastic service.

Socially significant trends appear as men lacking in lineage reached prominent office alongside those of highborn lineage. Some thirty-one men or nearly 41 percent had fathers who held the fifth rank or higher, and about two-thirds of that group also had grandfathers who had reached the same rank. Although this figure is comparable to those from earlier periods, there is an increase in the number of men who came from obscure, inferior, or otherwise undistinguished backgrounds. Individuals like Yi Ŭimin, Pak Sunp'il, Ch'oe Sebo, and Cho Wŏnjŏng all came from humble backgrounds that would have barred them from holding high rank in earlier reigns.[6] When recalling the strict social legislation that marked Koryŏ rule prior to 1170, the rise to prominence of men of socially inferior origin is a significant trend that had an immediate—and negative—impact on the quality and effectiveness of the dynastic government.

The composition of the State Council reflects these trends. Although the Council of Generals assumed many of the functions of the State Council, generals held concurrent posts in both agencies, indicating that the functions of these two bodies were merging at this time.[7] The Council of Generals also called upon the State Council to legitimize its decisions and summoned it to meet with the king to approve policy devised by the generals. Of thirty-five state councillors during this period, sixteen (slightly less than half) were military officers, while eighteen were clearly identified as civilians. Given that until 1170 only civilians entered the State Council, the effects of the coup are immediately clear. The social change is equally dramatic as men of socially humble backgrounds, men like Pak Sunp'il, Ch'oe Sebo, and Yi Ŭimin, also took positions in this prestigious body. Slightly less than half of the men (fourteen) had fathers who held the fifth rank or higher. This too represents a decline from the earlier reign.

In reviewing the general composition of those holding offices in these posts, other trends emerge. Military officers occupied many positions, nearly equaling the number of civilians in the Security Council, the Censorate, and a number of ministries. But civilians continued to monopolize such offices as the Ministry of Rites, the Royal Secretariat–Chancellery, and the Office of Examiner *(Chigonggŏ)*. As the Ministry of Rites oversaw ceremony and upheld Confucian learning, civilian officials naturally occupied posts there. Similarly the Office of Examiner conducted the state Confucian examinations, a function little suited to military officers. In the third to seventh rank of the Royal Secretariat–Chancellery, there were no military officers according to this survey. Of those members identified, all but one had passed the state examination. At this level, much of the actual drafting and reviewing of government measures occurred. Although the Council of Generals together with the State Council determined policy, this lower group oversaw much of the preliminary work and assessment of policy. These tasks demanded men of proven bureaucratic ability.

The men occupying these offices during Myŏngjong's reign reflected the new trends marking the period. Although civilians held a majority of administrative posts and a high percentage of them had passed the state examination, military officials shared authority. As service barriers eroded, so too did the rigid class distinctions that had prevented men of inferior origin from assuming key posts. As men with less administrative experience began to govern, the results led to serious problems for the kingdom—problems that might have been even more troubling if not for the dedicated leadership of certain civilians and military personnel during the first decade or so after the coup. But the actions of these talented men, as we shall see, were not sufficient to prevent the chaos that ensued by the mid-1180s.

Struggles Within the Military

The leaders of the coup had many internal difficulties to overcome. Of the three men, Yi Ŭibang, Yi Ko, and Chŏng Chungbu, Chŏng was a general whereas both Yis were at the lower rank of executive captain (*sanwŏn,* senior eighth grade). Yi Ko and Yi Ŭibang, along with Ch'ae Wŏn, were key people who aggressively pushed for a coup; Chŏng Chungbu and other generals were more moderate in their designs. It was Yi Ko and Yi Ŭibang, in fact, who elicited Chŏng's support in the mid-1160s to draw upon his contacts with other key military officers.[8] It did not take long for the tensions between these men to explode. Within four months of the 1170 coup, Yi Ko had killed several military leaders who criticized his behavior. Immediately after this incident, Yi Ŭibang murdered Yi Ko. Four months later, a jealous Yi Ŭibang killed another military officer, Ch'ae Wŏn.[9] Realizing their vulnerability, Yi Ŭibang and Chŏng Chungbu concluded a pact of amity that lasted until 1176, when Chŏng's son Kyun suddenly assassinated Yi Ŭibang. After Chŏng and his son eliminated Yi Ŭibang, men of more moderate temperament took charge. But in the process ordinary soldiers who had hopes of advancing to positions of importance saw their dreams smashed.

Tensions split the kingdom when, a year later, Kyŏng Taesŭng, a young general in his twenties, murdered Chŏng Chungbu and his son Kyun. Kyŏng Taesŭng, indignant at the failures of the military leadership, vowed to restore full power to the monarch and expel evil from the kingdom. Although, like his immediate predecessors, he embarked on policies that attempted to moderate conditions emerging out of the 1170 coup, this action won him the enmity of many. Within five years he was dead, a victim of strain and anxiety.[10]

Kyŏng Taesŭng's short rule is noteworthy for several reasons. First, although he vowed to restore civil rule, the Council of Generals continued to determine policy.[11] Second, he developed a special guard detachment called the Tobang. This was an innovation that Kyŏng Taesŭng had devised to bring together loyal followers to act as a personal bodyguard. The histories note that after Kyŏng Taesŭng had killed Chŏng Chungbu, "in fear he summoned a suicide squad of some hundred and ten people and stationed them at his house. Calling them the Tobang, he used them as a personal guard."[12] Finally after Kyŏng Taesŭng died, a new man, Yi Ŭimin, seized control of the kingdom.

Yi Ŭimin, the son of a slave, embodied the treachery that rapidly engulfed the kingdom. Initially attracting the attention of Ŭijong, Yi Ŭimin found his way into the capital army where he won the king's favor because of his skill in the martial arts and quickly advanced to the rank of subcolonel (*pyŏlchang*, senior seventh grade). With the military coup, he became senior colonel (*chungnangjang*, senior fifth grade) and then general. Enjoying support especially from Yi Ŭibang, Yi Ŭimin's arrogance saw no limits. In 1173, he murdered Ŭijong. Despite this criminal act, Yi Ŭimin advanced to the highest military ranks and helped suppress some of the more dangerous rebellions of the age.[13] When Kyŏng Taesŭng came to power, Yi Ŭimin, suddenly out of favor, retreated to his home region in Kyŏngju and waited for a change in the political environment. Once Kyŏng died, Yi Ŭimin returned to the capital.

Myŏngjong's weakness as a monarch is exposed in his ties with Yi Ŭimin. Fearing that Yi Ŭimin might cause a rebellion if he remained in Kyŏngju after Kyŏng Taesŭng's death, the king welcomed him to the capital. Because of Yi Ŭimin's physical size, he threatened Myŏngjong and, emboldened by sycophants eager for power, took charge of the country. Nevertheless, Yi Ŭimin recognized that by maintaining friendly ties with the king he would be free to pursue his own interests and gain royal patronage at the same time.[14] As Yi Ŭimin's autonomy grew and he became the sole arbiter in the kingdom, he brushed aside such institutions as the Council of Generals and used the civil bureaucracy to carry out his will. He and his sons plundered the kingdom from 1184 until 1196. In that year another general, Ch'oe Ch'unghŏn, assassinated him.

There was considerable unrest during Myŏngjong's rule as new power relationships developed and rivalries erupted among the various military leaders. To secure their positions and back their designs with force, a number of military officers began to cultivate followers known as *mungaek* (retainers). Private military units had been a source of strength for earlier autocratic civilian leaders like Yi Chagyŏm,[15] and once the 1170 revolt was over the private forces expanded rapidly. When Ch'ae Wŏn was murdered shortly after the 1170 coup,

many of his own soldiers died with him. Similar deaths followed Yi Ŭibang's assassination in 1176.[16] Besides these ringleaders, men like Cho Wŏnjŏng formed their own clique of attendants who were little more than bodyguards.[17]

Kyŏng Taesŭng's guard unit, the Tobang, institutionalized these trends and reveals the operation of private forces. Kyŏng Taesŭng had about a hundred and ten men in his Tobang. With this group stationed at his home for protection, he had them guard on alternating days. He provided them with pillows and blankets and even slept with them under the same blankets to show his commitment to them.[18] The bonds of loyalty between leader and retainer were so strong that once this tie was severed, leaderless retainers posed a threat. After Kyŏng Taesŭng died, for example, Kim Chagyŏk, the commander of his Tobang, tried to collect funds to cover a proper funeral and later falsely reported that the Tobang planned a rebellion. The authorities, sensing a threat to order, dismantled Kyŏng Taesŭng's Tobang by banishing or executing most of his soldiers.[19] The widespread use of private forces contributed to the disarray in the political structure and the disorder of the day.

Men of civilian ranks added to the turmoil that followed the coup when they launched several abortive countercoups. The first occurred in 1173 with the revolt of Kim Podang, a military commissioner for the northeastern district. After being demoted to executive of the Ministry of Public Works (kongbusirang, senior fourth grade) in 1171, Kim Podang grew antagonistic toward the new military leaders. Finally, in 1173, he mustered troops in northeastern Korea with the intent of killing Yi Ŭibang and Chŏng Chungbu and restoring the king to full authority.[20] Although the military leaders suppressed this revolt within a month, another civilian, Cho Wich'ong, an official at the Western Capital (Sŏgyŏng), mobilized troops in the northwest with the same goal the following year. Cho Wich'ong had been minister of military affairs (pyŏngbusangsŏ, senior third grade) at the end of Ŭijong's reign and most likely was dismissed with other civilians at this time. Smarting over the setbacks to civilians, he eluded the military for a year and a half before they captured him.[21] These two revolts—occurring in the north and led by men with similar motives—dramatically revealed the hazards confronting the new military leaders. The north had been the site of Myoch'ŏng's rebellion in 1135, and because it bordered the frontier was especially vulnerable to foreign threats. These two incidents also reflect a disdain that had built up in the north toward the central government. When summoned effectively, this attitude would challenge the new military leadership.[22]

Koryŏ society slowly disintegrated in the last decades of the twelfth century. Despite the efforts of the new military leaders to consolidate power under the Council of Generals and to retain a semblance of administrative coherence through the operations of the civil dynastic structure, the central government lost its ability to rule. The rise of men who lacked administrative training—some of them soldiers, others of humble origins—undoubtedly contributed to mismanagement. Power struggles among the top military leaders did not just bring individuals to blows, but also sparked contests among their military followers. Angered by the overthrow of civilian power, civilians too revolted. These revolts were followed shortly by massive peasant and monk uprisings. When Yi Ŭimin, denounced by later Confucian scholars for being the son of a slave, took over in 1184, all restraints disappeared and plunder and theft became the standards of the day.

1170–1196: Ch'oe Ch'unghŏn's View

Shortly after Ch'oe Ch'unghŏn led his coup in 1196, he reflected on the tragedies of Myŏngjong's reign. In a ten-point proposal for reform, he denounced the misgovernment of the previous two decades.[23] He attacked the bureaucracy, the powerful families, the Buddhist hierarchy, and the monarch himself for ineffective policies that had pushed the kingdom close to total collapse. Through these proposals he touched on the chaos engendered by peasant revolts, the disturbances caused by monks, and the perfidy of slaves. The Ch'oe reform agenda gives us insight into the turmoil of Myŏngjong's reign, but it must be studied with caution. Many of the criticisms of the period and the king are cited to justify Ch'oe's action. Furthermore, when the compilers of the *Koryŏsa* in early Chosŏn sought to depict this age, they latched onto these proposals as a means to reiterate their own indictment of military misrule. Nevertheless, Ch'oe's list offers a window into the growing anarchy that marked this age.

To Ch'oe Ch'unghŏn, the bureaucracy was at fault. In four of the ten points, he berates officials for their lax management of government affairs and their self-aggrandizement while letting the kingdom slip toward political and social bankruptcy. In Proposal 2, he claims that the inordinate number of officials is creating fiscal havoc:

> 2. Lately there has been an excess of people in the two departments (*Munhabu* and *Ch'umirwŏn*) and various ranks. The salaries are insufficient and evils have spread.

Ch'oe Ch'unghŏn wanted to reform the entire dynastic apparatus. In 1184, twelve years before he wrote this memorial, the Council of Generals had made a similar appeal, attempting to curtail in particular the number of civil offices.[24] Besides the excessive number of civil officials, Ch'unghŏn attributed many of the problems of Myŏngjong's reign to corrupt officials. In Proposals 4, 5, and 7, he discusses this issue:

> 4. Rents from private and public land all come from the people. If the people are in poverty, how can enough payments be collected? The clerks are no good. They only seek profits and harass and injure the people. The slaves of powerful houses fight to collect land rents and the people all groan: anxiety and pain flourish.

> 5. The various circuit (*to*) commissioners ought to investigate conditions, but they do not. Rather they demand exactions, and on the pretense of presenting them to the king they burden the stations to transport them. Sometimes, however, they pocket them for private expenses.

> 7. Many functionaries in the provinces are greedy and their behavior is shameless. The various circuit commissioners who are sent out do not question this. When people are honest they do not commend them. They allow evil to continue and honesty to be of no benefit. How can one reprove vice and promote goodness?

In Proposal 8, Ch'oe Ch'unghŏn criticizes the bureaucrats for their ostentatious behavior:

> 8. Today court officials are neither frugal nor thrifty. They repair their private houses, make their clothes, and decorate them with precious materials. They adore the exotic. Their customs have degenerated and soon they will be in disarray.

Unhappy with the dynastic officialdom, Ch'oe Ch'unghŏn believed that an increase in talented men would assure reform. As we have seen, prior to his coup there had been an increase in the number of men in high dynastic positions who came from obscure, inferior, or otherwise undistinguished backgrounds. Yi Ŭimin and others of humble origins would have been barred from holding important posts during earlier reigns. Besides men of low status, eunuchs took positions of power where they too abused their authority and committed crimes.

Men of slave ancestry achieved new freedoms during Myŏngjong's reign. Some used these rights to gain manumission and others to achieve economic security. In 1188, an instructive incident occurred:

> Executive (p'yŏngjangsa) Kim Yŏnggwan's house slave P'yŏngnyang once lived in Kyŏnju. Through hard work at farming, he became rich and influential. He was manumitted from his low (ch'ŏn) status and became a commoner (yangmin) with the position of executive captain (sanwŏn tongjong). His wife was the house slave of deputy director (sogam) Wang Wŏnji. Wŏnji's house was poor, however, so he entrusted his family to P'yŏngnyang. P'yŏngnyang generously consoled him, urging him to return to the capital. Secretly with his wife's brothers, Inmu and Inbi, they then killed Wŏnji's wife and children.[25]

Although the Censorate ultimately intervened and banished P'yŏngnyang, he had used his money and influence to raise his status to that of a commoner. It is impossible to ascertain how many other slaves broke social barriers through money and influence, but during this period slaves played many roles. This passage also shows that wives of slaves occasionally lived apart from their husbands and belonged to different masters. Slave owners, as in the case of Wang Wŏnji, might even attach themselves to former slaves for security.

Slaves assisted their masters in amassing property and wealth. In 1177, Yŏm Sinyak's slave, who had been dispatched to collect grain from Yŏm's field, had an altercation with another slave that ultimately cost Yŏm his post.[26] Of interest here is the fact that Yŏm used his slave to manage his fields and collect profits. Masters also sent slaves on official missions to China. Song Yuin's slave, relying on Song's power, went to Chin against the orders of the man heading the mission and was not stopped until Chin authorities refused him entry.[27] Slaves would help their masters accumulate goods and wealth from these profitable missions.

The relation between master and slave was close. Slaves could implicate their masters through their actions. Yŏm Sinyak lost his post because of his slave's deportment, as did Wang Kong when his slave fought with another slave over commodities. And when a master lost, his slaves also suffered. After assassinating Yi Ŭimin, Ch'oe Ch'unghŏn dispatched officials to the countryside to punish Yi Ŭimin's slaves and attendants.[28] Even though slaves were somewhat vulnerable, during much of Myŏngjong's reign the slave's life was improving. Given this broad emancipation, it is not surprising that slaves participated in only one major disturbance during this period. They had no reason to challenge the new order, for they were advancing and enjoying a considerable degree of mobility in their new status.

Other members of the humble classes experienced a similar rise in fortune at this time. Eunuchs, traditionally of low social rank, assisted in determining policy. They surrounded the king and through royal favors influenced many events. On one occasion eunuchs and high-ranking officials in the Censorate met for bathing and drinking.[29] Coupled with this relaxation in codes related to social behavior came changes in the customary limitations (hanjik) for bureaucratic advancement. Cho Wŏnjŏng, the son of a jade artisan and government slave, could not advance beyond the seventh rank during Ŭijong's reign, but with the 1170 coup he took the highest offices. Yi Chunch'ang offers a similar case:

> Yi Chunch'ang's mother was the daughter of one of Yejong's palace women. According to the old precedents, concubines were of mean status and their children and grandchildren were limited in their official advancement to the seventh grade. Only those who passed the state examination reached the fifth grade. Chunch'ang was appointed to the third grade.[30]

Slaves, eunuchs, and others of low status advanced into positions of importance. Witnessing the declining caliber of the Koryŏ officialdom, Ch'oe Ch'unghŏn believed this development was directly responsible for the growing peasant unrest.

Recognizing that the unbridled activities of slaves, eunuchs, and unscrupulous officials afflicted the peasantry, he complained that "all the people groan: anxiety and pain flourish." More than a dozen peasant revolts broke out across the kingdom during Myŏngjong's

reign. Throughout Korean history peasants have revolted during
times of hardship. Some hoped merely to correct the injustices of
their age; others sought to establish a new social order. During
Ŭijong's reign, peasant unrest had become serious. In 1162 and then
in 1168 disturbances forced the central government to dispatch
troops and officials. These uprisings could often be traced to poverty.
Perhaps more than military officials, the most oppressed groups were
the peasants and the socially restricted. Poverty was overwhelming
among the peasants: in one incident corvée workers, who were usually farmers, had to provide their own provisions while working on
state projects. One laborer was too poor even to provide this, however, and depended on his comrades for food:

> One day his wife came with food and said, "Please ask your friends
> to come and eat." The worker said, "Our family is poor. How did
> you provide food? Did you have relations with another man to get
> it, or did you steal it?" His wife replied, "My face is ugly, with whom
> could I be intimate? I am stupid, how could I steal? I simply cut
> my hair and sold it." Then she showed her head. The worker
> sobbed and could not eat. Those who heard this were very sad.[31]

High taxes, loss of property, and poor land administration also took
their toll, forcing peasants off the land. During the reigns of both
Ŭijong and Myŏngjong, the luxurious lifestyle pursued by the king
and his associates exacerbated this situation by enervating the court
and slowing its response to peasant discontent.[32] Ch'oe Ch'unghŏn
criticized this behavior in his reform proposals.

To stabilize the peasantry, sound administration was imperative.
In the first years after the 1170 coup, the central government sought
to assert its authority over the various regions and in fact intensified
its attempts to govern rural Korea. Throughout the 1170s, the
dynasty established district offices in many new areas. In 1178 it reor-
ganized and expanded the Western Capital office system.[33] During
the same period, the office of the royal commissioner for inspection
(ch'albangsa), which had not been used since Injong's reign, was
reactivated by dispatching officials to the countryside to inquire into
the people's livelihood. To expedite rural administration, the leadership made the office of royal commissioner for the promotion of
agriculture (kwŏnnongsa) a joint appointment with the royal inspector (anch'alsa).[34]

This expanded system did not work. Judging from the excessive criticism Ch'oe Ch'unghŏn leveled against regional administrators in his ten proposals, honest local officials were scarce. To support the new district offices, moreover, the dynasty needed vitality to enforce its commands. But because of the spreading political chaos, the kingdom was unable to assure uniform administration or enforce its directives. Peasants might have objected to expanded government control, in any case, for it meant more interference and more expense without added protection. To give special voice to their grievances, they were able to take advantage of regional loyalties and the political aspirations of regional military officers.[35] If regional policy had been firmer and the administration better coordinated, peasants would not have had the opportunity to vent their grievances. But the opposite occurred and peasant rebellions rocked the kingdom.

By the middle of Myŏngjong's reign, as the central authority withdrew its agents to the capital, much of rural Koryŏ was left to itself. Local leaders or randomly dispatched central officials assumed command and then arrogated revenues to themselves, thus depleting the dynastic treasury. When the latter was finally exhausted in 1186, the court looked first to officials at regional administrative divisions (mok) to provide loans. Profits from the land were available, but local officials, not the court, pocketed most of the benefits. Ch'oe Ch'unghŏn berated such behavior.

Ch'oe Ch'unghŏn also criticized the Buddhists. Buddhism had been a powerful religious force as well as an influential dynastic institution. Buddhist temples had been the destination of many of Ŭijong's excursions, and monks had close ties to aristocrats and the royal family. During Myŏngjong's reign princes often became monks while still remaining at court to participate in Koryŏ politics.[36] In Proposal 6, Ch'oe Ch'unghŏn discussed the debilitating consequences of such behavior:

> 6. Now only one or two monks are mountain dwellers. Monks loiter around the royal palace and enter the royal sleeping quarters. Your Majesty, lost in Buddhism, on each occasion has allowed them to do this. The monks already abuse your good graces, and through their activities tarnish your virtue. But Your Majesty has aided them by commanding the palace attendants (naesi) to take charge of the three jewels [Dharma, Buddha, and Sangha], and they use grain to collect interest [through loans] from the people.

The evils from this are not trivial. Only Your Majesty can expel the monks and keep them away from the palace and refuse interest on grain loaned to the people.

In addition to the interference of monks in politics, Ch'unghŏn decried the proliferation of Buddhist temples built by high-ranking government officials. Becoming in effect private foundations, individual donors used these temples to arrogate power to themselves. Ch'unghŏn attacked them in Proposal 9:

> 9. In T'aejo's day, temples were constructed taking into account favorable and unfavorable topographical features. This, accordingly, made the country peaceful. In later ages, ministers, generals, ranking officials, and unreliable monks, without examining the topographical conditions, built Buddhist buildings and named them their prayer halls. Injuring the earth's vital system, they often produced calamity. Please, only Your Majesty can make the geomancy officials investigate and remove any structures not built by the dynasty. Do not let yourself become an example of ridicule for later generations.

The Buddhist establishment was an independent power whose activities threatened the realm as well as military officials like Ch'unghŏn. In 1174, more than two thousand monks from Chunggwang temple, Hongho temple, Kwibŏp temple, and Honghwa temple gathered in an attempt to assassinate the military leader Yi Ŭibang and his brother. These temples were affiliated with the Doctrine (Kyo) Buddhist school, which numbered among its clergy many members of the royal family. Because of this association, the school had wielded significant political and economic power. As one of the major landowners of the age, the Doctrine school also depended on the integrity of the land system. Thus the military's seizure of power challenged this school's economic position.[37] The Doctrine clergy participated in revolts against the generals with the goal of restoring the supremacy of the king and the traditional order in order to protect their economic interests.

The royal family itself may have instigated the Doctrine school's revolt in 1174. This is indicated by the monks' demand, immediately after the assassination of Yi Ŭibang in 1176, for the dismissal of Yi Ŭibang's daughter, who had been thrust upon the crown prince as a wife. Yi Ŭibang's attempt to intermarry with the royal family had enraged the court and forced it to look to the clergy for help. Since the king's brother was a monk at Hungwang temple, a prestigious Doctrine site, and he generally had amicable relations with the school, the court may have turned to the Doctrine temples for aid in reestablishing its authority by reducing the power of the new military leadership and killing men like Yi Ŭibang. Using Buddhist influence to maintain its own authority, the court continued to be an active patron of Buddhism throughout Myŏngjong's reign. Members of the royal family joined the Buddhist clergy and established themselves at famous temples. Monks in turn protected royal buildings and joined dynastic armies.[38] Monks were a potent instrument of royal will. As demonstrated in their complicity in the assassination attempt on Yi Ŭibang, they interfered in politics and contributed to the instability of the era.

The royal family's association with the Buddhist hierarchy and its involvement with the conspiracies of the day caused Ch'oe Ch'unghŏn great concern. As head of the kingdom the monarch was the major legitimizing force in the dynasty. It was inconceivable for the military leaders to rule without a king selected from the royal Wang clan. Furthermore, the royal succession had to be explained to China and its approval obtained before enthronement officially took place.[39] Much legislation mandated royal approval. Even though the military leaders often controlled Myŏngjong, using him as a rubber stamp for their policy, the king was able to select officials and recruit his own associates into the dynastic service. The king established the moral climate of the kingdom. If he were a just ruler and scrupulous in his deportment, officials too would have to be circumspect in their behavior. But Myŏngjong—whether he was encouraged by military officers or was similar in character to his brother Ŭijong—took little interest in court affairs. He concerned himself with wine and women. He discussed appointments with eunuchs and favorites and allowed unruly competition and bribery to become common practice.[40] Royal offspring, using temples as their official residences, returned to the court and interfered in politics through their concubine mothers. All of these nefarious activities associated with the court especially concerned Ch'oe Ch'unghŏn, who aimed to build his authority through the legitimacy of the monarchy.

Fiscal irresponsibility, as we have seen, depleted the king's treasury and forced the dynasty in 1189 to borrow from local officials. Court officials not only ignored royal finances but disregarded general state policy. Ch'oe Ch'unghŏn attacks this neglect in Proposal 10, asking the king to seek wise advice and accept remonstrance:

> 10. The officials of the Royal Secretariat–Chancellery and Censorate have a duty to speak out on state affairs. If the king has deficiencies, they should admonish him regardless of danger to themselves. At present they all flatter, abase themselves, and blindly agree without discretion.

In this proposal Ch'oe calls for resuscitation of the Censorate, which had fallen into disuse, and thereby signals his future use of remonstrance as an instrument of change.[41]

The king's failure to return to his official palace created additional problems. In Proposal 1, Ch'oe Ch'unghŏn warns that this negligence will lead to dynastic disorder:

> 1. T'aejo . . . built a great palace so his descendants as rulers would live there for myriad generations. A while ago the palace was burnt and then rebuilt in a grand style. But because of beliefs in the theory of divination, for a long time it was not occupied. How can one just rely on yin and yang? Only your majesty on a proper day can enter to occupy it and follow the eternal heavenly commands.

To Ch'oe Ch'unghŏn and others, Myŏngjong bred instability.

In Proposal 3, Ch'oe Ch'unghŏn criticizes the arrogance of clans seeking their own self-enrichment:

> 3. Those in office, however, have become very greedy and have snatched both "public" and "private" land and held them indiscriminately without distinction. A single family's holdings of fertile land may extend across districts, causing the nation's taxes to decline and the military to wither.

Individuals not only increased their power through illegal landholding. As noted in Proposal 9 and seen in the case of Yŏm Sinyak, they also sent slaves to the countryside to enlarge their economic holdings by unethical means. Ch'oe Ch'unghŏn argued that these abusive activities weakened the dynasty's fiscal structure by curtailing government revenues. The perpetrators of these illegalities, powerful officials in particular, had to be purged.

All ten proposals reiterate the same theme: the governmental machinery must be revitalized and the excesses of Myŏngjong's reign checked. Special attention is focused on the problems of the common people and the social and political conditions that left the people and government vulnerable to the unethical. The chaotic conditions were to some extent the product of a weakened administration, an ineffective monarch, excessive Buddhist influence, and avaricious individuals. But equally damaging were the numerous revolts and counterrevolts that occurred throughout Myŏngjong's reign. The dynasty needed leadership to contain these destructive, centrifugal elements and to reassert authority over the kingdom. Ch'oe Ch'unghŏn was determined to provide that leadership.

Yi Ŭimin and the Rise of Ch'oe Ch'unghŏn

To Ch'oe Ch'unghŏn, the problems of Myŏngjong's reign were epitomized by the rise to power of Yi Ŭimin.[42] Because of his unusual physical strength, Ŭijong had initially summoned Yi from his home in the Kyŏngju area and placed him in the capital army, where he advanced to the post of supreme general. Notorious for his murder of Ŭijong, Myŏngjong called Yi Ŭimin to the capital after Kyŏng Taesŭng died. The king, fearful of Yi Ŭimin's strength, appointed him to positions that allowed him into the State Council. For twelve years, from 1184 to 1196, Yi Ŭimin was a virtual dictator ruling by whim and plundering the state to suit his greed. The Council of Generals, which had provided a center for military rule, all but disappeared from the dynastic records under Yi Ŭimin. By stifling the Council of Generals, he was able to quiet opposition to his power ploys by other military leaders and thereby place himself in a much more dominant position than earlier military men. Yi Ŭimin eliminated the consensus decision making that had characterized traditional Koryŏ civil and military administration. Thus even though Yi Ŭimin's command of the dynasty was relatively brief, he initiated changes that facilitated the rise of autocratic rule. In the short term, however, this action further inflamed the anger of military personnel like Ch'oe Ch'unghŏn, who were being isolated from positions of influence. In his ten injunctions, as we have seen, Ch'oe Ch'unghŏn spelled out the disasters invited by Yi Ŭimin.

Peasant unrest plagued Yi Ŭimin's rule. Without dynastic leadership and with the kingdom rocked by coups and countercoups, the peasants, now free from close scrutiny, struggled to liberate themselves. The constant abuse of power by Yi Ŭimin and his sons further aggravated discontent. When a certain general sought to pacify a local disturbance but was foiled in every attempt, he discovered that Yi Ŭimin's son Chisun had conspired with local bandits. As soon as Chisun learned of the general's strategy, he would alert the bandits in exchange for a share of the spoils. The general, realizing justice was impossible, committed suicide.[43] Flagrant offenses like this compounded the political, social, and economic disintegration that characterized Myŏngjong's reign. Only the assertion of judicious, authoritarian control could reestablish order. Yi Ŭimin, of base social origins, uneducated except in the politics of greed, failed to build a permanent structure that could foster social and political stability. That task remained for others—especially Ch'oe Ch'unghŏn.

For Ch'oe Ch'unghŏn, as for many other military and civilian officials, the years following the 1170 military coup were difficult and disappointing. Instead of curtailing the mismanagement and corruption that had characterized much of Ŭijong's administration —as his ten-point reform proposal described—the new military leadership aggravated those conditions. There were attempts to rectify the ills of the age, of course, but these were short-lived and erratic. Then, in 1196, Ch'oe Ch'unghŏn assassinated Yi Ŭimin and, in consolidating his power, proceeded on paths distinct from the earlier attempts to rule by Chŏng Chungbu, Kyŏng Taesŭng, and Yi Ŭimin.[44]

The initial cause of Ch'oe Ch'unghŏn's seizure of power, incredible as it may seem, was a dispute over chickens. The dynastic records recount that Ch'oe Ch'unghŏn's younger brother Ch'oe Ch'ungsu complained that he was fed up with Yi Ŭimin and his family—and the last straw was that not only did they steal his chickens but they tied him up when he went to complain. Although Ch'oe Ch'unghŏn was cautious, when confronted with Ch'oe Ch'ungsu's determination to fight he agreed to join a plot. When Yi Ŭimin went off to a mountain retreat, Ch'oe Ch'unghŏn, Ch'oe Ch'ungsu, and several Ch'oe kinsmen attacked. After Ch'ungsu's initial attempt to stab Yi Ŭimin failed, Ch'unghŏn stepped in and beheaded Yi. In shock and fear, Yi Ŭimin's followers fled as Ch'oe Ch'unghŏn and his men raced to report their success and enlist broad support for their cause.[45] Although an altercation over chickens might conceivably have been an impetus to assassinate Yi Ŭimin, there were other motives impelling Ch'oe Ch'unghŏn toward this course of action. The end of the twelfth century was an age of desperate intrigue. During the twenty-six years since the 1170 coup, the general who struck first frequently emerged the victor. And as Yi Ŭimin's atrocities were especially severe, it was inevitable that some military officer would plot a coup. It was Ch'oe Ch'unghŏn's good fortune that the timing and denouement of his attempt were successful.

To the Ch'oe family, Yi Ŭimin represented an inferior level of Koryŏ society. As the son of a slave and a salt merchant, Yi Ŭimin not only came from base origins himself; he also violated the strict Koryŏ social order by elevating others of humble status, such as slaves, into positions of prestige. Ch'oe Ch'unghŏn, by contrast, had a distinguished past. A member of the Ubong Ch'oe lineage, Ch'unghŏn's father, Wŏnho, had been a supreme general. His mother's lineage was of equally important military rank. His maternal grandfather, from the Chinju region in the south, became a supreme general. Ch'unghŏn, taking advantage of his father's rank through a protective *(ŭm)* appointment, took an entry-level post in a civil office. Unhappy after several transfers, he switched to a military post where he could gain greater fame.[46] At the start of Myŏngjong's reign, he achieved recognition for bravery in quelling antimilitary revolts, advanced to be a leader of special patrol troops *(toryŏng)*, and became a commander in the capital divisions. Although his prospects for advancement initially looked promising, additional appointments came slow. His duties during the middle years of Myŏngjong's reign are largely unknown. For a short duration he was a royal inspector in the Kyŏngsang area, from where he returned to the capital, apparently angered by the corruption of powerful officials.[47]

Ch'oe Ch'unghŏn had many grievances. Not only had he failed to advance under Yi Ŭimin's rule but also, as enumerated in his tenpoint proposal, Yi Ŭimin's tyranny had a disastrous impact on the kingdom. To Ch'oe Ch'unghŏn and his family, Yi Ŭimin embodied all that was evil in the current system. Ch'oe Ch'unghŏn's brother called Yi Ŭimin's sons "the country's bandits," and Ch'oe Ch'unghŏn launched his 1196 revolt against Yi Ŭimin both to restore order to the kingdom and to secure his own position of authority.

Yi Ŭimin was a formidable foe. His power was so great that once the assassination plot was hatched, Ch'oe Ch'unghŏn and his brother Ch'ungsu had to move with deliberate speed. They summoned a small cadre of relatives and followers to discuss strategy in secret—thereby catching Yi Ŭimin unaware as he was leaving a mountain pavilion.[48] Once they had executed Yi Ŭimin, the Ch'oe group raced to the capital to forestall reprisals. Although Ch'oe Ch'unghŏn anticipated that the discontent of the populace and officialdom would swing in his favor, he depended upon several key officials such as General Paek Chonyu. Meeting Paek Chŏnyu on the streets of Kaegyŏng, the Ch'oe group urged him to summon the capital guards to support Ch'oe Ch'unghŏn's cause. Assured of backing from these forces, Ch'oe Ch'unghŏn then went to Myŏngjong for royal sanction. On Myŏngjong's approval, Ch'oe's aspirations became the kingdom's cause, enabling him to enlist government forces to defeat Yi Ŭimin's supporters and begin to consolidate his own authority. This operation, completed in less than a day, was a prelude to Ch'oe Ch'unghŏn's total mastery over the kingdom, a process that occupied the ensuing months.

After the Coup

With Yi Ŭimin's forces eliminated, Ch'oe Ch'unghŏn pursued a deliberate, well-planned strategy to secure his command. The greatest threat to his authority came from other military officers who controlled forces capable of leading countercoups reminiscent of the unrest during the 1170s. Within the first eighteen months of Ch'oe rule, Ch'unghŏn purged at least ten generals, six grand generals, and six supreme generals—more than half the leadership of the nearly moribund Council of Generals—thus neutralizing the power of this council and replacing suspect generals with men loyal to his cause. In the first two years of his rule, he removed at least fifty-five people. Thirty-three of these men were from military backgrounds; others in this group included monks, concubines, and people of undetermined social status; five were civilian officials.[49]

Ch'oe Ch'unghŏn generally treated people of civil background with greater leniency. Isolated from ultimate policymaking decisions for more than twenty years, civilian officials were much weaker than military men and offered little threat to the new regime. Perhaps it was his experiences at the start of his career in civil office that made him more favorably inclined to them. Furthermore, Ch'oe Ch'unghŏn encouraged civilians because of their potential in building his authority. Civilians possessing administrative skill and experience were the core of the entire governmental structure. Civilians and civil institutions had to be maintained for the government to operate efficiently. By expanding the role of civilians, who conferred a sense of continuity and legitimacy essential to political stability, Ch'oe Ch'unghŏn balanced the power of the military and thereby reintroduced into the political arena another force—the civil administration—with which any future opponent of the Ch'oe regime would have to contend.

The policies that Ch'oe Ch'unghŏn pursued demonstrate the favored position of civilians. Men with civil backgrounds held many of the key positions in the dynastic structure. Moreover, Ch'oe Ch'unghŏn emphasized the civil service examination. Three months after he assumed power, he held a formal examination that was successfully completed by thirty-seven men—one of the largest groups to pass the examination during the Koryŏ dynasty. The Ch'oe leaders subsequently held more frequent examinations, which were passed by larger groups than in previous years when civilians were in total control.[50] By creating a cadre of followers among civilian officials of the dynasty, incorporating into the system a group of men trained in the classics and Confucian ideology, Ch'oe Ch'unghŏn benefited the dynasty as well as himself.

Although eager to promote men loyal to his rule, Ch'oe Ch'unghŏn had to assure his control over civil institutions. To achieve this, he assumed many civil positions himself. Two months after assassinating Yi Ŭimin, Ch'oe Ch'unghŏn had himself appointed to several positions, including acting chief censor (ch'iŏsadaebu, senior third grade). By taking an office in the Censorate, Ch'oe Ch'unghŏn was able to occupy a position that would enable him to forestall criticism and at the same time attack opponents through formal dynastic mechanisms. Ch'oe Ch'unghŏn was careful not to take the highest civil stations of prestige. He preferred honorary appointments that exalted his merit in eliminating the tyranny of Yi Ŭimin and elevated his reputation as an esteemed leader.

After a year, Ch'oe Ch'unghŏn accepted an appointment as supreme general—the highest military office in the dynasty—but still demurred from taking prominent civil positions. In this subtle consolidation, he joined the Security Council as an administrator of memorials (chijusa, senior third grade)—a position from which he could directly influence this office and its deliberations on military policy. It was not until two and one-half years later that he took charge of the civil ministries of personnel affairs and military affairs. With the dual appointment of administrator of civil personnel (*chiibusa*, junior third grade) and minister of military affairs (*pyŏngbu sangsŏ*, senior third grade), Ch'oe Ch'unghŏn personally assumed command over appointments and promotions within both the military and civil sectors of the dynasty. From these positions he influenced policy without having to resort to measures outside the normal dynastic framework. Playing by the traditional rules of the game, he was able to assure himself of being not only the most powerful player but also the umpire. In subsequent years, Ch'oe Ch'unghŏn continued to attain the highest posts in the civil structure, reaching offices reserved for senior statesmen. Throughout this entire process he was slow and deliberate, avoiding rash moves that could incur criticism and condemnation. Even though some might have opposed him in private, Ch'oe Ch'unghŏn was wise enough to silence this group by cloaking his actions and thus advanced into the top stations of civilian power with legitimacy and prudence.

The same pattern emerges when one studies the marriage ties that Ch'oe Ch'unghŏn established for himself and his family (Figure 2).[51] Marriage links had always been an important means to advance one's political power in traditional Korean society. Kin other than patrilineal relatives were significant in Koryŏ. The founder of the Koryŏ dynasty, Wang Kŏn, alone had twenty-nine wives from all parts of the country. Through his own marital unions, Ch'oe Ch'unghŏn attempted to win the favor and respect of the leading families. When he seized power in 1196, his wife was the daughter of General Song Chŏng. Ch'oe Ch'unghŏn had apparently married into a family of strong military tradition much like his own. Once ensconced in power, he turned his eye toward the prominent clans of the old ruling structure. Of Ch'oe Ch'unghŏn's two new wives selected after 1196, one was a member of the Chŏngan Im descent group. This lineage carried considerable influence during Injong's reign. The mother of kings Ŭijong, Myŏngjong, and Sinjong (r. 1197–1204) was a member of this family, which continued to play a significant role throughout the entire military period. For his next marriage, Ch'oe Ch'unghŏn turned to the court and married the daughter of Kangjong (r. 1211–1213). Through these marriages he was able to associate himself and his authority with one of the most prestigious aristocratic lineages, as well as the royal Wang clan.

Ch'oe Ch'unghŏn pursued very similar stratagems in selecting spouses for his children. One of his daughters married a Chŏngan Im and two of his sons married into the royal family. Ch'oe Hyang married the daughter of Hang, Prince of Such'un, and Ch'oe Song married King Hŭijong's daughter. Ch'oe Ch'unghŏn's immediate heir, Ch'oe U, on the other hand, married the daughter of Hadong Chŏng, Chŏng Sukch'ŏm. This family, like the Ch'oe clan, had established itself as a military household. They first gained recognition during Ŭijong's reign when one of their lineage, Chŏng Sonip, was a grand general in one of the capital units. Just before Ch'oe

Figure 2. Genealogy of the Ubong Ch'oe Lineage

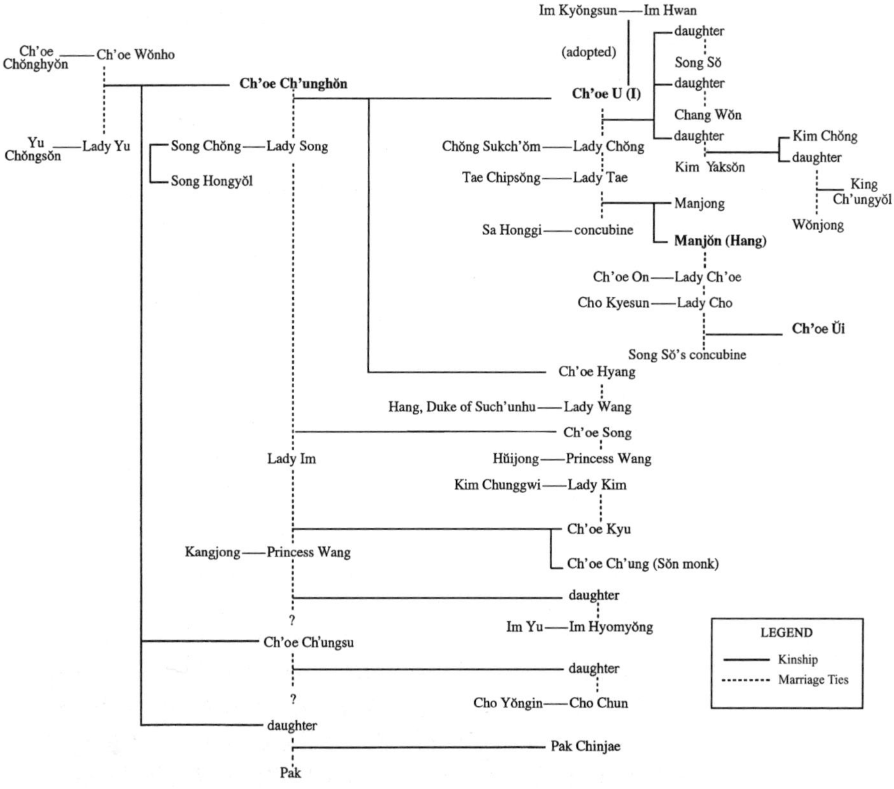

Ch'unghŏn toppled Yi Ŭimin, the Chŏng family clashed with Yi and a number of its members were removed. Benefiting from this early opposition to Yi rule, the Hadong Chŏng lineage, through its ties with the Ch'oe family, sustained its prominence and influence during most of this period. Through these varied marriage ties, one can see Ch'oe Ch'unghŏn's goals quite clearly. He was seeking to bring respect and dignity to the Ch'oe family in status-conscious Koryŏ society through marriages with the court and aristocratic lineages. In establishing ties with prominent military households, he was also assuring himself of additional sources of armed strength and an expanded geographical base of support.

In the years immediately following his rise, however, Ch'oe Ch'unghŏn failed to contain the aspirations of his immediate family. Ch'unghŏn's brother Ch'ungsu, despite Ch'oe Ch'unghŏn's stubborn objections, decided to marry his own daughter to the crown prince in 1197. Although Ch'oe Ch'unghŏn's opposition might have stemmed from jealousy over his brother's attempt to become father-in-law to the crown prince, there is a more probable explanation: he did not wish to violate the rigid social mores of Koryŏ society so soon after his seizure of power, when his authority was not yet absolute. Realizing that marrying one of his family members to the royal heir apparent would incur widespread indignation and foil his plans for consolidating his authority, he tried to block Ch'oe Ch'ungsu. Moreover, Ch'oe Ch'ungsu's action, coming shortly after Ch'oe Ch'unghŏn had forced Myŏngjong to abdicate, was ill timed. Caution and compromise are what Ch'oe Ch'unghŏn advocated when he addressed his brother on this issue:

> Although our power extends throughout the country, our lineage was originally poor and without influence. If your daughter married the crown prince, would we not be criticized? An ancient once said, "If the front carriage falls, the rear carriage should be careful." Earlier Yi Ŭibang married his daughter to the crown prince, and then Yi was killed. Do you want to follow this precedent?[52]

When Ch'oe Ch'ungsu continued to pursue the marriage, Ch'oe Ch'unghŏn fought him on the streets and killed him. The picture is clear: Ch'oe Ch'unghŏn was circumspect and paid close attention to each step lest it be imprudent. Even if Koryŏ social mores permitted

Ch'oe men to marry with prominent lineages, marriage to the crown prince at this stage would have been politically unwise.[53]

Ch'oe Ch'unghŏn approached the royal family with caution. He forced Myŏngjong to abdicate in 1197, one year after his coup, when he had secured his authority, by compelling Myŏngjong to claim illness. The king vacated the throne to his younger brother Sinjong. Fifteen years later, Ch'oe Ch'unghŏn drove Hŭijong into exile. Although he treated these two royals as mere figureheads, he balanced these abrupt acts with measures of respect toward other monarchs. The royal family remained the ultimate source of legitimacy throughout the military period, as the king's approval sanctioned major activities. When kings worked to forward the Ch'oe agenda, Ch'oe Ch'unghŏn responded with lavish rewards and stately ritual to elevate royal prestige.

Ch'oe Ch'unghŏn was deliberate in securing his rule. He purged a number of military officers because they threatened his regime and challenged his system. To those guilty of crimes—such as Ch'oe Pi, who once had intimate relations with a royal concubine—he was especially strict. When Myŏngjong tried to punish the girl, his action was thwarted by Ch'oe Pi's enlistment of Yi Ŭimin. But Ch'oe Ch'unghŏn, after coming to power, banished Pi and others like him to remote parts of the kingdom. He also forced many of the royal princes and monks to return to their resident temples and leave court politics to those trained in administration.[54] Some of these men were among the fifty-five people Ch'unghŏn purged in 1196 and 1197.

Prudent and decisive action enabled Ch'oe Ch'unghŏn to initiate much-needed reform. His stated goals, as well as his performance, show that change and growth were part of his scheme to restore order. Suggestive of his success is an incident occurring at a Buddhist celebration in the eleventh month of 1196, some seven months after Ch'oe Ch'unghŏn had seized control. The *Koryŏsa* reports:

> When Cha Ch'ung saw the superintendent of the Royal Archives, *p'anhammunsa* Wang Kyu, he made a low bow but did not prostrate himself. The officials censured him for his lack of propriety. ... When Cha Ch'ung first left his own town, he addressed the commandant, saying: "When the country summons us, it has something definite in mind. When I enter the court, I want to test

it with a trivial matter. If they punish me, the court has the right
people; if not, then they would be cowed by me."[55]

As indicated, Cha Ch'ung was punished, showing that the court had
the right people.

Ch'oe Ch'unghŏn, schooled by experience during the chaos of
Myŏngjong's reign, charted a new course for Koryŏ. As he outlined
in his ten injunctions, the mismanagement and corruption of the
dynasty's leadership would have to end if peasant unrest and political turmoil were to cease. Furthermore, the military leaders of
Myŏngjong's reign had been unable to find a new equilibrium
between those with military power and those who upheld traditional
civilian norms and dynastic legitimacy. Ch'oe Ch'unghŏn was determined to be the leader to resolve these pressing problems. Through
decisive action in the waning days of Myŏngjong's reign, he set out
to rebuild the dynasty, restore social codes, and at the same time
innovate with new institutions of his own.

3

The Ch'oe House
Military Institutions

With the purge of his major opponents completed and a new monarch, Sinjong, on the throne, Ch'oe Ch'unghŏn set out to build a structure that would assure his family control over the dynasty for the next sixty years. The result was a dual administration that permitted the traditional dynastic organs to function while building an auxiliary series of private agencies that were directly answerable to his commands. These mechanisms of government served him and his immediate successors: his son U (also known as I), his grandson Hang, and finally his great grandson Ŭi. In this manner he initially depended on the dynastic armed forces—the two armies and six standing guards—to support his regime and then slowly enlarged his private force. He pursued an identical strategy in refashioning the civil arm of his command by gradually supplanting dynastic offices with private agencies.

Military might was the foundation of Ch'oe Ch'unghŏn's authority. As we have seen, Ch'oe Ch'unghŏn depended both on his personal followers and on the dynastic units in the capital when he destroyed Yi Ŭimin. At the start of his rule, the capital forces clearly outnumbered Ch'oe's supporters. This state of affairs posed an institutional dilemma: although he needed the military force provided by the capital units, their inherent power meant they could be rallied to destroy him. The very organization of the capital forces balanced military authority among a number of generals, thus making it more difficult for one person to take full control of the military. Furthermore, since it left many people vying for influence, it could lead to renewed instability, as at the start of Myŏngjong's reign. Finally, because the ultimate loyalty of the capital forces was supposed to be directed to the king, not to another political or military figure, Ch'oe Ch'unghŏn's authority was vulnerable. So long as Ch'oe legitimacy was tied to the functioning of the dynastic organs, the Ch'oe rulers would be institutionally exposed. Ch'oe Ch'unghŏn's solution was to support the dynastic military units while at the same time enfeebling their authority and building up his private forces.

Dynastic Forces

After the assassination of Yi Ŭimin and his supporters, Ch'oe Ch'unghŏn paraded the dynastic troops and inspected them several times in 1196 and 1197. As the king's army, these forces gave a stamp of legitimacy to Ch'oe Ch'unghŏn, demonstrating that he had royal favor. Given that his own private forces were too small to assure the kingdom's security, the dynastic military troops were vital to his rule. When his brother tried to overthrow his authority, the capital units championed Ch'oe Ch'unghŏn and guaranteed his victory. But their prominence in the Ch'oe structure was ephemeral.

The Council of Generals (Chungbang), which had all but disappeared under Yi Ŭimin, experienced a quick revival in the first years of Ch'oe's rule and was charged with overseeing the operations of the dynastic troops. Resuscitating the council helped bring a sense of legitimacy to military endeavors. This policy may also have won the favor of reluctant military officers who attached significance to the rehabilitated council. But in reviving this traditional office, Ch'oe Ch'unghŏn took steps that enabled him to command its decisions. The purge of leading generals at the start of his consolidation neutralized opposition to his control and enabled him to fill vacant positions with men loyal to his cause, thereby eviscerating potential opposition to his authority within the Council of Generals. Gradually he relegated the council, which he had packed with relatives such as Chŏng Sukch'ŏm, to ceremonial roles and bypassed it when deliberating major decisions.

When Sinjong ascended the throne in late 1197, the Council of Generals assumed minor ceremonial functions. Rather than administering problems of law and order, it discussed issues related to the nation's topography, the kingdom's foundation, geomancy, and rituals. Although these matters were important to twelfth-century Koryŏ society, they were not customary areas of council responsibility, nor was the council allowed to determine policy. Furthermore, the Council of Generals frequently met with the State Council. No longer a center to determine dynastic policy, the Council of Generals fulfilled an honorary function reserved for senior military officers and did not carry much influence. When an emergency arose, rarely did the council deliberate. When Sinjong died, for example, the authorities called the State Council into session but the Council of Generals never appeared.[1] Furthermore, to assure that the Council of Generals would never attempt to circumvent his leadership, Ch'oe Ch'unghŏn put key relatives there, men who were central to his rule, like kinsman Kim Yakchin or in-law Chŏng Sukch'ŏm.

Ch'oe U continued his father's policy of curtailing the influence of the Council of Generals. Neither Ch'oe leader wished to pursue the extreme strategies of Yi Ŭimin, who had all but eliminated the council. But in 1223, when several generals in the council plotted to murder all civilian officials, U responded at once by banishing all conspirators.[2] The incident is instructive, for it shows that the Council of Generals could be a source of opposition to Ch'oe rule. Several years later, after 1230, the council totally disappears from the histories, a sign of its political and military collapse.[3] The demise of the Council of Generals, moreover, coincided with the disappearance of the capital armies that had been under its control. Ch'oe U, far less dependent on dynastic troops for protection, formed the capital units into an honorary guard that he selected personally.[4] Denied financial support and bypassed in recruitment, the dynastic troops slowly withered.

The emergency armies, which traditionally had been formed throughout the kingdom whenever a domestic or foreign crisis threatened, suffered a similar fate. Toward the end of Ch'oe Ch'unghŏn's rule, Khitans and then Mongols began to plunder Koryŏ's northern border. To meet this threat, Ch'oe Ch'unghŏn mobilized and dispatched three emergency armies in 1216. Within a month, it became apparent that these forces were insufficient. The authorities then formed two additional units, but the army's commander, Chŏng Sukch'ŏm, discovered that his forces were composed of the old and weak.[5] To control these special forces, Ch'oe Ch'unghŏn placed trusted followers like General Chŏng in charge of them.

When there were victories, he summoned the generals back to the capital, rewarding those loyal to his cause and passing over potential opponents.[6] Moreover, in selecting the leaders of these expeditions he prevented any single clique from dominating and often sent civilians as deputy commanders, thereby diluting the leadership.[7]

As northern attacks became severe in the 1220s, Ch'oe U reluctantly released the central army to check the invaders. Again in 1226 and 1227 he dispatched another army, but by this time regional troops defending their home area became more essential in meeting the assaults. The continuing battles and lack of Ch'oe interest so weakened the dynastic troops that when the Mongols commenced their attacks, the Ch'oe House—drained by earlier fights, perhaps aware of the ferocity of the Mongols, and uncertain of its own political position—was even less eager to organize resistance. In 1231, U and his son-in-law, Kim Yakson, summoned their well-trained house troops to protect them, leaving weak troops or young boys and girls to guard the capital.[8] Growing losses ultimately convinced the military leaders that escape to Kanghwa Island was a better defense.

Kanghwa Island, resting just offshore from the estuaries of the Han and Imjin rivers, was a half-day journey from Kaegyŏng. Circled by some of the highest tides in the world, Kanghwa became an excellent haven from the land-bound Mongols. In 1232 the court and the Ch'oe House fled to Kanghwa. The *Koryŏsa chŏryo* relates:

> At that time there was frost and rain for ten days and mud filled the roads sinking people to their shins. People and horses died. Even wives of high officials and rich households went barefoot and carried their loads on their heads. The crippled, widowed, orphaned, and homeless lost their way and cried out. Their numbers were countless.[9]

After the 1232 retreat to Kanghwa Island, the capital units and the emergency armies disappear from the histories (along with the Council of Generals) and no central dynastic force is mentioned until the end of Ch'oe rule. Except for the military commissioners who made occasional appeals for aid, the defense of the kingdom seems to have been relegated to special patrols *(pyŏlch'o)* that offered sporadic guerrilla tactics in an effort to foil Mongol maneuvers.[10] Regional forces waged valiant defenses of their own areas. Coordinated, central resistance surfaced only in random forays by some of the Ch'oe troops onto the mainland to harass the Mongols. The Mongol invasions, by destroying the dynastic armies, completed the job that Ch'oe Ch'unghŏn had commenced through institutional mechanisms.

Ch'oe Troops

The destruction of the dynastic armies did not leave the kingdom defenseless. For as Ch'oe Ch'unghŏn and his son U presided over the depletion of the dynastic units, they recruited soldiers loyal to their cause. Ch'oe forces evolved into three overlapping units: general Ch'oe House troops; an elite guard detachment known as the Tobang; and patrols called Yabyŏlch'o. The practice of military leaders surrounding themselves with private forces had already emerged in Myŏngjong's reign, when generals like Kyŏng Taesŭng formed their private guard detachments. Ch'oe Ch'unghŏn inherited this tradition and refined it to new levels.

When Ch'oe Ch'unghŏn defeated Yi Ŭimin, his base of support came from relatives like his brother Ch'ungsu, nephew Pak Chinjae, and others, including No Sŏksung and Kim Yakchin. The next year, when Ch'oe Ch'unghŏn and Ch'ungsu clashed, Ch'unghŏn marshaled more than a thousand men to his banners and Ch'ungsu commanded a smaller following. Although the dynastic forces fell in with Ch'oe Ch'unghŏn and assured his victory, the real battles took place between the private forces of the two men. These were the men that both Ch'oe Ch'unghŏn and Ch'ungsu depended on for victory. When Ch'oe Ch'ungsu realized that he was greatly outnumbered and without hope of success, he wanted to run. But his followers admonished: "We are your retainers because you have great potential to sway the world. Now, however, to be a coward like this [and not fight] means the extermination of our clans. We beg you to let us fight to decide the winner and loser."[11] The troops and retainers, dependent on their master's fortune, fought not only for their master's life but for their own futures and thus became trusted confidants and active participants in the power structure. Family ties were another bond that transformed private forces into cohesive units.

Over the next twenty years, Ch'oe forces continued to grow rapidly. During this period there were several attempts to assassinate Ch'oe Ch'unghŏn. In each case he was rescued by the quick thinking of his retainers and the loyalty of his troops. King Hŭijong, for example, had long resented Ch'oe Ch'unghŏn's domination of Koryŏ. Encouraged by his aides, he set out on an ill-conceived plot to assassinate Ch'oe Ch'unghŏn. After inviting Ch'oe Ch'unghŏn deep into the palace, monks attacked Ch'oe Ch'unghŏn and his escorts. At first Ch'oe Ch'unghŏn pleaded to Hŭijong for help; rebuffed, he hid and was rescued only when his guards reached him.[12] The histories note that after Hŭijong's failed attempt to kill Ch'oe Ch'unghŏn, Ch'oe private forces increased to such an extent that when they went out on review, they stretched for several *li*. At the start of the Khitan invasions in 1216, Ch'oe's house troops, including those of his son U, numbered more than ten thousand men.[13]

Men flocked to join the Ch'oe forces. In return, they were well treated and lavishly rewarded. When troops marched in review, their weapons were richly decorated with silver to recruit more men. On occasion, *kisaeng* came and offered words of praise after rigorous training sessions or Ch'oe Ch'unghŏn gave out silver vases and fine silk.[14] With such support, Ch'oe soldiers willingly defended Ch'oe interests. When Khitan troops threatened Kaegyŏng in 1216, Ch'oe Ch'unghŏn mobilized his troops to escort him and protect his family. It was this patronage of Ch'oe private forces that caused Chŏng Sukch'ŏm to lament the waning strength of the dynastic troops he was asked to lead.

The transfer of power is always a difficult process and one that Ch'oe Ch'unghŏn consciously planned. Aware that the structure he had erected would not survive a bloody power struggle, Ch'oe Ch'unghŏn began to groom his son U to succeed him and take control of his troops. Ch'oe U emerges in the dynastic records in 1202. Already a general by the middle of Hŭijong's reign, he conferred with the king and performed such ceremonial roles as presenting vases to successful examination candidates.[15] When Ch'oe Ch'unghŏn was approaching death, he summoned U to warn him of a possible incident and instruct him not to attend him during his illness. Ch'oe U followed his father's advice and dispatched Kim Yaksŏn, his son-in-law, to attend to Ch'unghŏn in his place. As the senior Ch'oe had suspected, several leading men in the government tried to trap the heir, but their plans were foiled by a well-prepared U. Thus Ch'oe Ch'unghŏn secured a relatively stable succession for his son. By enabling U to participate in government affairs, build his own private army, and then prepare for counterrevolts, Ch'oe Ch'unghŏn assured the continuation of many of the polices and dreams he had for thirteenth-century Koryŏ society.

Ch'oe U confronted the challenges posed by his enemies and quickly consolidated his succession by checking all opposition. The first casualties of the new rule were the men who attempted to kill Ch'oe U at the time of Ch'unghŏn's death. They had been among the closest military supporters of Ch'oe Ch'unghŏn's authority. But fearing that Ch'oe U's ascendance would leave them without any influence in the government, they chose rebellion and met death.[16] In addition to these men, Ch'oe U purged twenty-eight other people during the first months of his rule, including high-ranking military officers, slaves, household servants, friends, and relatives of Ch'unghŏn. By checking the authority of Ch'oe Ch'unghŏn's closest associates, U demonstrated his determination to take total mastery of the Ch'oe House and tolerate no competition. Sensing treason, he even exiled his own brother Ch'oe Hyang. To Ch'oe U, the greatest threats to his power were men of military background, who were accordingly dismissed in greater numbers than civilians during U's rule.

At the center of Ch'oe U's power structure were his house troops, which he used primarily to protect the Ch'oe family and then to meet other emergencies as conditions permitted. Ch'oe U pursued policies identical to those of his father by carefully drilling these troops and then granting them generous rewards.[17] Their immediate responsibility was to protect the Ch'oe leaders. If fires or attacks threatened the capital, Ch'oe U enlisted Ch'oe troops to protect him and his family rather than meet these dangers. Dynastic concerns were not necessarily ignored, however, for in 1223 Ch'oe U used his troops as a corvée labor force to repair the outer wall of the capital. Ten years later, in 1233, as the government troops neared collapse after continual battles with the Mongols, Ch'oe U dispatched his own private soldiers to pacify a rebellion in Sŏgyŏng.[18] Once ensconced in Kanghwa Island, Ch'oe U allowed his forces to travel to distant regions of the country to reestablish peace. Although their prime function was to protect the Ch'oe House, Ch'oe soldiers assumed responsibility for defending the capital and became the unchallenged arm of Ch'oe authority as the dynastic units atrophied.

As the strongmen in the country, Ch'oe Ch'unghŏn and Ch'oe U amassed the largest private forces but they did allow others to have their own personal troops. Pak Chinjae, Ch'oe Ch'unghŏn's nephew, Kim Yaksŏn, U's son-in-law, and Tae Chipsŏng, U's father-in-law, each maintained private forces as personal bodyguards. As all were relatives and presumably loyal supporters of the Ch'oe House, the Ch'oe leaders could count on the private troops of these men to augment their own. Pak Chinjae's soldiers may have assisted Ch'oe Ch'unghŏn in his early consolidation. The function and size of these private units are not known. But beyond keeping them as personal bodyguards and escorts, the Ch'oe leaders were unwilling to allow them to grow too large or to assume too many duties. Moreover, there is no record of any individual not associated with the Ch'oe power structure supporting private forces. And those who did quarter their own soliders were kept under constant scrutiny by the Ch'oe leaders.[19]

Tobang and Yabyŏlch'o

Two additional units—the Tobang (including its special horse patrol known as the Mabyŏlch'o) and the Yabyŏlch'o—assured Ch'oe control over the kingdom.[20] The primary task of the Tobang (private guard detachment) and the other Ch'oe units, as noted, was to protect the Ch'oe family. The Yabyŏlch'o, however, concentrated on controlling banditry and ventured to remote parts of the kingdom to fight the Mongols. The Tobang was especially vigorous in defending Ch'oe rule at the start of the Ch'oe climb to power, giving way later to the Yabyŏlch'o, which formed a core of the Ch'oe defense. Men in the Tobang as well as the Yabyŏlch'o occasionally held dynastic ranks concurrent with their Ch'oe responsibilities, and some officers held simultaneous positions in both Ch'oe military units.

Modeled on Kyŏng Taesŭng's Tobang, Ch'oe Ch'unghŏn developed this private guard detachment after several attacks on his life. The histories recount:

> Ch'unghŏn feared an incident he could not fathom. From the high and low civil and military officials and reserved officers (hallyang) to the rank and file soldiers, he assembled the strong and powerful and divided them into six units. Changing daily as guards at his residence, they were called the Tobang. Whenever Ch'unghŏn entered and left his house, they joined like an escort going into battle.[21]

Ch'unghŏn personally drilled the Tobang and rewarded them with special favors. Many of the men he recruited into the Tobang came from the elite of the king's palace guards, thus hastening the evisceration of the dynastic forces.[22]

When King Hŭijong plotted to kill Ch'oe Ch'unghŏn in 1211, the Tobang rescued him. Because Ch'oe Ch'unghŏn had carefully recruited and nurtured this group, its loyalty was unshakable. When Ch'oe Ch'unghŏn found himself surrounded and under attack, the Tobang responded immediately. The sources describe the crisis:

> Ch'unghŏn's relative, Supreme General Kim Yakchin, and Ch'oe U's father-in-law, Administrator of Memorials (chiju) Chŏng Sukch'ŏm, were in the Council of Generals. Hearing of the [Hŭijong] incident, they immediately entered the inner palace and helped Ch'unghŏn exit. Ch'unghŏn's followers Instruction Officer (chiyu) Sin Sonju, Ki Yunwi, and others fought with the monks. The six units of Ch'unghŏn's Tobang all assembled outside the palace walls. They did not know if Ch'unghŏn was dead or alive. One Royal Chamber of Recreation (Tabang) member No Yongŭi . . . cried in a loud voice: "Our master is not harmed." Thereupon the Tobang fought to enter and aid him.[23]

Ch'oe Ch'unghŏn's relatives, Kim Yakchin and Chŏng Sukch'ŏm, in addition to their affiliation with the Council of Generals, might also have been associated with the Tobang. Certainly their swift response, coupled with the mobilization of the Tobang, saved Ch'oe Ch'unghŏn's life. Contacts with the royal staff, as seen in No Yongŭi's assistance, also aided the Tobang in its rescue.

On taking over from his father, Ch'oe U incorporated many of the men in his father's Tobang into his own by dividing his guards into inner and outer units. The outer units, comprising primarily Ch'oe Ch'unghŏn's Tobang, protected Ch'oe relatives; the inner Tobang became U's personal defenders.[24] Ch'oe U expanded the Tobang into thirty-six divisions, including the Mabyŏlch'o, which first appeared in 1229 as a unit of specially trained, highly mobile horsemen that doubled as an elite escort and honor guard.[25] During times of peace, the Mabyŏlch'o paraded in fine armor and elaborate saddles; but deployed in an emergency as a crack cavalry unit, it overpowered opponents. After the retreat to Kanghwa Island, the Tobang acquired new duties when Ch'oe U commanded it in 1232 to construct his private residence. This was not customary work for an elite guard like the Tobang. But given the crisis atmosphere and the urgency to build protected quarters for the Ch'oe leader, the Tobang's work on construction was not entirely anomalous. As a military unit, it could easily be mobilized and directed to handle this type of situation.

The Yabyŏlch'o, the third unit in Ch'oe private forces, emerged under Ch'oe U's rule and eventually evolved into the Sambyŏlch'o (Three Patrols).[26] Sometime before 1232, Ch'oe U established the Yabyŏlch'o by selecting brave soldiers and having them patrol and prevent crimes at night. Its proximity to the Ch'oe power structure was evident in 1231 when Ch'oe U discussed with his advisers the feasibility of moving the capital to Kanghwa Island. In the middle of the meeting, a leader of the Yabyŏlch'o entered to offer his unsolicited advice.[27] Ch'oe U, and later his son Hang, sent men in the Yabyŏlch'o to investigate crimes and interrogate prisoners. In this capacity, the Yabyŏlch'o played a dual role by helping to remove both political and military enemies. Before the court moved to Kanghwa Island, the Yabyŏlch'o supported dynastic peacekeeping by suppressing domestic disturbances. After the move, it also performed functions expected of a private guard.[28]

As the power of the dynastic troops faded, the Yabyŏlch'o became the primary force to defend the kingdom against the Mongols and pacify the country when rebels threatened the domestic order.[29] The Mongol invasions were among the most serious threats the Koryŏ dynasty ever confronted, and the burden of resistance fell almost entirely on the Ch'oe family. Unwilling to risk his personal security by dispatching his highly trained private forces into battle, Ch'oe U supplemented his troops with the Yabyŏlch'o. The Yabyŏlch'o assumed the responsibilities abandoned by the shattered dynastic armies. When rebels appeared in the deserted capital of Kaegyŏng, the Yabyŏlch'o advanced; when there were rumors of Mongols, the Yabyŏlch'o would investigate.[30] Beyond these duties, the Yabyŏlch'o continued to function as a personal investigative force for the Ch'oe House. When Ch'oe Hang sought to eliminate an antagonist to his rule, he sent a member of the Yabyŏlch'o to drown the man. On another occasion, it was a member of the Yabyŏlch'o who personally interrogated a prisoner.[31]

During this period, the Yabyŏlch'o gradually transformed itself by merging its responsibilities with those of the Tobang. When Ch'oe U died, the Yabyŏlch'o and the Tobang assembled to bolster the authority of Hang, the new Ch'oe leader. The similarity in their functions and importance is revealed by the fact that both organizations were under the command of one general. On the collapse of the Ch'oe House in 1258, the Tobang again joined the Yabyŏlch'o as royal escorts for the king and as an armed force to support the new leaders in their attempt to consolidate power.[32]

By the end of the Ch'oe House, the Yabyŏlch'o had further evolved into the Sambyŏlch'o. When Ch'oe Hang died, the Yabyŏlch'o, which included a right and left division, joined with the Tobang and another new group, the Sinŭigun (Divine Righteous Troops), to keep the peace.[33] The Sinŭigun included soldiers who had escaped capture by the Mongols and formed a highly skilled group after returning to Koryŏ. Battling Mongols and protecting the key figures of the period, the Sinŭigun combined with the two divisions of the Yabyŏlch'o to form what became known as the Sambyŏlch'o.[34] Korean schoolchildren today regard the Sambyŏlch'o as fervently loyal soldiers who refused to surrender to the Mongols, choosing instead a heroic death while trying to preserve the independence of the Koryŏ kingdom. The more tempered view is that the Sambyŏlch'o realized that surrender to the Mongols spelled doom to their privileges and lifestyle and therefore choose to revolt. The Sambyŏlch'o were the remnants of the same forces that had first been soldiers of the Ch'oe House. When that house collapsed, the new military leaders commanded them until the combined Mongol and Koryŏ forces captured them in 1273.

The size of the Tobang and Yabyŏlch'o is difficult to estimate. At one point thirty-six units comprised the Tobang, but the number of men in each unit is not stated. We know that the Yabyŏlch'o was divided into a right and left division, but few additional details emerge. In 1253, the king escorted by eighty armed Yabyŏlch'o troops met with Mongol leaders. In the next year, the histories report that eighty Yabyŏlch'o came from both Kyŏngsang and Chŏlla to guard the capital. Earlier in 1235, a leader in the Tobang and Yabyŏlch'o received one hundred and sixty men to attack the enemy. Based on this scant evidence, combined with the knowledge that the Yabyŏlch'o assumed increased responsibility for the defense of Koryŏ, the Yabyŏlch'o together with the Tobang might have numbered in the thousands—perhaps as many as five thousand men. This figure is based on a hundred men in each Tobang unit, for a total of thirty-six hundred men, plus at least six hundred men in each Yabyŏlch'o division. Given the figures that appear in the account of the Sambyŏlch'o revolt, these estimates seem plausible. When the rebellion first erupted in 1270, Koryŏ initially sent two thousand men to subdue the rebels. This would have been a sufficiently large force if the Tobang and Yabyŏlch'o troops who revolted had been half the estimated force, or about two thousand. When this deployment was not sufficient to end the rebellion, Koryŏ increased the force to ten thousand troops. In 1273, Koryŏ dispatched more than ten thousand soldiers to wipe out the remaining rebels, who came to include women and children.[35]

The Ch'oe House employed different techniques to assure the loyalty of each of its forces: the general house troops, the Tobang, and the Yabyŏlch'o (Sambyŏlch'o). A number of key figures in the Yabyŏlch'o emerged from poorer families. Enjoying Ch'oe patronage and wealth, they willingly pledged their support.[36] Many of the men in these units retained dynastic ranks with nominal positions in the kingdom's capital units. Thus even though the dynastic armies had all but disappeared as a military force during this age, the Ch'oe House still used the rank system to finance Ch'oe military personnel. A number of Yabyŏlch'o officers held dynastic ranks such as commandant (toryong), instruction officer (chiyu), or lieutenant (kyowi).[37] Furthermore, as special rewards, the Ch'oe leaders distributed rations from the public granaries and tapped other dynastic revenues. The Ch'oe House also relied on its personal resources to augment salaries and showered its troops with rewards and other inducements.

Retainers

Many of the men in these Ch'oe units are also referred to as retainers (mungaek). Men called retainers first appeared shortly after the military coup of 1170 as the new military leaders protected themselves with small cadres of followers. Ch'oe Ch'unghŏn dramatically expanded the number of his personal retainers into the thousands, and other men at this time had retainers as well.[38] Although this retainer phenomenon was so short-lived that the histories provide little discussion, retainers were immensely important to the Ch'oe House rule.[39]

The idea of pledging allegiance to another person is not unique to Korea. Medieval Europe and Japan both developed forms of vassalage that carried the notion of subordination and service between two people. Japan's version, much more informal than the European model, gradually evolved between the ninth and fourteenth centuries, with the relationship based on unwritten or oral contracts specifying individual duties and privileges.[40] A "consensus of common behavior" regulated both parties, but duties remained vague. A pattern of fictive or natural kinship practices formed the underlying principle of the lord/vassal relationship. Although the allegiance of the vassal rested ultimately on the lord's military strength, there was often a bond of personal feeling cemented by material rewards such as land rights.[41] To secure his command, Minamoto Yoritomo placed his followers in various strategic posts in the local government. Through them he was able to control the country. Followers would often serve the personal needs of a lord in his residence, and on a higher level they would aid the lord through public service. This order did not reach its maturity in Japan until the fourteenth century.

Korea in many ways paralleled Japan's medieval development, but the lord/vassal relationships formed there were much less common and less involved than those found in either Japan or Europe. Instead of vassals, men had retainers. These lord/retainer ties began to appear in Koryŏ during the military period. But cut short by the collapse of the Ch'oe House and the return to the strict Confucian bureaucratic system, they never developed into an intricate hierarchy. Much more like the feudal relationships that marked Carolingian France or twelfth-century Japan, those in Korea were not distinguished by written contracts or elaborate ceremonies during the Ch'oe period. Although being a retainer carried the idea of subordination and service, Koryŏ retainers had no promises of benefices (tenements held on easy terms).[42] The pattern of fictive kin relations that characterized Japanese lord/retainer ties was also present in the terminology of the time. Ch'oe retainers were called *mungaek* (house guests) or *chokin* (family persons), but only during the initial stage of growth. If the military period had continued for another century beyond 1270 and the Ch'oe House had not depended so extensively on civil institutions, Koryŏ too might have developed a much more elaborate lord/retainer nexus. But this did not occur.

As seen in Myŏngjong's reign, many of the key figures had retainers who were little more than close confidants. Yet men like Yi Ŭibang and Yi Ŭimin were able to use them to bolster their authority and construct a personal power structure. Retainers were often joined by other men—such as house slaves *(kadong)* who performed menial functions—and together they served the needs of their lords.[43] The fate of retainers, like general followers, depended on the success of the lord.

The retainer system expanded with Ch'oe Ch'unghŏn's consolidation of power. Ch'unghŏn alone had some three thousand retainers, and his nephew Pak Chinjae is reported to have had a significant number as well. Retainers, in offering unquestionable loyalty to the Ch'oe House, became the primary agents of its authority. As trusted confidants they would meet with the Ch'oe leaders to determine policy; as holders of rank in the Ch'oe forces, they executed decisions. In this way, the Ch'oe House efficiently transferred directives to the various military organizations and channeled communications among its units. This system helps explain the overlapping functions of the Ch'oe private military units.

Retainers, found in all of the Ch'oe units, were also dispatched on special missions such as protecting favored monks. Ch'oe U, for example, sent his retainers to guard his ailing favorite, National Tutor *(kuksa)* Chonggak. When he needed to explore the notion of relocating onto Kanghwa Island, Ch'oe U first sent his retainers along with the Tobang to prepare the new capital for inhabitation.[44]

Initially, under Ch'oe Ch'unghŏn, retainers were military personnel; but during U's domination, a number of retainers came from the civilian ranks. Both scholars and retainers could be found in the Chamber of Scholarly Advisers (Sŏbang) and the Personnel Authority (Chŏngbang), where they performed administrative functions. They were well educated: some had even been dispatched to temples by Ch'oe leaders to study under erudite monks.[45] Others, like Ch'oe U's lead retainer *(sanggaek)*, Kim Ch'ang, took charge of recommendations and promotions. Kim Ch'ang, who oversaw the state examination, selected one Han Yusŏn, who had written an especially fine essay, to be one of Ch'oe U's retainers.[46] Like their military counterparts, civilian retainers offered total loyalty to the Ch'oe House and in this way advanced through officialdom, holding titles in the dynasty as well as positions of power in the Ch'oe organization.

The lord/retainer relationship that emerged in Koryŏ in the twelfth and thirteenth centuries was distinct from the lord/vassal ties that appeared in Kamakura Japan in the same period. It is from this time that Korea and Japan pursued increasingly divergent paths institutionally. And the key to this development is the location of power and authority. Koryŏ continued to be governed from the center as the military leadership controlling the king determined policy. In Japan, however, power became much more dispersed. The new Kamakura *bakufu* situated itself hundreds of miles east of the emperor's seat in Kyoto and established a system of governance not completely dependent on the emperor. A much more decentralized regime developed as the vassals *(gokenin)* of the Kamakura shogunate exercised considerable authority in their own locales and regional autonomy became an accepted part of life. Slowly in Japan the values of the samurai became the norms of society. In Koryŏ retainers never achieved the autonomy that the Kamakura vassals enjoyed but remained bound to their acknowledged lord. And these lords, as seen in the Ch'oe leaders, protected their authority by manipulating the central government in the capital. Furthermore, as we shall see in later chapters, it was the values of the civilian, the literatus, that reclaimed prominence in Koryŏ.

Dispersal of Power

From the founding of the Koryŏ dynasty in 918, the military had always played a prominent role in governance. Beyond consolidating royal power in the face of regional opposition, the military rendered a crucial function in defending Koryŏ from attack along its northern borders. Northern defense mandated a strong, well-prepared central army. And this in turn required a powerful, central government. One of the great ironies of Koryŏ is its persistence in exalting civil values over martial norms despite the need for a strong military posture—as well as the lessons learned from Sung China's own weak military stance and consequent defeat by the Jurchen Chin. A strong military arm could pose an internal problem, however. And in fact when the Koryŏ military felt too aggrieved to endure their hapless state, it was the king's palace army that led the revolt in 1170. The ensuing years of Myŏngjong's reign witnessed a struggle to find a new balance between the needs of the military leaders and some sort of orderly governance. Given the anarchy of this period, no solution was forthcoming. When Ch'oe Ch'unghŏn took power, he initially sought to reassert the authority of the central state as the surest route to bring order.

Given the nature of the dynastic institutions, in which the monarch was the focus of all loyalty, Ch'oe Ch'unghŏn had to side-step the established military structure and devise his own machinery. The military organs that he and his descendants designed were hastily formed over a period of several decades to meet the emergencies of the time. They were novel departures from the recognized norm, but in serving the Ch'oe House they became effective extensions of its power. As time passed and the dynastic troops gradually weakened, the Ch'oe forces had to defend the kingdom as well as the Ch'oe family. To assure the uncontested loyalty of this new structure, the Ch'oe House cultivated the support of retainers. These private Ch'oe forces and retainers evolved into a new system of authority. Men no longer achieved their influence through personal family ties and bureaucratic positions alone. Instead, retainers could advance through judicious relations with strategically placed officials. Prestige and influence no longer rested solely with the king and the dynastic structure, but shifted to individuals. The Ch'oe House encouraged this change by constructing a dual administration of dynastic and private offices—and the confusion and cries of urgency following the collapse of the dynastic military institutions sped these developments.

4

Civil Structure and Personnel
Ch'oe Ch'unghŏn and Ch'oe U

In the early Koryŏ period, prestige and authority rested with men who held civil positions in the dynastic structure. Even though Ch'oe Ch'unghŏn placed considerable emphasis on constructing a solid military base, he also nurtured and won the support of the civilian elite. In effect, the Ch'oe House ruled the kingdom by drawing upon civilian administrative talent as well as military force. Parallel to its use of existing military institutions, the Ch'oe leadership at first depended on the dynastic bureaucracy but gradually constructed its own private agencies. In the end, the Ch'oe House superimposed its own units, both military and civil, on the formal dynastic structure to act as a brain trust at the nucleus of the entire Ch'oe system. This chapter analyzes the operation of the Ch'oe House's manipulation of both the civil dynastic structure and its new administrative institutions. We begin by examining the men who assisted the Ch'oe House and enabled it to govern. The composition of the ruling structure reveals new trends distinct from those established during Myŏngjong's reign. Although the Ch'oe House recruited men who had bureaucratic ability, it also sought to secure its position in society by employing men with prestigious social backgrounds. The Ch'oe House did not encourage men of humble social origins to participate in this new ruling structure.

Ch'oe Ch'unghŏn

Ch'oe Ch'unghŏn, as he commenced his consolidation of power, depended heavily on the established dynastic order. Rather than erect a completely new administrative body, he used traditional channels to govern. During the preceding tenth and eleventh centuries the dynastic structure had evolved to meet the challenges of the Koryŏ kingdom. It would have been foolish to eliminate these units, for through them Ch'oe Ch'unghŏn began to inaugurate the changes and reforms that he envisioned. Furthermore, if he had tried to eliminate the established centers of control in the early years of his rule, he would have encountered the united objections of the civilian officials.

Dynastic Administration

The civilian officials, trained in Confucian ideology, believed that the preservation of the dynastic structure was tied to legitimacy. These men had been instrumental in the establishment of military rule and the administration of the kingdom during Myŏngjong's reign and thus looked to Ch'oe Ch'unghŏn to remedy the abuses perpetrated under Yi Ŭimin. Ch'oe Ch'unghŏn spent considerable time and effort placating this group and winning it to his cause. Alienating them unnecessarily at this stage would only have hindered his long-range goals. Ch'oe Ch'unghŏn was essentially a conservative man who depended on compromise as a means to co-opt opposition and gain followers. He demonstrated his support for the civilian leadership by using the traditional dynastic structure. Furthermore, he realized that his own position was still insecure. By linking his cause to that of the dynasty, he would be able to use Confucian ideological foundations to bolster Ch'oe authority.

The dynastic system of offices and ranks also provided a force of legitimacy, much like the monarch, which the Ch'oe House could use to sustain its policies when handling domestic and international problems. Moreover, it played an integral role in meeting Ch'oe fiscal needs. Ch'unghŏn would pay for his own troops and administrators from dynastic funds simply by assigning dynastic titles to men in his power structure. With a formal office and rank, the Ch'oe official was eligible to receive revenue from a prebendal allotment under the land stipend law (*chŏnsikwa*). Rather than depleting his own wealth to support his bureaucracy, Ch'oe could simply depend on the present system of allotments and stipends to meet many of his financial obligations. Although it was in Ch'oe Ch'unghŏn's interest to maintain the integrity of traditional land relations and the land stipend law to support his officials, he aggressively pursued strategies to build up his private wealth.

CIVIL OFFICIALS

Each of the Ch'oe leaders—Ch'unghŏn, U, and Hang—cultivated close ties with civilian elites and the civil structure. (Ch'oe Ŭi's rule was too short to provide substantial evidence.) As noted earlier, Ch'oe Ch'unghŏn established a pattern whereby each of the Ch'oe leaders assumed the highest civil positions of prestige and, moreover, allowed men with civilian backgrounds to dominate the dynastic structure. Eighty men were found to be holding positions in the top offices of the civil dynastic structure during Ch'oe Ch'unghŏn's rule from 1196 to 1219.[1] These are the men who held offices in the Royal Secretariat–Chancellery, the Security Council, the Censorate, and the six ministries and acted as official examiners for the state examination. The background of these men is presented in Table 1.

The most obvious development is the heavy infusion of men with military backgrounds into the civil dynastic structure. Nevertheless, even in this age of "military domination," civilians occupied a majority of the offices, accounting for at least 54 percent (forty-three men) of the people in these offices. Similarly, the state examination remained an important entrance for civilians. At least twenty men

Table 1. Civil Composition: Ch'oe House Rule (1196–1219)

Background	Number
Total	80
Civilian	43 (54%)
Civilian?	10
Military	16 (20%)
Both	3
Unclear	18
Examination	20 (25%)
Protective appointment	5
One ancestor fifth grade or above	32 (40%)
Two or more ancestors fifth grade or above	13 (16%)
Ch'oe family members	6

(25 percent) passed the civil examination—and quite possibly many of the forty-three civilians listed here may have passed the examination as well. As noted earlier, examinations under Ch'oe Ch'unghŏn were held at frequent intervals and the numbers of men passing each year show a dramatic increase.[2]

If merit remained a criterion for advancement, lineage too continued to play a role. Thirty-two men (40 percent) had at least one ancestor who had served in the government at the fifth rank or higher and thirteen men (or 16 percent) had two or more such ancestors.[3] Five people entered the government via protective appointments. Finally, six of the men in the civil structure were members of the Ch'oe family. As mentioned earlier, the paucity of source materials hinders our analysis of the lives of these men. Since many of these totals represent minimums, an even larger percentage of examination passers may have had ancestors in government service. In summary, then, these figures indicate that birth definitely facilitated the advancement of some people. But the greatest change was the increase in the number of military men in the social composition of the civil structure. Similar patterns are evident under Ch'oe U and Ch'oe Hang.[4]

ADMINISTRATIVE OFFICES

The monarchical system posed a unique dilemma to the Ch'oe rulers. As the supreme authority, the king theoretically controlled all policy and embodied political legitimacy. It was he who personified the political, social, and ideological structure of the kingdom. The legitimacy of all acts and the privileges and duties of all men depended on the sanction of the king. Ch'oe Ch'unghŏn's problem was to devise a method to divest the monarch of authority while still maintaining the symbolic fiction of royal leadership.[5] By building his own private structure to meet emergencies and administer the government, Ch'oe Ch'unghŏn would be able to control Koryŏ and govern more efficiently. There was nothing novel about this idea. "Kitchen cabinets" are not unique. Ch'oe Ch'unghŏn and his descendants merely formalized their kitchen cabinets into a private organization that acted as a brain trust for the Ch'oe House—a power behind the throne.

Other families in the past, such as the Kyŏngwŏn Yi lineage, had tried to encroach on royal authority. Ch'oe Ch'unghŏn's action, however, was unique for several reasons. He was a dictator, a military official, and not from a civilian family. He chose to institutionalize his private administration rather than controlling the dynasty by having his children marry the monarchs. Where other families had failed to establish their power, the Ch'oe leaders supplemented the normal dynastic operations with their personal organization. By superimposing their own offices on top of the dynastic administration and having Ch'oe loyalists control major dynastic operations, the Ch'oe rulers diverted royal power from the monarch to themselves and thereby secured a position of supreme authority in the kingdom. In this way the Ch'oe leaders appropriated some of the authority of the civil bureaucracy that prior to the 1170 coup had similarly struggled to check the power of the monarch.

Ch'oe Ch'unghŏn commenced this process by totally dominating the civil structure, as evidenced through his assumption of civil titles. He also placed close followers in the top civil offices, assuring their dominion over the dynastic apparatus. Within four years of coming to power, Ch'oe Ch'unghŏn was appointed concurrently to the command of the Ministry of Civil Personnel (Ibu) and Ministry of Military Affairs (Pyŏngbu). Dual appointments were not uncommon in Koryŏ political life. In taking charge of these two ministries, he was able to control the appointment and promotion of every man in the civil and military branches. Ch'oe Ch'unghŏn also decided at this time that he would perform his official duties at his private residence. From his home he would recruit and select civil and military officials and then present his roster to the king for approval.[6]

By doing this, Ch'oe Ch'unghŏn introduced a striking change into the established structure, for he radically altered ministerial procedures to implement his needs. Dynastic officials still met in government buildings. Their administrative functions remained intact. But decisions were determined at the Ch'oe House, with Ch'oe Ch'unghŏn himself directing affairs and deciding who was fit for advancement. Thus, by compromise and the utilization of established agencies, Ch'oe Ch'unghŏn won the support of many officials and tapped dynastic institutions for effective administrative purposes. At the same time, he maneuvered himself into a dominant position of power within this whole structure. Even so, Ch'oe Ch'unghŏn was not totally satisfied with the operation of the formal dynastic structure.

When Ch'oe Ch'unghŏn announced his reform proposals soon after taking power in 1196, he stated his dissatisfaction with bureaucratic inefficiency and ostentatious behavior. Bureaucratic inertia is not a modern phenomenon. Ch'oe, a man impatient to enact his will, wanted to streamline his administration and settle conflicts quickly. Furthermore, he would never be able to exercise total control over the kingdom so long as he remained dependent on the formal structure.

His next step in devising a private authority came with the establishment of the Directorate General of Policy Formulation (Kyojŏng Togam) in 1209. Directorate generals were ad hoc dynastic agencies vested with extraordinary power to handle emergencies. This was Ch'oe Ch'unghŏn's first cautious move to bypass the king and traditional decision making. But once it was established, Ch'oe Ch'unghŏn quickly transformed this supplementary dynastic office into a permanent arm of his administration. Following a 1209 assassination attempt, Ch'oe Ch'unghŏn fashioned the Directorate General to formulate internal defense policy and take up police functions.[7] Six years later, an official named Yun Seyu boldly and unwisely requested he be made a special commissioner for policy formulation (kyojŏng pyŏlgam) to investigate several people plotting treason.[8]

Ch'oe U further developed the Directorate General into taking charge of recruitment policies and ultimately fashioned it into overseeing major policy formulation. The sources reveal:

> Ch'oe U had the Directorate General of Policy Formulation dispatch messages instructing all high-ranking and court officials to recommend those with ability who had passed the state examination but had not received a post. Earlier Ch'unghŏn had established the Directorate General of Policy Formulation. All that was done was carried out from the Togam. U also did this.[9]

The responsibilities of the Directorate General for Policy Formation were extensive. In addition to its defense, police, and recruitment functions, it also deliberated on financial issues: in 1250, for example, it called for a reduction in taxes throughout the country. The powerful even tried to use its authority to reprimand disobedient officials, as in 1228 when Tae Chipsŏng tried to do just that.[10] The military influence on this council was omnipresent. The position of the special commissioner (pyŏlgam), who headed the Directorate General, was a military title similar in status to that of general. The Ch'oes themselves, all generals, each held this post.[11] There is further evidence, too, demonstrating the Directorate General's martial qualities: it was formed after an attempt on Ch'oe Ch'unghŏn's life, and initially its functions replicated those of the Tobang.

As the Council of Generals and the State Council became less vital to Ch'oe policy, the Directorate General emerged as the supreme legislative, executive, and judicial body through which the Ch'oe leaders and their key retainers sought to resolve government affairs.[12] Retaining the consensus-building mechanisms of these two dynastic agencies, the Directorate General enabled the Ch'oe House to gain wide support for its policies.[13] Through sessions that came to include both military and civilian officials, the Ch'oe House determined policy and, in turn, executed these decisions through the efforts of the individuals in this agency. The men in the Directorate General and other Ch'oe units, often referred to as retainers, held posts simultaneously in both the Ch'oe and dynastic offices. In theory they pledged their ultimate loyalty to the Ch'oe leader, however, not the king. The Ch'oe House controlled the dynastic structure by means of the Directorate General at the top and by the loyalty of the retainers who worked within it at other levels of the structure. So vital were the operations of this office to the functioning of the government that the successors to the Ch'oe regime continued to use it until 1270.

The second most important Ch'oe agency was the Personnel Authority (Chŏngbang), which supervised recruitment and promotions. Its roots can be traced back to Ch'oe Ch'unghŏn's effort to dominate the selection process when he brought the Ministries of Civil Personnel and Military Affairs to his home in order to deliberate policy. Ch'oe U completed this transition by selecting civil scholars to establish the Personnel Authority and charging them with recommending people for official appointments. In 1225, the *Koryŏsa* notes: "U established the Personnel Authority in his private house. To propose official appointments, he selected civilian scholars to be in charge of it."[14] This agency was organized, like most dynastic offices, with specific ranks and titles. Again the sources relate:

> Ch'oe U established the Personnel Authority in his private residence to make recommendations and select civilian scholars. It was called the Pijach'i. . . . After Ch'unghŏn took power, he set up an Administration (Pu). Privately he set policy and made recommendations and appointments. He took men from his group and made them transmitters (*sŭngsŏn*), calling them "politically colored" transmitters (*chŏngsaek sŭngsŏn*). Those with administrative responsibility were of the third rank and called "politically col-

ored" ministers *(sangsŏ)*. Those of fourth rank and below were called "politically colored" deputy directors *(sogyŏng);* they handled writing. Below them, those who managed general affairs were called "politically colored" drafters of documents *(sŏje)*. The place where they met was called the Personnel Authority.[15]

Ch'oe U needed a way to institutionalize his private means to recruit, select, and promote officials. He delineated authority within the agency and borrowed dynastic titles to provide it with additional legitimacy. He called his officials transmitters, a prestigious office title within the Security Council and possibly usurping some of those functions.[16] Although the actual number of men who served here is unclear, the high caliber of the appointees can be gleaned from the list of those identified with the agency. Civil scholars who passed the state examination dominated the Personnel Authority. Of the six men identified in Table 2, all passed the state examination, three were identified as Ch'oe retainers, and all held high-ranking dynastic positions in the ministries. Two were directly responsible for recommendations and personnel matters. One was in the Royal Confucian Academy.

The elite of the period found positions in the Personnel Authority. The Ch'oe leaders considered personnel matters of such importance that they established this agency separate from the Directorate General. Undoubtedly some men served simultaneously in both offices, although the Personnel Authority was subordinate. The fact

Table 2. Personnel Authority

Name	Entrance	Ch'oe Relation	Dynastic Office
Kim Ch'ang	Exam	Retainer	Dept. of Ministries
Kŭm Ŭi	Exam	None	Dept. of Ministries
Pak Hwŏn	Exam	Retainer	Minister of Punishments
Song Kukch'ŏm	Exam	None	Minister of Punishments
Yu Kyŏng	Exam	None	Royal Confucian Academy
Yu Ch'ŏnu	Exam	Retainer	Executive Minister of Civil and Military Personnel

Note: Cho Kyut'ae, "Ch'oe muin chŏnggwŏn kwa kyojŏng togam ch'eje" (Ch'oe military rule and the Kyojŏng Togam), in *KMC*, p. 93, identifies Sŏn Inyŏl as a member of the Personnel Authority. I did not find enough information to make this link.

that many of these same men also occupied key offices in the dynastic structure facilitated Ch'oe mastery over the kingdom's formal structure. The Personnel Authority was a vital link in the Ch'oe House's dual administration in that it allowed the Ch'oe leaders to control personnel decisions without dynastic intervention. The Personnel Authority was afforded some degree of independence inasmuch as it was established not by royal command, as in the case of the Directorate General, but by Ch'oe U himself. Ch'oe U, in a much more secure position than Ch'oe Ch'unghŏn, did not depend so heavily on royal fiat. So when he needed to establish an agency to oversee personnel matters, he simply created his own organization. The Personnel Authority continued until the end of Koryŏ. In the fourteenth century, because it was used by powerful cliques, it became a source of controversy.

The Chamber of Scholarly Advisers (Sŏbang) was another Ch'oe agency that first appeared during Ch'oe U's rule. Like the Personnel Authority, it comprised civil scholars whom Ch'oe U personally trusted and made his retainers. Moreover, it was not a dynastic institution but was created by Ch'oe fiat. The *Koryŏsa* states:

> Ch'oe I's [U's] retainers were all famous Confucian scholars of the age. They were divided into three divisions: the Ch'ebang, Sukpang, and Chamber of Scholarly Advisers (Sŏbang).[17]

By the time Ch'oe Hang died in 1257, the chamber comprised three divisions that patrolled with Ch'oe military units to maintain peace. As loyal Ch'oe followers, the men in the Chamber of Scholarly Advisers helped to devise military policy, conceivably meeting in the 1240s and 1250s to formulate military responses to the Mongol invasions. The chamber may also have usurped certain functions of the Hallim Academy, which had traditionally drafted documents for the king.[18] The chamber also maintained law and order when unrest threatened the capital on Kanghwa Island and its members appeared as escorts and honor guards when Ch'oe leaders died.[19] The size of this office, the number of people who participated, and even its possible membership remain obscure. As an agency for Ch'oe retainers, many of the people who served in the Personnel Authority and the Directorate General may also have been active in the Chamber of Scholarly Advisers.

The chamber's activities reflect the merging of military and civilian values that came to epitomize the Ch'oe period. Although the leadership assembled the men in the chamber to march during transitional stages in the Ch'oe period and to act as an escort, there was a much more pressing need for them to apply their civil abilities to resolve military issues. Serving as a center for military strategy, the chamber may well have been formed by Ch'oe U to chart a sound defense against the Mongol onslaught. Throughout Koryŏ, civilian scholars had been called upon to devise strategy during war and domestic unrest. Since classical treatises on war, which scholars frequently studied as a matter of course, were the basis of much battlefield planning, Ch'oe U may well have been prompted to gather scholars, his civil retainers, to meet in the chamber to plan tactics. Although this development may have blunted the military's power to exercise total mastery over military policy, it also signaled a new era of military/civilian cooperation. Ch'oe U and his descendants were bridging the barriers of social difference and suspicion that had divided early Koryŏ society.

CH'OE CH'UNGHŎN'S GOVERNANCE

Ch'oe Ch'unghŏn had both the dynastic institutions and his own innovative agencies to help him master the kingdom. But in addition to these institutional mechanisms, he filled these offices with capable men who provided both the expertise and the wisdom to help him govern. The civil dynastic structure, as we have seen, was a blend of both civilian and military officials in high-ranking government positions. Men who had passed the state examination filled the ranks as well, among whom were many descended from previous officeholders. A number of these same men also held posts in the Ch'oe private administration.

Although Ch'oe Ch'unghŏn governed through this dual organization, there was a cadre of about ten men who represented his closest confidants (Table 3). An analysis of this brain trust yields further insight into the dynamics of the period and the quality of leadership at this time. Because of their positions in the central hierarchy, family ties with Ch'oe Ch'unghŏn, and other references, these men are believed to be the top Ch'oe leaders. Presumably this group of six military officers and four civilians helped Ch'oe Ch'unghŏn chart policy and deliberated in the Directorate General. Seven had fathers who held the fifth rank or higher, and each of the civilians had passed the state examination and represented the civilian elite of the day.

Men who had helped Ch'oe Ch'unghŏn consolidate his power in 1196 were key players. Kim Yakchin and No Sŏksung (both relatives) and Paek Chonyu, the general who had thrown support to Ch'unghŏn just after Yi Ŭimin's assassination, played important military roles for Ch'unghŏn. Kim Yakchin helped rescue Ch'unghŏn during Hŭijong's ill-timed assassination attempt. Paek held a variety of positions. Not only a supreme general, he was also a military commissioner, a figure in the Security Council, and a member of the State Council. Chŏng Sukch'ŏm was an indirect Ch'oe relative, as his daughter married Ch'oe U. He helped Kim Yakchin rescue Ch'oe Ch'unghŏn in the assassination plot, and he later led the dynastic troops against the Khitans. In addition, he occupied a number of key civil offices in the State Council. Chŏng Sukch'ŏm's success story is not without blemishes, however. Implicated in a plot in 1217, he was banished by Ch'oe Ch'unghŏn to his home in Hadong. Only his relation to Ch'oe U spared him from the death penalty.

Two military officers, Ki Hongsu and Chŏng Kŭgon, winning respect from both civilian and military officials alike, had already earned recognition in Myŏngjong's reign. Shortly after Ch'oe Ch'unghŏn killed Yi Ŭimin, Ki Hongsu accepted his first major pro-

Table 3. Ch'oe Ch'unghŏn's Brain Trust

Name	Service	Ancestors	Office	Miscellaneous
Kim Yakchin	M		Supreme general	Ch'oe relative
No Sŏksung	M			Ch'oe relative
Ki Hongsu	M	A	State Council	
Paek Chonyu	M		State Council	
Chŏng Kŭgon	M	AA		Merit subject
Chŏng Sukch'ŏm	M	A	State Council	
Ch'oe Sŏn	C/Ex	AA	State Council	Merit subject
Im Yu	C/Ex	AA	State Council	Merit subject
Cho Yŏngin	C/Ex	A	State Council	Merit subject
Kŭm Ŭi	C/Ex	A	State Council	Merit subject

Note: M: military; C: civilian; Ex: examination; A: one ancestor fifth grade or above; AA: two or more ancestors fifth grade or above.

motion, perhaps because of his special skills. The histories note that "when Hongsu was young, he was good in reading and skilled in writing. On becoming an adult he put aside writing and followed the military."[20] Ki Hongsu, active in the Ministry of Civil Personnel, joined Ch'oe Ch'unghŏn to discuss affairs. When Sinjong asked to abdicate because of illness, Ch'oe Ch'unghŏn turned immediately to Ki Hongsu for advice. Chŏng Kŭgon of the Chŏnju Chŏng lineage, the son of a grand general, brought status, merit, and respect to Ch'oe Ch'unghŏn's organization. So significant was his leadership that he was commemorated in Kangjong's royal shrine.[21]

The civilian advisers possessed even more prominent social backgrounds and records of proven ability than their military counterparts. Im Yu, the son of Wŏnae and uncle to kings Ŭijong, Myŏngjong, and Sinjong, was the most esteemed. Holding important offices in Myŏngjong's reign, Im Yu advanced into the State Council after Ch'oe Ch'unghŏn took over. Playing a prominent role in supervising the state examinations, he recruited and recommended many men to the Ch'oe leaders.[22] Im Yu's son married one of Ch'oe Ch'unghŏn's daughters, further solidifying the relationship between these two families. Furthermore, Im Yu's sons all served the Ch'oe House. The Chŏngan Im lineage, one of middle Koryŏ's aristocratic houses and one of the families that Ŭijong had isolated from power, played a prominent role before and after the rise of the military in 1170 and continued in this capacity throughout the Ch'oe period.

Ch'oe Sŏn, of the Tongju Ch'oe lineage and son of Yuch'ŏng, duplicates many of Im Yu's experiences. Although the court banished Ch'oe Sŏn for his impeachment of a royal monk during Myŏngjong's reign, Sŏn quickly advanced into the State Council after Ch'oe Ch'unghŏn's assassination of Yi Ŭimin. When Ch'oe Ch'unghŏn discussed Sinjong's abdication with Ki Hongsu, Ch'oe Sŏn was there. Ch'oe Sŏn's family maintained its prominent status throughout the military period.[23]

Cho Yŏngin and Kŭm Ŭi were two more scholars who were also in the State Council. Cho, of the Hoengch'ŏn Cho lineage and a son of Sion, took charge of the Ministry of Civil Personnel after Ch'oe Ch'unghŏn came to power. His son Cho Ch'ung also achieved recognition under Ch'oe Ch'unghŏn and became a merit subject like his father. One relative also married a daughter of Ch'oe Ch'unghŏn, revealing this family's intimate links with the Ch'oe House.

Kŭm Ŭi passed first in his class on the state examination in 1184. Under Ch'oe Ch'unghŏn, he entered the Censorate and then the State Council. Kŭm, like Im Yu, recruited many talented men into the Ch'oe House and later, under Ch'oe U, worked in the Personnel Authority.[24]

All of these men played vital roles in the Ch'oe House. Some served in formal dynastic offices in the Ministry of Military Affairs or the Security Council overseeing military matters; others selected and recruited men of talent into the Ch'oe structure. Eight were in the State Council. Most, especially the civilians, came from elite lineages but frequently held inconsequential posts in Myŏngjong's reign. This group in many respects reflects the trends first seen in the composition of the men who held the general dynastic offices. Through this cadre of followers, Ch'oe Ch'unghŏn maintained contacts with the many varied elements vying for influence in Koryŏ society. By bringing together Ch'oe family members, military leaders, and accomplished civilian personnel, Ch'oe Ch'unghŏn assured the success of his rule.

Ch'oe U

Under Ch'oe U the Ch'oe House reached maturity. Once he stabilized his power, Ch'oe U pursued policies that marked new directions, even while continuing many of the themes of his father's rule. He addressed some of the excesses that occurred under Ch'oe Ch'unghŏn by introducing changes to land and fiscal policies that improved the management of the kingdom. He also pursued social-political reform by eliminating men with poor administrative records and removing those who had advanced through irregular means. Of the twenty-eight men purged at the start of his rule, at least twelve were guilty of official misdeeds. Noting that Ch'oe U sought to end the practice of gaining office through purchase, the histories reported in 1220—only three months after U came to power—that "the custom of giving bribes for office gradually diminished."[25]

SOLIDIFYING CONTROL

The marriage ties Ch'oe U chose for himself and his children were quite similar to those forged by Ch'unghŏn and demonstrate U's desire to maintain contacts with a broad range of people. (See Figure 1.) After the death of his first wife, the daughter of Chŏng Sukch'ŏm, Ch'oe U married the daughter of Tae Chipsŏng, another man of military heritage. Once Tae Chipsŏng married his daughter to Ch'oe U, he became exceedingly arrogant and used this relationship for personal gain. Ch'oe U benefited from both the Chŏng and Tae marriages by incorporating two military households into his power structure. In addition to these women, Ch'oe U also had several concubines. One, the daughter of Sa Honggi, bore him two sons, Manjong and Manjŏn (Ch'oe Hang). Sa Honggi was a civilian who, as a state councillor, was a minister of civil personnel.

In choosing spouses for his children, Ch'oe U selected children of the leading Koryŏ civilian lineages. Ch'oe U's daughter married Kim Yaksŏn of the Kyŏngju Kim clan. Ch'oe U seems to have selected this man, who could boast of Silla kings as ancestors, to be his heir and went to great extremes to promote him into positions of influence. When Kim Yaksŏn became embroiled in a dispute that led to his banishment and execution, Ch'oe U turned to his own son Hang, who had been sent to live in a temple, as a potential heir.[26] Summoned back to lay life and groomed as a successor, Ch'oe Hang married Ch'oe On's daughter. Ch'oe On, a member of the Tongju Ch'oe lineage, had passed the state examination and was the son of Chongjae who had been a censor and examiner during Ch'oe U's rule. Through marriage ties with the Tongju Ch'oe family, Ch'oe U was reinforcing the support of an old ally and esteemed Koryŏ clan. In expanding his family ties, Ch'oe U also adopted Im Hwan, the son of the Chŏngan Im family member Kyŏngsun. As noted earlier, this lineage was one of the most powerful civilian families during much of the Ch'oe period. Through these ties, Ch'oe U was not only offering some of the more prominent civilian and military families in the dynasty a chance to play an influential role in his administration. He was also guaranteeing their support for his regime.

Even though Ch'oe U was in a much stronger position from the start of his rule than his father had been, he was still cautious. To solidify his control over the bureaucracy, he followed his father's method of advancing slowly through the bureaucracy into the top civil positions. Ch'oe U had already achieved the rank of general by 1217. In the following year, he assumed the civilian post of administrator of memorials (*chijusa*). After his father died in 1219, Ch'oe U entered the Security Council. By the end of 1221, one and a half years after his own consolidation of power, he took a number of positions that gave him supreme control over personnel appointments and promotions.[27] He also appropriated command of the Censorate and, as a state councillor, became one of the ranking policy formulators in the Royal Secretariat–Chancellery. Although the appointments he received paralleled those of his father, unlike his father Ch'oe U assumed ranking positions almost immediately. In subsequent years Ch'oe U received one honor after another, but by the second year of his rule he was able to cloak his real power with all the legitimacy and prestige of the leading dynastic offices. In this way he could use the established dynastic institutions as additional support. He would not have to fight tradition. Instead, he could use it to effect his strategies for power.

Ch'oe U employed many civilians in his structure (Table 4). Of ninety-six men found to have held dynastic civil ranks (from 1219 to 1249), sixty-nine (71 percent of all officials) were men with civilian backgrounds. (See Appendix 6.) This was an increase from the 54 percent found during Ch'oe Ch'unghŏn's regime. Twenty-four men (25 percent) were military officers, and the background of three men is unclear. Although the military officers were in the minority, they were definitely a force that had to be considered in the administration. At least forty-three men (45 percent) were found to have passed the state examination—a sizable increase from the figure for

Table 4. Civil Composition: Ch'oe U's Rule (1219–1249)

Background	Number
Total	96
Civilian	69 (71%)
Civilian?	10
Military	24 (25%)
Unclear	3
Examination	43 (45%) (62% of all civilians)
One ancestor fifth grade or above	46 (48%)
Two or more ancestors fifth grade or above	28 (29%)
Lowborn	1

Ch'oe Ch'unghŏn's period. Of the civilians, at least 62 percent passed the examination—a much higher percentage than during Ch'oe Ch'unghŏn's rule. Like his father, Ch'oe U sought to improve the quality of the men appointed. In meeting this goal, Ch'oe U continued to rely on the state examinations, maintaining a regular schedule for their completion. He venerated scholars and expanded the ceremonies to honor those who passed the state examination.[28] Ch'oe U also encouraged respect for civilian officials and institutions by reverting to a greater dependence on Chinese traditions. In 1225 he memorialized: "I request that our dynastic institutions and rites of music emulate Chinese systems." At the same time, the histories report that Ch'oe U permitted men who came from China to enter important dynastic offices, selecting them on the basis of their talent. Realizing that good administration begins with the recruitment of able men, Ch'oe U sought continually to achieve this goal.[29]

The social background of the men who entered the dynastic structure at this time appears to parallel that during Ch'oe Ch'unghŏn's rule. At a minimum, forty-six men (48 percent) had fathers who held the fifth *p'um* rank or higher in the dynasty. And over half of these men (at least twenty-eight) could also claim to have had grandfathers who held the fifth *p'um* rank or above. In other words: at a minimum 29 percent of the people who held dynastic office could claim this distinction. This increase from Ch'oe Ch'unghŏn's rule might be attributed to the maturity of the military rule. By Ch'oe U's regime, twenty years had elapsed since Ch'unghŏn came to power and close to fifty years had passed since the 1170 military revolt. Authority was becoming entrenched in established families. This trend is revealed in the fact that only one person was found to have come from humble origins. And that one man, An Sŏkchŏng, received his post because of special ties with Ch'oe U (and in the face of widespread objections).[30] Compared to the period just after the 1170 coup, when at least four men of low social status reached positions of political prominence, a limitation of social mobility is evident. Birth and ability, as in Ch'oe Ch'unghŏn's period, remained important criteria for recruitment and promotion into positions of power during Ch'oe U's leadership.

In no single office did military officers exercise prime control. Instead, military men appeared throughout the entire system, though they tended to congregate around the most prestigious agen-

cies. Twelve of the thirty-eight men in the State Council were originally military officers. Nearly one-third of the lower offices of the
Security Council (Ch'umirwŏn), the Ministry of Civil Personnel, and
the Ministry of Military Affairs included military officials. Over the
preceding fifty years, these agencies had already had many military
officers and Ch'oe U continued the pattern. Several military officers
were also found in the Ministry of Rites—a ministry that previously
had been reserved almost exclusively for civilian officials who had
completed the state examination. The lower offices of the Royal Secretariat–Chancellery, however, remained under civilian auspices.
This was a traditional center of civilian officialdom and perhaps
administratively the principal agency in the dynastic bureaucracy.
Membership in the Department of Ministries, usually extended as an
honor to an established personage, also seems to have been filled
exclusively by civilian officials.

In terms of successful examination candidates and prestigious lineages represented, the composition of the State Council is a microcosm of the entire dynastic structure. The social and political prestige of this elite group does not seem to have diminished during
Ch'oe U's rule. Men of elite social backgrounds and ability were present. The state councillors continued to meet to discuss state affairs
and were summoned to attend many Ch'oe functions. Men who
held positions in the State Council also retained concurrent posts in
the ministries or other dynastic agencies.

Institutionally, some offices appear to have been more critical
than others. The State Council, for example, remained at the apex
of the civil administration, as well over half the men located there
served in other dynastic offices. The six ministries were an excellent
training ground for future state councillors. Nearly all the men who
held office there also advanced into other posts within the dynasty.
Similarly, more than half the men in the Censorate held other
appointments. Of the twenty-three examiners, all but four are
recorded as holding other positions. The fact that much of officialdom held a number of different offices contributed to the high caliber of administrative effectiveness that characterized Ch'oe U's
regime. The dynasty in general functioned in much the same manner as when Ch'oe Ch'unghŏn was in command. Although all major
decisions were made in the Ch'oe units, the dynastic structure
remained essential in forwarding Ch'oe policy by providing both a
measure of legitimacy and a rationale for financial security.

Ch'oe U's Inner Council

The men who filled the Ch'oe offices were often the same men who held dynastic ranks. There is no exact record of who all these personages were, but there are indications that certain men—all possible candidates for membership in the Directorate General for Policy Formulation—were prominent in Ch'oe U's administration. Of twelve men discerned to be in this category, four were military officers and eight were civilians. Two, Pak Hwŏn and Song Kukch'ŏm, also served in the Personnel Authority. All but three, Song Kukch'ŏm, Chu Suk, and Pak Hwŏn, were identified as coming from families with previous government service. As in Ch'oe Ch'unghŏn's inner council, all of these men were chosen as possible members of Ch'oe U's elite group on the basis of their prominence in the Ch'oe structure and their personal ties with U (Table 5).

The military confidants included Kim Yaksŏn, Kim Kyŏngson, Kim Ch'wiryŏ, and Chu Suk. Two of these, Kim Yaksŏn and Kim

Table 5. Ch'oe U's Brain Trust

Name	Service	Ancestors	Office	Miscellaneous
Kim Yaksŏn	M	AA	Supreme general	In-law
Kim Kyŏngson	M	AA	Security Council	In-law
Kim Ch'wiryŏ	M	AA	State Council	Merit subject
Chu Suk	M		Grand general	Affinal ties
Pak Hwŏn	C/Ex	A	Ministry of Punishments	Retainer; Personnel Authority
Song Kukch'ŏm	C/Ex		Ministries	Personnel Authority
Kim Ch'ang	C/Ex	AA	Security Council	
Yi Kyubo	C/Ex	A	State Council	
Ch'oe Chongjun	C/Ex	AA	State Council	Affinal ties
Ch'oe In	C/Ex	AA	State Council	Affinal ties
Im Kyŏngsuk	C/Ex	AA	Ministry of Punishments	Relative
Kim Yanggyŏng	C/Ex	A	Security Council	

Note: M: military; C: civilian; Ex: examination; A: one ancestor fifth grade or above; AA: two or more ancestors fifth grade or above.

Kyŏngson, were brothers from the esteemed Kyŏngju Kim lineage. Ch'oe U made Kim Yaksŏn his son-in-law—demonstrating, as in Chŏng Sukch'ŏm's case, the importance of marriage ties in the Ch'oe structure. During the early years, Ch'oe U promoted Kim Yaksŏn, as his heir apparent, to serve in the Security Council, but he later exiled and killed him. Kim Kyŏngson, another relative of Ch'oe U through Kim Yaksŏn, in his capacity as a general held positions in the Censorate and then in the lower offices of the Security Council. He played an important role in the Ch'oe power structure until Ch'oe Hang banished him in 1250.[31] Kim Ch'wiryŏ, a member of the Onyang Kim lineage, the son of Ministry of Rites official Kim Pu, was an important commander and adviser. As a state councillor with an office in the Security Council, he held a concurrent post in the Ministry of Military Affairs.[32] For his service the king subsequently named him a meritorious subject. These three men obviously had elite backgrounds, but one Chu Suk, who was simultaneously the commander of the Yabyŏlch'o and Tobang, came from obscure origins. As a supreme general, a member of the lower offices in the Security Council, and one directly responsible for Ch'oe private troops, Chu was a key member of the inner circles of Ch'oe power. Furthermore, he was indirectly related to Ch'oe U, for they had both married daughters of Tae Chipsŏng.[33] Ch'oe U used each of these men in his own inner structure and simultaneously gave them appointments in the dynastic agencies. As military officers, they were all active in the Security Council, an office that came to administer much of the dynasty's military policy.

The civilian leadership was an equally distinguished group. Three of them, Pak Hwŏn, Song Kukch'ŏm, and Kim Ch'ang, have already been mentioned in relation to their roles in the Personnel Authority. Pak Hwŏn, a scholar from a Kongju family, was a Ch'oe House retainer. Besides passing the state examination and serving in the Ch'oe units, Pak also became a minister of punishments. Song Kukch'ŏm, a Chinju Song, came from a family that had close links with the Ch'oe House, as a number of its men held ranking posts under both Ch'oe U and Hang. Song Kukch'ŏm, active in the Censorate, in the lower offices of the Royal Secretariat–Chancellery, and in the Ministry of Punishments, held administratively important posts in the dynastic structure. These offices were vital in coordinating the dynastic and Ch'oe bureaucracies. Kim Ch'ang—an Andong Kim and descendant of the Silla royal family—handled recommendations. Many saluted him for his strong memory and ability to recall all the names of those he had recruited into the Ministry of Civil Personnel and Ministry of Military Affairs. He also participated actively on the Security Council.

Other men of similar experience and lineage joined this elite group. Although it is impossible to state whether they joined the Personnel Authority, it is quite probable that they occupied important positions there and in other Ch'oe units. Yi Kyubo is perhaps the most renowned member of Ch'oe U's administration. One of Koryŏ's foremost writers and poets, Yi Kyubo did not receive a prominent post until Ch'oe Ch'unghŏn came to power, even though he had passed the examination during Myŏngjong's reign. Ch'oe Ch'unghŏn, discovering his literary talent, employed him in a number of different functions. And when U inherited the leadership, Yi Kyubo continued in the administration, first as a member of the lower offices of the Security Council, then as executive. Yi Kyubo had a brilliant literary style: his written appeals for a cessation to invasions are said to have brought tears to the Mongol emperor. Yi Kyubo influenced dynastic policy as a state councillor, and he also supervised the examinations several times, bringing many talented people into the Ch'oe administration.[34]

Ch'oe Chongjun, Ch'oe In, and Im Kyŏngsŏk were all members of civilian families that had achieved prominence during Ch'oe Ch'unghŏn's rule and now were active in U's administration. Ch'oe Chongjun and In, both members of the Tongju Ch'oe family, were successful in the examination and were related to Ch'oe U through marriage. Ch'oe Chongjun, who was a military commissioner when the Khitans invaded in 1216, became a transmitter (chwa sŭngsŏn) in the Security Council and then became a state councillor with a concurrent position as minister of civil personnel under Ch'oe U. Ch'oe Chongjun, like the others, was an important official in both the Ch'oe and dynastic ranks. Ch'oe In, who also played a prominent role in Hang's regime, was a transmitter and then a state councillor. While holding these posts, In was also supervising recruitment as an examiner (chigonggŏ). Im Kyŏngsuk of the Chŏngan Im lineage epitomizes the membership of this elite Ch'oe group. As a relative of the Ch'oe House, an examination passer, and an official in the high Koryŏ ranks, he served as a minister of punishments and in the lower

offices of the Security Council during Ch'oe U's rule. He managed
the examination four times. Within a few years, of those who passed
under him, ten had received dynastic posts, three were generals, and
one was a junior colonel. One final person, Kim Yanggyŏng (In-
gyŏng), must be mentioned. Kim, another member of the Kyŏngju
Kim clan, successfully completed the state examination and advanced
to serve on the Security Council as a minister of punishments and as
a state councillor.[35] Like most of the other men mentioned here, he
also assisted in the administration of examinations and recruitment.

The composition of this group, which comprised the closest associates of Ch'oe U, shows the overwhelming weight of the old civil
families, many of whom could be labeled aristocratic. Kyŏngju Kims,
Chŏngan Ims, and Tongju Ch'oes all played prominent roles in the
top echelon of the power structure. Equally conspicuous is the role
of marriage ties. Six members of this group (half the total) had some
sort of family link to the Ch'oe House. Eight of these associates—all
of the civilians—were also examination passers. This group, which
held top posts in the formal dynastic structure and seems to have
been equally prominent in the Ch'oe House organization, reflects
the general composition of the Ch'oe administration. But here even
more than in the lower levels, birth was an important criterion. And
if a man could complement his birth with ability, he achieved even
greater success in the system that Ch'oe U developed. Like his father,
Ch'oe U ensured the participation and prominence within his system of these two groups by placing into his highest ranks men with
military support and civilian prestige. And in so doing he fostered a
blurring in distinctions between military and civilian. He further
guaranteed the support of these blocs by binding them to himself
through marriage ties. He had made the Ch'oe House an integral
part of Koryŏ society at the very center of both political and social
influence. By this he also assured the successful transfer of power to
his son Hang.

Confucian Scholarship

Both Ch'oe Ch'unghŏn and Ch'oe U forged amicable ties with Confucian scholars and became the leading patrons of learning, both
Confucian and Buddhist. Their support for Buddhist scholarship is
addressed in Chapter 7. But they actively promoted Confucian learn-

ing, too, and championed the civil service examination, which became an important vehicle of recruitment.

Not all scholars embraced the Ch'oe House. Han Yuhan, who lived in the capital, concluded that trouble would soon follow when he saw Ch'oe Ch'unghŏn usurp authority. Taking his wife and sons, he hid in the Chiri Mountains and refused to return despite Ch'oe Ch'unghŏn's pleas.[36] Of greater fame than Han Yuhan were the "Seven Worthies of the Bamboo Grove." This exclusive group of scholars—O Sejae, Im Ch'un, Yi Illo, Cho T'ong, Hwangbo Hang, Ham Sun, and Yi Tamji—took their name from a group of earlier Chinese poets and prided themselves on their knowledge and understanding of the Chinese classics. Many of these scholars purposely distanced themselves from the Ch'oe leaders, and others were passed over in selection. Of the seven members, only Yi Illo and Cho T'ong actually occupied civil posts. That only two of the seven joined the Ch'oe House was unusual. For at least five of them had passed the state examination and many of them came from esteemed families. Some of the men, such as Im Ch'un, wished to have no ties with the military. Not only did Im refuse to sit for the state examination, but he harbored resentment over the murder and purging of many of his family members during the 1170 coup. Alienated from the military leadership, Im Ch'un chose to wander and write poetry with men of similar inclinations.[37] O Sejae, on the other hand, passed the state examination and was even recommended for posts by Yi Illo. Yet he never received an appointment. In disgust he too joined this famed group, indulged himself in wine and good poetry, and ultimately retired to his maternal grandfather's home in Kyŏngju.[38] The literature they produced departed from early Koryŏ works in that it revealed a much closer affiliation with the countryside and the life of the peasant. It also lacked the idealism that characterized writings from previous centuries and instead pushed an escapist mentality.[39] Once the military period ended, writers who did not join the Ch'oe House were acclaimed, while men such as Yi Kyubo, who had close links especially with Ch'oe U, were censured.[40]

Although there were tensions between scholars who allied themselves with the Ch'oe House and those who did not, most scholars, even a few of the Seven Worthies, worked in support of the Ch'oe power structure. Yi Kyubo, a Ch'oe supporter who was one of Koryŏ's most eminent writers, was offered O Sejae's vacated seat among the

Seven Worthies, indicating the degree to which relations with the Ch'oe House and its supporters had moderated.[41] Ch'oe Ch'unghŏn, in an earnest effort to support the arts and foster literature, held writing contests to which he invited all scholars, both those who did and those who did not collaborate with the Ch'oe House. In 1205, when Ch'oe Ch'unghŏn constructed a garden pavilion, he summoned Confucian scholars for a poetry contest. Similar events occurred repeatedly during his rule.[42] Recognized scholars without any position in the government also participated in these affairs.

Through these acts, Ch'oe Ch'unghŏn established himself not only as the dominant political force in the kingdom but also the chief patron of the arts. In recalling the vast amount of literature written at this time and still extant today, one can only marvel at the productivity of the age.[43] Even though a few men chose to remain aloof, many more scholars had either formal political ties or less regulated literary contacts with Ch'oe Ch'unghŏn. Ch'oe U perpetuated these links and seems to have been even more successful in attracting leading scholars to his authority. In fact, by Ch'oe U's regime there were few Confucian mavericks divorced from the power structure. The famed scholars of the day were co-opted into supporting Ch'oe U's system.

There were other intellectual undercurrents as well. Some scholars, such as the Seven Worthies of the Bamboo Grove, devoted themselves almost entirely to the pursuit of literary endeavors, all but disavowing active political life.[44] Many of these men, like Yi Illo or Im Ch'un, regarded with nostalgia the former reign of Yejong when the writing of poetry and knowledge of the Confucian classics was an avenue to success. Bound by a Han–Tang literary style, these men affirmed the unity of Buddhism and Confucianism.[45] There was also the emergence of a *komun* literary tradition—stressing the idea that through literature a person could cultivate morality. Ch'oe Cha (d. 1260), viewing himself as a successor to Koryŏ's Confucian tradition and an admirer of Chinese *kuwen (komun)* Confucianists, criticized men who concentrated exclusively on writing verse. Ch'oe Cha called for greater political involvement. He also questioned the close links between Buddhism and Koryŏ's political leadership, especially the military rulers. Ch'oe Cha, a scion of the aristocratic Haeju Ch'oe lineage and a senior executive at the end of the Ch'oe rule, in some of his writings also displayed a tinge of resentment toward military rule and asserted the superiority of civilian norms.[46]

The Ch'oe House fostered scholar-officials and Confucian learning in many ways. Besides the expansion of the examination system and the enhanced role of the civil official, Ch'oe Ch'unghŏn endeavored to champion education. When confronted with student complaints over the possible loss of a hall that had been sold to a general illegally, Ch'oe Ch'unghŏn settled the matter quickly by fining and imprisoning the accused.[47] Presumably the students recovered their hall; but in any case Ch'oe Ch'unghŏn's popularity soared. Under Ch'oe Ch'unghŏn's rule, men with the position of academician *(haksa)* received an additional promotion. In 1200, the Royal Secretariat–Chancellery memorialized:

> In the old system, if those who were in the academician post did not hold a censorial *(taegan)* or examiner *(chigonggŏ)* office, they could not participate in the ranks of the leading officials. We request that from now on all those who have the position of academician at the same time be permitted to attend royal audiences at the rank of royal attendant.[48]

When this proposal was accepted, the prestige of the academician increased further. Continuing this trend, Ch'oe U accorded the civil Confucian scholar benefits and respect, openly acclaiming Confucian institutions as the foundation of the Koryŏ dynastic structure.

Both Ch'oe Ch'unghŏn and Ch'oe U openly embraced civil officials and their traditions. By sustaining scholarly interests and Confucian ideology, they were able to co-opt this influential group into their structure, thereby ruling Koryŏ more effectively. The smooth operation of the Ch'oe House and the Koryŏ kingdom at this time was assured by the presence of able administrators who played dual roles within the private Ch'oe agencies and the formal dynastic structure. It was the manipulation of this dual administration that made the first phase of Ch'oe rule so successful. And it was the Ch'oe search for civil talent to assist in their operation that helped make these years a record of institutional and intellectual achievement.

5

Civil Structure and Personnel
Ch'oe Hang and Ch'oe Ŭi

There is a clear division, both in the operation and the tenor of the
Ch'oe House, that is marked by the rise to power of Ch'oe Hang.
Ch'oe Ch'unghŏn and Ch'oe U had been institutional architects.
They freely improvised and adjusted Koryŏ conventions to enhance
their command over the kingdom. They were effective administrators and at the same time decisive leaders. They left a definitive stamp
on Koryŏ institutions and dominated Koryŏ's cultural life. Moreover,
under their leadership Koryŏ doggedly endured the Mongol invasions. The decline of the Ch'oe House began with Ch'oe Hang's rise
to power. Its final collapse came shortly after Ch'oe Ŭi succeeded
Hang. These last years of Ch'oe rule are tragic not only because of
the immense destruction wrought by the Mongols, but also because
a mountain of evidence reveals that the new Ch'oe leaders were incapable of addressing the key issues of the period. Both Ch'oe Hang
and Ch'oe Ŭi become pawns of events rather than the molders of
change.

Ch'oe Hang

As Ch'oe U approached his twenty-fifth year in office, he realized
that it was time to secure an heir. After exiling his son-in-law Kim
Yaksŏn, Ch'oe U considered his grandson Kim Chŏng as a possible
successor, but early in 1243 he also banished the younger Kim.[1]
Then Ch'oe U decided on Hang as his new heir, placing him under
the tutelage of several leading scholars and promoting him to the

post of minister of revenue. Ch'oe Hang did not become a state councillor, but he did take charge of one of the ministries. In this position, Ch'oe U probably intended that Hang be trained for dynastic politics. Within a year, Ch'oe Hang had entered the lower ranks of the Security Council. At the same time, Ch'oe U sought to enhance Hang's military position by giving him five hundred of his own personal house soldiers.[2] Thus, before he died, Ch'oe U clearly demonstrated through support and promotion that Hang was his successor. At Ch'oe U's death in the eleventh month of 1249, the Ch'oe bodyguards immediately went to guard Hang's house.

RISE TO POWER

On succeeding to power, Ch'oe Hang embarked on policies quite reminiscent of those of his father. Quickly he isolated and removed from office all opponents, including men and concubines who had been loyal to Ch'oe U. Officials who had supported Kim Chŏng as Ch'oe U's heir were special targets of attack, as was Ch'oe U's second wife's family. As the Tae family had covert ties with Kim Chŏng, Ch'oe Hang sought to eliminate this clique completely. In his campaign to establish absolute control over the kingdom, Ch'oe Hang also neutralized the power of many key men who had been in Ch'oe U's Personnel Authority.[3] Even though this policy might have been an honest attempt to check possible opposition, Ch'oe Hang purged respected civilian officials who would have been invaluable in his consolidation of power. He also exiled people such as Min Hŭi and Kim Kyŏngson simply because they were popular.[4]

With the rise to power of each new Ch'oe leader, significant changes occurred as established officials left the power structure. This pattern suggests that each leader had created a cadre of people who were loyal to the Ch'oes as individuals but held little allegiance to the Ch'oe House itself—a situation indicating that loyalty was still very much a personal bond. Fidelity could be established between individuals—in this case the Ch'oe leader and his followers—but few men were loyal to the Ch'oe system. This must have posed a serious dilemma to the Ch'oe House, for the very success of Ch'oe rule would then depend on the ability of each new Ch'oe leader to consolidate his followers rapidly and firmly. Part of this problem undoubtedly rested in the fact that since the dynastic structure had never been eliminated, the Ch'oe House was never able to make a clean break with the old order. In the Koryŏ context, it appears that men could be loyal to individuals and to the monarch—the embodiment of the dynastic order—but most people found it difficult to be loyal simultaneously to individual Ch'oe leaders and the Ch'oe House in addition to the king and his administration. The ramifications of this dilemma, as we shall see in Chapter 9, were manifold.

Hang had sufficient political knowledge to realize that he would have to make some sort of accommodation with the civilian elite if he were to govern effectively. Consequently, he made overtures to the king, who was instrumental in conferring legitimacy on this new Ch'oe regime. Shortly after Hang inherited his father's position, the king declared:

> Since my father and then I have occupied the throne, the Duke of Chinyang [Ch'oe U] has assisted us and worked for the Three Hans [Korea]. Now suddenly he has died without appointing an heir. His son, Deputy Commissioner of the Security Council (ch'u-mirwŏnbusa) Hang, has inherited the responsibilities and protects all. He should be summoned and given the position of minister.[5]

Some may claim that the king was only a figurehead, speaking at Ch'oe's command, but this sort of declaration enabled the monarch to add his voice and provide royal sanction and legitimacy to bolster Ch'oe Hang's newly acquired authority. For this aid the king received Ch'oe blessings and a number of treasured gifts over the following years.[6] Ch'oe Hang also held parties for royalty in an additional effort to win broad support for his regime. Throughout the early months of 1252, Ch'oe Hang entertained the royal family continually.[7]

Unlike his father or grandfather, who were reluctant to marry with ranking civil lineages at the start of their careers, Ch'oe Hang early in his secular life married into the highest civilian families. Ch'oe U had arranged for Hang to marry Ch'oe On's daughter. Ch'oe On was a member of the Tongju Ch'oe lineage, and after the fall of the Ch'oe House he would become an elder statesman in the kingdom. When this marriage failed because of the girl's constant illnesses, Hang selected a new wife—the daughter of Cho Kyesung. Cho, a member of the Hoengch'ŏn Cho lineage, had a social background and prestige similar to that of Ch'oe Hang's first father-in-law, Ch'oe On. Cho Kyesun, the son of Ch'ung, was a respected civilian official and for years his family had been closely associated with the Ch'oe House. Through these two marriages, Hang was binding the prominent civilian households into supporting his power structure.

Hang's advancement in the dynastic structure, although reminiscent of his two immediate predecessors, was much more rapid and comprehensive. Even before he became sole master of the kingdom, he had already reached a post in the lower ranks of the Security Council. Shortly after his father died, Hang promoted himself into the top civil positions in the dynasty when he became in effect head of the Security Council, the Ministries of Civil Personnel and Military Affairs, and the Censorate. In the following year Hang advanced further by becoming chancellor *(munhasijung)*, a post traditionally reserved for ranking elder statesmen.

CIVIL OFFICIALS

This new leader depended extensively on civilian officials. Thirty-five men were located in the dynastic offices, fewer than during Ch'unghŏn's and U's regimes. But given that Hang ruled for only eight years while the other men served more than twice as long, the smaller number is reasonable. Of these thirty-five men, twenty-six (74 percent) came from civilian families and seven (20 percent) from military families; the background of two men could not be discerned. These were about the same percentages that obtained during Ch'oe U's rule, demonstrating that there had been little shift in the balance between civilian and military forces (Table 6).

As under Ch'oe U's rule, there was no single sector of the administration where the military was especially strong. Rather, they were spread thinly over the entire administration. When one remembers the high positions they had achieved at the start of the military period, it is clear they were playing a reduced role in Ch'oe Hang's dynastic structure. Perhaps tensions between the military and civilian elements had lessened. Certainly the civilians were playing a positive military role in their work in the Chamber of Scholarly Advisers. After more than sixty years of ultimate military control, the differences between these two divisions had been diluted. After two generations in power, the Ch'oe leaders were less martial in outlook. Ch'oe Hang, for example, had been trained in a Sŏn monastery and learned military tactics only late in life. Men who chose the military profession now even passed the state examination, which had once been reserved for civilian scholars. The aristocratic Kyŏngju Kim lineage had members who were military and civilian officials; the Hadong Chŏng lineage, once a prominent military family, now had family members passing the state examination. For whatever reasons one can submit, distinctions between military and civilian officials were becoming blurred. And the scholar-official was again achieving a prominent role in the kingdom's administration.

Ch'oe Hang and his advisers recruited men of talent. Twenty-two officials (63 percent) passed the state examination. Stated another way: at least 85 percent of all the civilians discussed here completed the examination successfully—a sizable increase from the earlier Ch'oe periods. During Ch'oe U's rule, the state examination had been held with much more frequency than before. When one compares the Ch'oe period and the three reigns preceding 1170, the Ch'oe period shows an increase both in the number of successful candidates and in the frequency of the examinations. During the reigns of Sukchong, Yejong, and Injong, a total of sixty-five years, some forty-seven examinations were held, in which a total of 1,039 people passed, for an average of 16 each year. From 1196 to 1258, during the rules of Myŏngjong, Sinjong, Hŭijong, Kangjong, and Kojong, a period of sixty-two years, some fifty-seven examinations

Table 6. Civil Composition: Ch'oe Hang's Rule (1249–1257)

Background	Number
Total	35
Civilian	26 (74%)
Military	7 (20%)
Unclear	2
Examination	22 (63%) (85% of all civilians)
One ancestor 5th grade or above	18 (51%)
Two or more ancestors 5th grade or above	11 (31%)
Functionary	1

Note: For details see Appendix 7.

were held, with 1,752 people passing, for an average of 21 per year—
a modest but significant increase of 25 percent. Even more dramatic
increases can be found when tallying figures on the Royal Confucian
Academy (Kukchagam) examination. During the Ch'oe period, on
average fifty-three men passed the examination every year, compared to the annual average of thirty-three during the preceding
period.[8] It is quite possible that Hang was reaping the benefits of the
expanded examination system.

The social background of the men in power reflects similar
trends observed during Ch'oe U's regime. None of the thirty-five
men was described as coming from humble or socially inferior families, while at least eighteen (51 percent) of them had fathers who
had served in a dynastic office of the fifth *p'um* rank or above, and
eleven (31 percent) also claimed grandfathers with this distinction.

CH'OE HANG'S INNER COUNCIL

Although the composition of the top ranks in the dynasty contained
many men of distinguished birth and academic ability, the men Hang
recruited into his private circle—his most trusted confidants—
appear to have come from a wider background (Table 7). Of those
who were Ch'oe Hang's closest associates, two, Ch'oe Yangbaek and
Ch'oe Yong, served in distinct military capacities at this time. Ch'oe

Table 7. Ch'oe Hang's Brain Trust

Name	Service	Ancestors	Office	Miscellaneous
Ch'oe Yangbaek	M		Subcolonel	Slave
Ch'oe Yong	M		Grand general	Retainer
Yi Sunmok	C/Ex		Senior executive	
Yu Kyŏng	C/Ex	AA	Personnel Authority	
Ch'oe In	C/Ex	AA	Asst. executive	
Sŏn Inyŏl	C			Retainer
Yu Nŭng	C	A		Retainer
Ch'ae Chŏng	C/Ŭm			Retainer
Cho Kyesun	C	AA	State Council	In-law

Note: M: military; C: civilian; Ex: examination; A: one ancestor fifth grade or above;
AA: two or more ancestors fifth grade or above; *Ŭm:* protective appointment.

Yangbaek was one of the first men of slave origins to reach the upper echelons of power in the Ch'oe House. Although Ch'oe Yangbaek's role in Hang's structure is not defined, the *Koryŏsa* indicates that he went to Hang shortly after Ch'oe U's death. Then, when Ch'oe Ŭi succeeded to power, Ch'oe Yangbaek continued as one of his confidants too. Ch'oe Hang appointed Ch'oe Yangbaek as a subcolonel, and Ch'oe Yangbaek proved his loyalty by aiding Hang's designated heir Ŭi. Ch'oe Yong, a grand general, was the other important military figure in Hang's power structure. As one of Ch'oe Hang's retainers who had distinguished himself in battle against the Mongols, Ch'oe Yong transmitted this dying leader's last testimony to others in the Ch'oe power structure. By his allegiance he enabled Ch'oe Ŭi to consolidate his command over the kingdom when Hang died.[9]

The civilian associates carried diverse credentials. Three of them, Yi Sunmok, Yu Kyŏng, and Ch'oe In, successfully completed the state examination. Yi Sunmok, who taught Ch'oe Hang to write after Hang had returned to lay life, was a renowned scholar of the age. Once Ch'oe Hang came to power, the *Koryŏsa* indicates that Hang "depended upon him for rites and selected him to be senior executive *(sangsŏ chwabogya)*, but before he could assume that office he died."[10] Although Yi Sunmok never handled the state examination, he did once supervise the examinations for entrance to the Royal Confucian Academy. He also advised Ch'oe Hang on a number of matters. Another leading civil scholar in Ch'oe Hang's rule, Yu Kyŏng, the son of Munhwa (Yuju) kinsman T'aek, served in the Personnel Authority and Hang treated him quite generously.[11] But once Ch'oe Ŭi came to power, Yu Kyŏng changed his stance and joined Kim Chun to set the stage for the assassination of Ch'oe Ŭi. Ch'oe In, the third man who completed the examination, was a member of the prominent Tongju Ch'oe family that had been so intimately involved with the Ch'oe House from Ch'unghŏn's time. During Ch'oe U's rule, Ch'oe In participated in recruitment and served on the Security Council. Once Ch'oe Hang was in authority, Ch'oe In, as assistant executive in Political Affairs *(ch'amjijŏngsa)* handled relations with the Mongols. Through his family ties Ch'oe In contributed a strong conservative influence and brought respectability to Ch'oe Hang's power structure.

The remaining civil officials include Sŏn Inyŏl, Yu Nŭng, Ch'ae Chŏng, and Cho Kyesun. The histories refer to all of these men, with the exception of Cho Kyesun, as retainers or confidants of Hang. Cho Kyesun was a member of the Hoengch'ŏn Cho lineage, which had figured so prominently in the earlier Ch'oe regimes. Once again this family played a significant function as Cho Kyesun assumed dual roles: first as father-in-law to Hang and member of the Security Council, then as a state councillor with the position of chancellor. Sŏn Inyŏl's part is unclear. Aside from being a confidant to Ch'oe Hang and participating with Yu Nŭng and Ch'oe Yangbaek in the transmission of Hang's last injunctions, there is little information on this man. Yu Nŭng, as one of Ch'oe Hang's retainers, was invaluable in securing Ch'oe Ŭi's succession to the Ch'oe seat of power. In Ch'oe Hang's regime, he was a trusted aide and continued in this capacity for Ch'oe Ŭi. The histories, however, draw a very unflattering picture of this man, claiming that "those whom Ch'oe Ŭi trusted were all like Yu Nŭng's group—mediocre and worthless." Ch'ae Chŏng, the final member of this group, first entered the bureaucracy through a protective appointment (ŭm). But there is no record of the positions he held or the duties he fulfilled until Wŏnjong's reign, after the fall of the Ch'oe House, when he served in the lower ranks of the Security Council and Censorate.[12]

As there is little material to delineate the responsibilities and functions of the men in Ch'oe Hang's inner council, we must be content to generalize from broad statistics. Four of the nine men came from families whose fathers had served in the fifth p'um rank or above; two were from the well-established Tongju Ch'oe and Hoengch'ŏn Cho lineages. Compared to the composition of Ch'oe U's inner group, there seems to have been a subtle decline in the quality and ability of the men Ch'oe Hang selected as his confidants. This is especially apparent when one notices that, by the end of Ch'oe Hang's rule, Yi Sunmok and Ch'oe In had died and many of the more eminent figures of Ch'oe U's rule, such as Pak Hwŏn or Yu Ch'ŏnu, had been dismissed from positions of authority and replaced by such "mediocre men" as Ch'oe Yangbaek and Yu Nŭng. Below the surface of Hang's power structure, there seems to have been a subtle deterioration. Although Ch'oe Hang undoubtedly attempted to include important Tongju Ch'oes and other prominent clan members, and he did recruit men who had passed the state examination, his inability to balance all the counterforces, his failure to recruit and promote top talent, and the disintegration of

his administration, in part owing to the severity of the Mongol invasions, further undermined his position, leaving his son Ch'oe Ŭi in
an untenable situation when the latter assumed the leadership of
the Ch'oe House in 1257.

APPRAISING CH'OE HANG

Ch'oe Hang lacked political talent. His policies were much more
rash, his actions much less elastic, and his personality more arrogant
than Ch'oe U's. This attitude is evident when the prestigious Board
of Astronomy (Sach'ŏndae) continued to present memorials on their
observations of the heavens. Unhappy with the statements, Ch'oe
Hang urged that the Censorate reject this unsolicited advice and dis-
miss two men from the board.[13] Hang took a similar attitude toward
the compilation of history. In order to assure his proper place in history, Ch'oe Hang made the unprecedented move of supervising the
compilation of the records.[14] This was a grave act not lightly accepted
by Confucian standards. The writing of history was in theory done
with total objectivity and free of personal prejudice. Tradition dic-
tated that not even the strongest monarchs might interfere with the
writing of their own official records. Ch'oe Ch'unghŏn and Ch'oe U,
showing respect for Confucian customs and institutions, do not
appear to have overtly attempted to control these matters (or at least
the dynastic sources do not single out such action). Ch'oe Hang,
coming to power some forty years after his grandfather Ch'unghŏn,
failed to realize the value of compromise and mutual respect.
Although depending on dynastic institutions, he was unwilling to sustain the traditional checks that remained even in the Ch'oe system.

Ch'oe Hang, ruling during the most desperate stage of the Mongol invasions, was unable to devise a strategy to strengthen his position. Perhaps no individual could succeed. But Ch'oe Hang was
incapable of providing even the leadership that his father and
grandfather had asserted. In 1253 the histories comment that he was
aloof and note a marked decrease in the number of formal occasions he met with his dynastic advisers. He allowed bribery to facilitate official promotions. He shied from appearing in front of the
populace and seems to have feared the will of the people. Some of
his policies even invoked guarded criticism.[15]

Although trained by his father and leading scholars, Hang lacked
the intelligence and the will to operate the Ch'oe system of rule

effectively. He became too power-hungry and failed to foster the military/Confucian consensus that lay behind the power of the Ch'oe House. He removed respected scholars, he curtailed civilian traditions, he alienated prestigious military men. He promoted slaves into positions of authority and depended on them to help him determine policy. Moreover, Ch'oe Hang's own low social status as the son of a concubine further tarnished his standing and credibility in Koryŏ society. Coupled with these limitations, Ch'oe Hang had to look for strategies that could sustain his regime despite the growing severity of the Mongol invasions. This third-generation Ch'oe leader failed to chart a course that would preserve the Ch'oe House.

Ch'oe Ŭi

When Ch'oe Hang died eight years after coming to power, the Ch'oe House was in a vulnerable position. Ch'oe Ŭi, Hang's son by a concubine, succeeded him in 1257. But he was even less adept than Ch'oe Hang at confronting the problems of the age. Still Ch'oe Hang's followers rallied to the Ch'oe heir, and together they initiated steps to correct the deteriorating conditions besetting the kingdom.

"Young, Foolish, and Stupid"

Within days of achieving power, Ch'oe Ŭi opened the granaries to feed the starving and paid the ranking officials each 30 *sŏk* of grain. Besides placating the populace and officialdom, Ch'oe Ŭi also returned some lands to the court and presented the court with rice, cloth, honey, and oil. Although he might have won some support through this action, Ch'oe Ŭi had poor advisers who presented shortsighted and conflicting policies. Six months after offering aid and land to the poor, the histories report that Ch'oe Ŭi had 3,000 *kyŏl* of Kanghwa land placed under his own control. Early the following year he dispatched a number of his associates to act as tax collectors *(suhoeksa)* on Kanghwa Island. These men seized any profits the peasants might have acquired.[16] The demise of Ŭi's regime was speeded by the alienation such policies inspired, coupled with the errors of his inexperienced and unenlightened associates and the trials of war.

Ch'oe Ŭi held a number of posts in the civil structure. Before Ch'oe Hang died, he appointed Ŭi to several offices and had him study with the leading scholars of the kingdom. Then, immediately

on Ch'oe Hang's death, Ŭi became a general and took charge of the
Directorate General for Policy Formulation. The former appointment was honorary, but the latter position was the most important
seat in the Ch'oe House government. Shortly afterward, Ch'oe Ŭi
assumed posts in the Security Council, ministries, and Censorate—
all offices that his forefathers had held as they advanced in the
dynastic bureaucracy and ranks that assured him of a dominant
voice in the formal administration. Several months later, Ch'oe Ŭi
advanced further in both the Censorate and the Security Council.
Although these two appointments were in lower-ranking positions,
such offices were quite important in the Koryŏ structure as seats of
political activity and decision making.[17]

Ch'oe Ŭi was in a precarious position. The son of a concubine, he
was inexperienced, unable to maneuver through a labyrinth of political intrigue, and surrounded by mediocre advisers who were most
concerned about amassing private wealth. The histories provide an
unflattering view. They describe Ch'oe Ŭi as

> young, foolish, and stupid. When meeting nobles to discuss con-
> temporary affairs, he was without propriety. Those whom he per-
> sonally trusted were like Yu Nŭng and Ch'oe Yangbaek's group.
> All were worthless and mediocre. His uncle Kŏsŏng Wŏnbal,
> together with Ŭi's own favorite concubine Simgyŏng, terrorized
> the countryside and in court slandered people and seized prop-
> erty without limit.[18]

Although there had been many attempts to assassinate the Ch'oe
leaders, all had failed. Ch'oe Ŭi, lacking support and ill prepared,
was not so fortunate. Opposition to him came from two segments of
thirteenth-century society that Ŭi had alienated most: Confucian
scholars, represented by Yu Kyŏng, and underprivileged military
upstarts, embodied in the leadership of Kim Chun.

OVERTHROW OF THE CH'OE HOUSE

Friction within the Ch'oe organization, which had begun a few
months after Ch'oe Ŭi succeeded his father, peaked with the dismissal of Song Kilyu. Song Kilyu, who first appears as a general during Ch'oe Hang's rule, was no hero but, rather, a treacherous officer
who never hesitated to abuse his power. When some of his more
extreme actions forced an inspector to censure him and refer the
matter to Ch'oe Ŭi, some of Song Kilyu's associates, Kim Chun in

particular, complained to the Confucian scholar Yu Kyŏng. Yu Kyŏng tried to intervene but invoked the ire of Ch'oe Ŭi, who accused the men of treason. Although the men escaped punishment, from this point on Kim Chun's disaffection from Ch'oe Ŭi became serious.

Two months later, Kim Chun and Yu Kyŏng led the coup that assassinated Ch'oe Ŭi and some of his closest supporters, such as Yu Nŭng, Ch'oe Yangbaek, and Ŭi's uncle Kŏsŏng Wŏnbal. Kim Chun, who emerged as the ringleader after Song Kilyu's exile, represents a whole group of men who had initially been brought into the Ch'oe command under Ch'oe Hang and had moved into vital positions of power within the Ch'oe House forces. With the rise of Ch'oe Ŭi and then the dramatic dismissal of Song Kilyu, this group realized it was being isolated from power in the new regime. Kim Chun first appeared in Ch'oe U's reign, when he was banished for having sexual relations with one of U's concubines. Although Kim Chun was a house slave, he was exceedingly ambitious. When Ch'oe Hang took charge, Chun maneuvered himself into an appointment as a subcolonel. From there he gained Ch'oe Hang's confidence and advanced into the Ch'oe power structure.[19]

Kim Chun represents two elements of Koryŏ society that were experiencing changes in status: soldiers and descendants of slaves. As a soldier, Kim Chun realized that military personnel under both Ch'oe Hang and Ŭi were playing a less significant role in the Ch'oe House. Ch'oe Hang never married a woman from a military household, for example, and within the dynastic civil structure there was a noticeable decrease in the number of men from military families. Men of humble origins, however, were becoming far more important in the military as well as in the Ch'oe House. Both Ch'oe Hang and Ŭi were the children of concubines. Moreover, no longer was it sons of generals alone who worked in the top positions of the Ch'oe House; descendants of slaves also held important posts. Kim Chun, representing both of these trends, longed for power. Watching Ch'oe Ŭi's refusal to fight the Mongols and alienated from Ch'oe Ŭi's inner circle, he led the coup. Disaffected house slaves, men who had played a key role in the Ch'oe structure, willingly abetted Kim Chun. Equally crucial to the coup's success was support from men in the Yabyŏlch'o and the Sinŭigun.[20]

Civilian elements, too, were central to the success of the coup. Kim Chun from the start worked closely with the Confucian scholar

Yu Kyŏng. Yu Kyŏng's father and grandfather had both held civil offices in previous years, other ancestors were officials prior to the 1170 coup, and Kyŏng had passed the state examination early in Kojong's reign. His real rise to prominence, much like other men in this group, starts with Ch'oe Hang's regime, when Yu Kyŏng worked in the Personnel Authority and received generous treatment from Hang. But, like Kim Chun, he sensed a loss of influence in the new rule and, disillusioned by the actions of Ch'oe Ŭi and his cohorts, he too championed change.[21] To help legitimize their overthrow, both Kim Chun and Yu Kyŏng agreed to ask the prestigious statesman Ch'oe On to lend his dignity to their coup and present their action to the king for his approval.

The coup was essentially a military plot. Ch'oe House slaves, the Yabyŏlch'o, and the Sinŭigun took the lead. While Kim Chun sought protection from the Sinŭigun, the Yalbyŏlch'o smashed down the entrance to the Ch'oe mansion. Ch'oe Ŭi's uncle Wŏnbal tried to protect the Ch'oe leader and help him flee, but Ŭi was too corpulent to escape over the walls. Once they had killed Ch'oe Ŭi, Kim Chun, accompanied by Yu Kyŏng and Ch'oe On, met with the king and proclaimed the righteousness of their deed. Although the new rule under Kim Chun preserved the balance between military and civilian officials that the Ch'oe leaders had secured, Kim Chun increasingly dominated Koryŏ affairs and treated the nation much as his own personal kingdom. His rule lasted until another coup led by one of Kim Chun's associates toppled him in 1268—only to collapse in turn by 1270, when civilians took complete charge of the kingdom and the court returned to the mainland capital at Kaegyŏng.[22]

New Consensus

The Ch'oe House, especially under Ch'oe Ch'unghŏn and Ch'oe U, labored to blunt the sharp dichotomies that had separated military from civilian officials. Besides having military officers fill civil dynastic ranks, the Ch'oe leaders brought civilians into their private structure to devise military strategy. Military officers passed the state examination, indicating a new era in which officers received training in Confucian learning and were well read in the classics. Civilian elites counted among their disciples both military officers and civilian scholars.[23] Through these policies the Ch'oe House succeeded in bridging the barriers and suspicions that had divided military and civilians. Ironically this strategy was so successful that soldiers and civilians joined to topple the ineffective Ch'oe Ŭi and destroy the Ch'oe House.

In addition to supporting civilian scholars, the Ch'oe leaders increasingly fostered Confucian ideas. To win support from the civilian elites, the Ch'oes had to become patrons of Confucianism, the ideology of the age. Moreover, the Ch'oe family promoted literary activities and presided over a cultural flowering. Ch'oe Ch'unghŏn hosted countless parties and banquets to which he invited the eminent literati of the day.[24] Scholars loyal to the Ch'oe House as well as those without any governmental position participated in these functions. Yi Kyubo, one of the dynasty's foremost writers, actively competed in literary events of the age. Others, such as Im Ch'un and Yi Illo, also became leading writers of the period.

There is a certain element of expediency in the Confucian rhetoric of this age. Ch'oe leaders, eager to win support from civil officials, paid lip service to Confucian ideology as a political device to co-opt civil opposition. One is left, therefore, to question the sincerity of the Confucian men who flocked to support the Ch'oe House. Certainly the Ch'oe leaders made it easy for them by constantly parading the king as the legitimate head of the kingdom. But a dogmatic Confucian would have had trouble supporting a situation in which the king was in fact subordinate to the Ch'oe leaders. Few civilians, however, upheld strict Confucian principle. Instead they preferred the comfort and security afforded by jettisoning the primacy of the monarch and aligning themselves with the Ch'oe leaders.

Ch'oe Ch'unghŏn and his descendants established new institutions and reshaped the dynasty to meet their needs. They initiated such agencies as the Directorate General of Policy Formation and placed enhanced importance on their personal military forces. They launched their own private administration—first to compete with and then to upstage the dynastic offices. Looking for able warriors and administrators, they recruited men to serve their own needs first. Under their direction, there is a significant change in the tenor of the kingdom as military institutions were put on an equal footing with civilian norms and generals participated in the highest echelons of decision making.

Despite the Ch'oe search to fashion a new age, they were never able to escape the traditions of Koryŏ. Civil norms still governed the culture, forcing Ch'oe Ch'unghŏn and his followers to embrace those values in order to gain acceptance in the kingdom. Furthermore, to govern effectively they had to depend on the administrative ability of well-trained civil officials. To guarantee a ready pool of educated men and to meet civilian expectations regarding the proper behavior of a ruler, the Ch'oe House was obliged to hold the state examinations at regular intervals. The Ch'oe leaders fell victim to the less noble traditions, as well, as they had to guard against conspiracies threatening their own lives and adjudicate disputes within the civil and military bureaucracy.

Through a dual organization, both dynastic and private, the Ch'oe House dominated Koryŏ. The relation of the Ch'oe House to the entire structure of government in the thirteenth century is clear. The Ch'oe leaders acquired powers that operated alongside—and only incidentally in competition with—those exercised by the court. The Ch'oe position was not a usurpation but a growth within the established dynastic order. Through this new system and the calculated support of its retainers, the Ch'oe House was able to superimpose its will on the dynasty. It was able, through this dual organization, to support Confucian ideology and the power of the king while simultaneously constructing its own independent authority.[25]

At the same time that Ch'oe Ch'unghŏn consolidated his authority in Korea, similar institutional changes occurred in Japan as Minamoto Yoritomo established his house rule *(bakufu)*. Both men, Ch'oe Ch'unghŏn and Minamoto Yoritomo, rose from military lineages and both used royal or imperial legitimacy to sustain their regimes. Both sought through strategic marriage ties with the civil elite of the country to enhance their social standing and thereby solidify their political position. Confronted with the limitations of the dynastic or imperial governing institutions, both Ch'oe Ch'unghŏn and Minamoto Yoritomo erected new institutions, preferring to rely on private agencies rather than the arms of the state to expand their power.

The authority that Minamoto Yoritomo constructed was much more independent of the central government but also much weaker than that of Ch'oe Ch'unghŏn. Minamoto Yoritomo chose to locate his rule in Kamakura, nearly three hundred miles east of the imperial center at Kyoto. And because of the growing decentralization that characterized Japan in the late twelfth century, he was unable to impose his authority throughout Japan as effectively as Ch'oe Ch'unghŏn in Korea. From the start of the Koryŏ kingdom there had been an urgent need to maintain a strong central army to defend the nation from foreign attack. This in turn mandated a strong central government. For Ch'oe Ch'unghŏn to govern, he had to sustain and dominate this central structure. From the beginning of his rule, in marked contrast to Minamoto Yoritomo's advance in Japan, he infiltrated the civil arm and took many titles there. A similar picture emerges in the military structure. Where Minamoto Yoritomo first relied on his private military forces to secure power, Ch'oe Ch'unghŏn needed support from the dynastic army to assure the success of his coup. And only after a number of years in power was he able to divert responsibility for both the pacification and defense of the country from government troops to his own private forces.

Although both men relied on retainers to consolidate their rule, the retainer system developed much further in Japan than in Korea. Client/patron relations had already been refined in the Heian period, providing a foundation for Minamoto Yoritomo to develop this system.[26] Yoritomo relied on vassals *(gokenin)* and another classification of men, called *zoshiki* and *bugyōnin,* placed in a somewhat subordinate, retainer-like relationship. The *gokenin* were essentially independent military lords who chose link up with Minamoto Yoritomo and enjoy the benefits of such an association. The *zoshiki* and *bugyōnin* were a "patrimonial dependence group" who represented the personal arm of Minamoto Yoritomo and were used by him to deal with the *gokenin.*[27] Ch'oe Ch'unghŏn's retainer system never developed the complexity found in Japan, and his retainers never achieved the autonomy or standing of the Kamakura *gokenin.*

Both Ch'oe Ch'unghŏn and Minamoto Yoritomo fought the centrifugal forces that challenge most regimes. Both men wished to protect their private authority. Ch'oe Ch'unghŏn used his retainers to serve his needs and prevent anyone from erecting a competing authority. Yoritomo, alert to the same problem, used his *zoshiki* to check the potential independence of his *gokenin.* In this way both men were able to maintain a viable and coherent center. The Ch'oe House continued to govern from the dynastic center. The Minamoto relocated to Kamakura where they secured an uneasy accommodation with Japan's imperial center.

6

Peasants and Lowborns

The century following the 1170 coup witnessed significant social change as the old aristocratic order began to give way to peasant unrest, slave rebellions, and a general erosion of social restrictions. The chaos that accompanied the rise of Yi Ŭimin and other men of humble origins during the last decade of Myŏngjong's rule has already been discussed. When Ch'oe Ch'unghŏn seized control of the kingdom in 1196 and passed power to his son and grandson, the Ch'oe leaders pursued two distinct policies. On the one hand, they rigorously maintained traditional class divisions and sought to limit both peasant and slave aspirations for political power. At the same time, they allowed their personal followers of lower-class origins to advance into positions of prestige and authority, if only to gain their loyal support. This chapter focuses on the events surrounding the peasant and lowborn classes during the Ch'oe rule. We will look at the social history of the period to understand the life of these people and see how the Ch'oe regime used both peasants and lowborns to its advantage. In addition, we will examine the local and regional power structure in relation to the peasantry and the Ch'oe House. The effectiveness of Ch'oe personnel and Ch'oe leadership can be seen in the implementation of Ch'oe policy and their interaction with the nonelites.

Traditional leadership in Koryŏ evolved from one of three social groups: powerful local lineages, central aristocratic lineages, or military officer lineages. Peasants and those of lowborn status were relatively unimportant, as social codes, Confucian ideology, and dynastic institutions curtailed their access to power. Although the term for lowborns *(ch'ŏnmin)* is elusive, generally it refers to people of inferior birth, lower than peasants, that the Koryŏ dynastic system had denied entry into high-ranking offices. Lowborns generally include such people as slaves *(nobi)*, eunuchs, ferrymen, station attendants, weavers, actors, and musicians.[1]

Peasants

Although subordinate to the politically powerful ruling elites (but above the lowborns), peasants performed important functions in Koryŏ society. It was their labors that fed this agrarian country and their taxes that financed its administration. The ruling elite restrained peasants from advancing politically and economically and thereby enjoyed a monopoly of power and prestige in the kingdom. Despite their desire for total authority, the Koryŏ leaders could not ignore the needs of the peasants. They acknowledged that their own fortunes ultimately rested on the tacit support of the peasants. This meant that the welfare of the masses, according to classical rhetoric, had to be considered in political decision making and that agriculture had to be encouraged. To this end, the government dispatched officials to ensure the proper management of local affairs and the integrity of its local operations. Peasants had to be protected from the depredations of the powerful. In short, conditions that might spark peasant wrath had to be alleviated to assure the efficient operation of the dynasty. Peasants were the foundation of the nation, as the Confucian dictum asserts. And if that base were upset, the dynasty would be in turmoil.

The central government did not assert itself directly in local affairs. It divided the country into circuits *(to)*, provinces *(mok)*, prefectures *(chu)*, and districts *(kun, hyŏn)*. When emergencies arose, the central government dispatched inspector generals *(sasimgwan)*, commissioners *(anch'alsa)*, and other ad hoc officials to address these problems. These, however, were temporary offices. The only central officials posted outside the capital for specified terms were the magistrates *(suryong)* at the *chu* level and the lesser magistrates *(kammu)* at the *hyŏn* level. The magistrate system covered only one-third of the localities, however, leaving vast areas of the countryside with indirect rule. To fill this gap the central government depended on the effi-

ciency of the local headman *(hojang)* and local magnates *(hyangni)* to
initiate and enforce policy.[2] These local leaders—together with officials appointed by the central government to inspect the local
administration, such as commissioners and inspector generals—generally attended to peasants' needs and thus averted uprisings. Society was stable. Peasants and lowborns acknowledged their subservient positions.[3]

During Myŏngjong's reign, however, this order began to crumble.
As we have seen, the local power structure changed fundamentally.
Starting as early as the beginning of the twelfth century, the central
government took a direct role in local politics by establishing many
new district offices and dispatching a plethora of central inspectors
to rural areas. With increased central supervision, the local leaders
had less responsibility for regional affairs. This transformation,
which peaked early in Myŏngjong's reign with the establishment of
still more district offices, might have succeeded had the central government been able to retain some vitality.[4] But just at this time the
breakdown in central leadership, coupled with resistance from peasants, monks, and civil officials, caused Koryŏ's once stable regional
system to disintegrate.

By the middle of the Myŏngjong period, the central administration seems to have abandoned its direct responsibility over local
affairs, leaving the rural areas leaderless and without support. With
local administration in shambles, there was little direction or order.
Peasants were left to manage themselves; drought and famine raged;
and hastening disaster, dishonest officials took advantage of the
uncertainties of the age. Equally significant developments occurred
in the central political and social structure as lowborns and peasants
began to reach senior dynastic positions and assume offices of
authority in the kingdom. Men who had been the children of slaves
and farmers challenged and cracked the monopoly of the ruling
elites.

After seizing command in 1196, Ch'oe Ch'unghŏn had to confront these new developments. He had to balance the centrifugal
forces that had stripped the central authority of its power in the
provinces. And he had to restructure Koryŏ society, if he could, to
make it more amenable to his control. Ch'oe Ch'unghŏn had to find
ways to alleviate the causes of peasant unrest, he had to resolve the
problems posed by the breakdown of the social system, and he had

to assert his authority over the kingdom. As we have seen, Ch'oe Ch'unghŏn opted for the most expedient move: he sought a restoration of the former dynastic order. Essentially he tried to reassert central authority over the local areas to allay peasant grievances and to reestablish the social hierarchy by limiting the mobility of lowborns. Violent opposition by peasants and lowborns, however, hindered the realization of these goals. A number of revolts erupted in the first decade of Ch'oe rule. They were both symptoms and causes of discontent. Understanding these revolts—their origins and the Ch'oe response to them—helps to clarify the conditions of the age. At first the Ch'oe House sought to co-opt the peasant and lowborn classes into supporting its new system. If resistance still flourished, however, it then marshaled more forceful means to crush opposition. In pursuing these policies, the Ch'oe House assured a greater degree of social mobility for only a few favorite slaves at the bottom of the social order who could serve its particular needs.

PEASANT REVOLTS

During the years Ch'oe Ch'unghŏn commanded the kingdom, at least eight peasant rebellions erupted in various parts of the country:

 1199: Kangnŭng–Kyŏngju

 1200: Kimhae

 1202: T'amna (Cheju)

 1202–1204: Kyŏngju

 1203: Kigye (near Kyŏngju)

 1208: Munŭng

 1217: Chinwihyŏn

 1217: Sŏgyŏng

The causes of these disturbances were far from uniform. The economic situation of the peasants, already desperate because of the fiscal collapse that occurred in the latter part of Myŏngjong's reign, is one possible factor. The economy did not immediately improve with the rise of the Ch'oe House. Ch'oe Ch'unghŏn acknowledged that part of the woes stemmed from the breakdown of the land order as peasants were plunged into bankruptcy and taxes were aggressively assessed. Proposal 3 of his ten-point reform of 1196 sought to restructure dynastic land relations to ensure the peasants a means of survival. This was a slow process. Ch'oe Ch'unghŏn could not restore economic vitality merely by redrawing land boundaries. The dynastic fiscal problems were too serious. Economic chaos continued as Ch'oe Ch'unghŏn came to power: many of the ruling elite, anxious to secure their own fiscal well-being, seized land and charged extortionate land fees, thus robbing the peasants of their livelihood.[5] Peasants, forced off the land and without recourse, would revolt if only to steal grain from central or local granaries.

A second cause may have been peasant resentment of the rapid rise of slaves and other lowborns in Myŏngjong's reign.[6] As men of humble origins like Yi Ŭimin started to dictate policy, peasants revolted to improve their lot. Not only did they suffer economic exploitation but they also harbored social ambitions. Peasants openly questioned why they should be blocked from improving their status. If men of humble birth, by this logic, could achieve prominent office, peasants too should no longer be forced to toil and accept humiliating positions as laborers. Furthermore, not only did they resent being ruled by slaves but they were appalled that many peasants had no choice but to abandon their commoner status and become slaves to escape starvation. Once the social system began to show signs of weakness, it could not contain all the various expressions of social aspiration.

Political developments in the kingdom, which played into the hands of malcontents, form a third set of factors. The forced abdication of Myŏngjong in 1197 agitated the peasants and opened the gates for new waves of social release. The removal of the monarch, who sat at the apex of the social order and personified many of the abuses of the system, afforded an incentive to peasants to rectify what they viewed as injustice. Thus peasants and lowborns were encouraged to rebel in order to establish a new society in which they too would have opportunities for wealth and political might. Peasants aggravated this unstable political environment by taking advantage of the fledgling Ch'oe rule. It required several years for Ch'unghŏn to build a stable order. Until he was able to demonstrate his absolute authority, peasants and lowborns challenged the regime in hopes of improving their lot.

A number of peasant revolts erupted from other causes. Most salient, perhaps, was the general breakdown in local government. When the disappearance of a strong central authority during the late Myŏngjong period curtailed state intervention into local matters, local leaders were able to assume more autonomy. Ch'oe Ch'unghŏn, in his endeavor to reassert central power, inevitably collided with local leaders or, having won the support of the local elite, then conflicted with the peasants, who were enjoying a relative degree of freedom from state meddling.

In Kimhae in 1200, for example, state and local leaders (hojok) joined to suppress peasants. At that time a group of men rebelled and tried to kill the local community leaders. The government official immediately assisted the local leaders in quelling the revolt. The peasants then complained to the official: "We wanted to eliminate the powerful and greedy to clean out our village. Why do you attack us?" Their pleas were to no avail, for the local leaders and dynastic official were working together. Judging from the peasant complaints about greed, the local elite must have drained considerable wealth from the countryside.[7] To bring a degree of stability and order to the kingdom, central leadership had to be reasserted. Often this meant working with the local elite. It was the peasants who resisted these changes, for they ended up paying more to state and local leaders as they lost their relative autonomy. Many of the revolts were especially severe in such areas as subordinate districts (pugok), where peasants were often burdened with especially onerous levies.[8]

Regional aspirations coupled with subtle political overtones were also apparent in some of the revolts. Four peasant revolts took place in southeastern Korea over a period of five years (1199–1203), and two slave insurrections occurred there during the same period. Although many of the conditions outlined here were present in this area, too, the region was unique for several reasons. First, it was the site of the former Silla capital. Because of this, Kyŏngju was made a subsidiary capital in the Koryŏ dynasty. Even after nearly three centuries, loyalty to the old Silla kingdom and Silla traditions remained latent in the Kyŏngju area.[9] Second, Kyŏngju was the power center of Ch'oe Ch'unghŏn's archrival, Yi Ŭimin. Yi Ŭimin had built on Silla sentiment in constructing his own power base during the latter part of Myŏngjong's reign. In 1193, Yi Ŭimin's son and one of his associates, Kim Sami, tried to revive pro-Silla localism to enhance their control. The fact that the associate was a local hoodlum indicates the degree to which Koryŏ power had waned.[10] Once Ch'oe Ch'unghŏn was in command, he made several attempts to eradicate any lingering vestiges of Yi Ŭimin's power and sent a number of expeditions to the Kyŏngju area. By removing Yi Ŭimin's clique, he was also attacking the local power structure in the Kyŏngju district, which Yi Ŭimin had used to dominate the area. Reiterating Yi Ŭimin's ploys, the rebels claimed: "The Koryŏ mandate is completely exhausted. Silla must be restored."[11] And third, it was relatively easy for Kyŏngju residents to consider revolt because of the area's distance from the capital at Kaegyŏng. It is significant that Ch'oe Ch'unghŏn asserted he was upholding Koryŏ dynastic legitimacy in his suppression of the area.[12]

In one of the revolts that erupted at the end of Ch'oe Ch'unghŏn's rule, there was still another factor that spurred peasants to resistance: foreign invasion. The uprisings in the Western Capital (in the north), while expressing peasant distress and antigovernment sentiment, would probably not have occurred without the turmoil caused by foreign attacks. This area, like others across the country, had been subjected to increased intervention and control from the central government. But through the Ch'oe House's more efficient administration, peasant discontent was gradually quelled. Now, suddenly, foreign invaders overran the north and laid waste to it. The initial shock of defeat left local administration in a shambles. The Ch'oe House was unable to stave off open insurrection. In the Western Capital region peasants, destitute from battle, without leaders, homes, or food, were easy prey to the urgings of malcontents. The Chinwihyŏn revolt in central Korea might have been caused by a similar administrative breakdown due to foreign attacks.

DEALING WITH DISSENT

From the start of his rule, Ch'oe Ch'unghŏn confronted the peasant disturbances by seeking a speedy solution. In his response he not only demonstrated a keen understanding of the opposing power configurations but also pursued ruthless means to suppress them. He also attempted to win the support of his antagonists through compromise and the amelioration of their grievances. The ten proposals Ch'oe Ch'unghŏn submitted to the king shortly after his seizure of power reveal his concern for peasant life, especially the vitality of local government. In Proposal 4, Ch'oe Ch'unghŏn recounted the harsh conditions facing the peasants because of corrupt clerks and officials. Before the nation can be ordered, he reasoned, the grievances of the peasant must be addressed. To alleviate these problems, Ch'oe Ch'unghŏn suggested that better administrators be dispatched, that the presentation of gifts be curtailed, and that ostentation and luxury be forbidden.

Immediately after Ch'oe Ch'unghŏn presented his reform proposals, he dispatched court officials to the various circuits in the kingdom to talk to the people and soothe their fears.[13] He also sent commissioners *(anch'alsa)* to the countryside on numerous occasions to inquire into the problems of the peasants.[14] Besides dispatching officials, Ch'oe Ch'unghŏn sought to raise the general integrity and administrative talents of officialdom. In the previous chapter we noted the high quality of the Ch'oe bureaucracy. As Ch'oe Ch'unghŏn reinvigorated the central dynastic institutions, he also reasserted central power over the local administration. This policy is particularly evident in his manipulation of area designations, such as *chu* and *hyŏn*, as a reward or punishment and in his constant dispatch of central officials to investigate outlying areas.[15] These officials, concerned with peasant needs, regulated government policy in a just manner by curtailing extortion and excessive taxation. In addressing the grievances of people living in *pugok*, the Ch'oe regime elevated the status of many of these regions to *hyŏn* or *chu*.[16] Furthermore, by restocking granaries to meet emergencies and encouraging agriculture, the Ch'oe House restored stability to the countryside.

Ch'oe Ch'unghŏn even used measures such as geomancy to curtail peasant uprisings and other disturbances. The Koryŏ histories report:

> Yi Ŭimin's gravel dike was destroyed. Earlier Ŭimin had constructed a dike from Nakt'a bridge to Cho bridge. Bordering the dike, he planted willow trees. People did not dare utter any criticism, but praised him as the "new road minister." Later, when the southeastern bandits had a great uprising and slaves planned to rebel, a diviner indicated this dike to be the cause. Therefore they destroyed it.[17]

Topographical abuses were held accountable for many problems.[18] The authorities also sought divine aid by praying to Buddha to resolve the constant uprisings. The king, for example, made at least one journey to Poje temple to pray for the extinction of bandits.

Reward and punishment were traditional methods employed to pacify peasants and suppress banditry. In 1199, the Royal Secretariat–Chancellery memorialized: "Even though the remaining cliques of bandit officials, Cho Wŏnjŏng and Sŏk Ch'ung, have received royal pardon, avoided banishment, and been freed, to reprimand bandits we request that they never again be given *chikchŏn* [office land]."[19] Although this measure did not bring an immediate halt to peasant trouble and banditry, the administration used promises of reconciliation to bring stability to the kingdom. When several bandit leaders surrendered in Sinjong's reign, the king gave them wine, food, and clothing and sent them home.[20]

Ch'oe Ch'unghŏn resorted to more extreme action when his temperate policies failed. On a number of occasions, he countered forceful resistance with decisive military attacks. He repeatedly dispatched troops during his early period of rule to quiet one uprising after another. In 1198, for example, Ch'oe Ch'unghŏn used soldiers to quell a slave revolt in the capital. In the following two years, 1199 and 1200, he again mobilized men to end uprisings in the Kyŏngsang area. He made additional dispatches in 1202 and 1204. In extreme cases he would demote an area's regional status.[21] His policies were fairly effective: after he died there was a lull of about ten years when few peasant uprisings or other domestic disturbances occurred.

Ch'oe Ch'unghŏn's descendants, U and Hang, continued these policies of stabilization. Ch'oe U sought to bring order to the peasants' life by sustaining the land system—both the land stipend law and private holdings—and returning land and tenants that Ch'unghŏn had seized to their lawful owners. Ch'oe U also attempted to restore the integrity of the tax structure and maintain the existing local administration. Between 1225 and 1246, Ch'oe U used the tax system to address peasant problems more than once: in 1225 he stopped the corvée tax around the country; in 1246 he waived both the corvée and tribute taxes in Sŏhae for seven years; earlier in 1242 he expressed concern about collecting taxes as peasants were unable to harvest their crops.[22] These measures would stabilize peasant society, Ch'oe U hoped, and assure a fairer distribution of responsibilities and economic burdens. This strategy was relatively successful at the outset. But when Ch'oe U moved the capital to Kanghwa Island in 1232, governmental neglect provoked a number of revolts. The first started in Kaegyŏng, when an official of low rank, who remained in the abandoned city, took advantage of the circumstances by inciting local hoodlums and slaves to rebel. Monks from neighboring temples, joining this nucleus, formed three army units.

On hearing of the disturbance, Ch'oe U dispatched troops who brought the uprising to a quick end. Several months later, at the end of 1232, people in the Western Capital also rebelled. But the Ch'oe House again responded by sending some three thousand of its own troops who pacified the revolt with the aid of the district military commissioner *(pyŏngmasa)*. After this, the histories report, the Western Capital became a wasteland. In the following year, when peasants rebelled in Kyŏngju, the Ch'oe House responded with equally decisive attacks.[23] Although peasants might have thought that the Ch'oe House, by withdrawing to Kanghwa, had lost its ability to maintain order, the regime demonstrated its vitality by rapidly pacifying revolts.

These revolts were random expressions of discontent, however, and not necessarily representative of the period. It should be emphasized that there were few revolts during this time of foreign invasions. Indeed, the peasants played a major role in resisting the Mongols.[24] Peasants, formed into local patrol units *(pyŏlch'o)*, executed guerrilla warfare against the Mongols, temporarily blocking their advances. When faced with the alternative of capitulating to foreign demands or fighting for their own land and kingdom, the peasants in most cases chose the latter course. Localism might have been one reason, but the Ch'oe House's adroit use of tax incentives and exemptions to secure peasant support was undoubtedly effective. From its new insular capital the Ch'oe House demonstrated its ability to maintain control over the peninsula. As peasant support was crucial to the success of the Ch'oe regime, it made considerable efforts to alleviate the burdens of the peasantry. Although Ch'oe Ch'unghŏn faced bleak prospects at the start because of constant domestic disturbances, the Ch'oe House competently countered the turmoil and retained the allegiance of most peasants during the Mongol invasions.

One reason for this impressive record can be traced to the Ch'oe House's ability to stabilize local government. It was the local township headmen *(hojang)* who were responsible for collecting taxes and

ultimately administering dynastic policy toward peasants. Although
the Ch'oe House curtailed the *hojang*'s power and that of the local
inspector general,[25] as the central government assumed greater
responsibility for local administration, the Ch'oe system seems to
have worked equitably and to have enlisted the support of much of
the populace.

Lowborns

Accompanying many of the peasant uprisings during this period
were slave revolts. Slaves, like peasants, were burdened with excessive
demands on their labor and received few social or economic benefits. Although slave revolts had occurred sporadically throughout traditional Korean history, during the military period they became
more frequent. Slave revolts and peasant unrest often evolved out of
similar causes. But the social discrimination leveled at the slave and
other lowborn people was much more severe. If the peasant's life was
toilsome, the slave's existence was desperate: the lowborn class was at
the bottom of the social scale, peasants in the middle, and aristocrats
at the top.

As we know very little indeed about other varieties of the lowborn, most of this discussion concerns slaves. Slave activity was so
striking during this period that some have come to believe they had
achieved a high degree of mobility. The term "slave," however, is not
a totally accurate translation of the word *"nobi."* To most Westerners,
a slave is considered property, subject to the will of one man, coerced
into labor and service, and denied individual and family rights. In
the American context, moreover, there are racist overtones and a
history of abject subordination. Korean *nobi,* by contrast, had much
greater control over their own existence, although few avenues of
social advancement were available to them and they were subject to
the ultimate demands of their owner. The size of the *nobi* population
in Koryŏ is debated: some estimate that perhaps 30 percent of the
population comprised slaves.[26]

Slaves appeared in two forms: public and private.[27] Public slaves
belonged to the state and performed menial tasks in government
offices or worked in shops that supplied essential commodities to
the court and the ruling elite. The government also supplied public
slaves to officials as attendants. The number of these slaves was fixed
according to the official's rank; often they acted as couriers or

escorts. All other slaves were privately owned—by kings, officials, or temples—and comprised two groups: ordinary slaves and out-resident slaves. Although the latter were slaves in name, the socio-economic position of some is believed to have been similar to commoner tenants.[28] They paid "personal tribute" to their masters in the form of 50 percent of their produce whereas tenants paid an equivalent in taxes to the state.

Men became slaves in different ways. Prisoners of war or criminals often became slaves. There are also examples of people selling themselves into slavery for survival or for religious purposes.[29] Whatever the origin, slave status was inherited. All members of a family often shared equally in the inheritance of slaves. In fact, the transfer of slaves was much more equal than the succession to land rights. It is believed that slave ownership was more common than private land-ownership at the start of the Koryŏ kingdom.[30] Manumission could be achieved either by purchase or by the will of the master.

During the twelfth century, some slaves achieved social recognition and escaped their humble status. Slaves were not immune to the problems confronting peasants and other elements of society, for they too had to work for their livelihood and perform services for their master. During the early twelfth century, however, some slaves took advantage of their owners' power in order to enhance their own status. Slaves freely helped augment their owner's wealth by acting as agents in land seizures and other means to expand aristocratic control. During Ŭijong's reign, the court relaxed restrictions by allowing slaves and eunuchs who had won royal favor to advance into low dynastic offices and carry out royal designs. Debauchery and governmental irregularities, sometimes caused by eunuchs and other lowborns in the administration, played a role in inciting the military revolt in 1170. The rise in the social, economic, and political position of slaves did not end with the onset of military rule. As seen in Chapter 2, during Myŏngjong's reign slaves achieved new levels of prominence in Koryŏ, usually cooperating with—and sometimes becoming—leaders of the new order.

SLAVE DISTURBANCES

Once Ch'oe Ch'unghŏn assumed power in 1196, there was a dramatic reversal in the official posture toward slaves that is best reflected in the increase of slave rebellions. During Myŏngjong's reign, there had been only one slave revolt. Then, within seven years of Ch'oe Ch'unghŏn's seizure of control, slaves participated in five major disturbances in different parts of the kingdom. There were two more major slave uprisings three decades later in 1232. These events were highly unusual. In the whole expanse of Korean history, there were virtually no slave revolts before or after this episode. These were the major slave disturbances during the Ch'oe House rule:

1196: Kaegyŏng

1198: Kaegyŏng

1200: Chinju

1200: Milyang

1203: Kaegyŏng

1232: Ch'ungju

1232: Kaegyŏng

This shift in the attitude of the slaves was not only a response to growing hostility from the ruling elite but also an expression of resentment toward the new policies of Ch'oe Ch'unghŏn.

The Manjŏk rebellion in 1198 sheds light on the causes of discontent among the slaves. Manjŏk was a private slave who, with other men of similar social status from the capital, joined to plot against the ruling elite. Manjŏk declared:

> Since the 1170 coup and the 1173 countercoup, the nation has witnessed many high officials rising from humble (ch'ŏn) status. How could these generals and ministers be different from us in origin? If one has the opportunity, then anyone can make it. Why should we still toil and suffer under the whip?[31]

Agreeing to rise up and kill Ch'oe Ch'unghŏn and their own lords on a prearranged signal, the slaves set a specified day to revolt. Finally, after burning their slave registers, they would become lords and generals themselves. On the appointed day, however, their numbers were insufficient so they postponed the revolt. But by then the plot had been revealed. The authorities seized and drowned Manjŏk and some one hundred slaves.

Was the major thrust behind the Manjŏk rebellion the quest for social liberation?[32] One cannot deny that by burning their slave registers and killing their masters, the slaves were seeking to improve their social status. They obviously felt that with Ch'oe Ch'unghŏn's administration in power just two years, they might be able to rally many to their cause and topple the Ch'oe authority. But if slave conditions were improving, as witnessed during Myŏngjong's reign, it would have been better for them to remain silent and not try to unseat the new government. Manjŏk rebelled, not to maximize rising aspirations, but in frustration at Ch'oe challenges to the political and social advances of slaves. Ch'oe Ch'unghŏn vigorously rooted out slave resistance. The fact that no additional slave revolts occurred from 1203 until the Mongols invaded demonstrates the success of Ch'oe suppression.[33]

Unlike the early military rulers, Ch'oe Ch'unghŏn seemed eager to restore the traditional social order and showed little sympathy for slave aspirations. His exclusion of men with inferior class origins from the dynastic structure has already been demonstrated.[34] Soon after he assumed power, his ten injunctions criticized the activities of the slaves: "The slaves of powerful houses fight to collect land rents, making the people groan in anxiety and pain." Once Ch'oe power was secure, there was no reference to harassment by slaves or their arrogance in economic endeavors. The slaves seem to have ceased their economic activities and reduced their involvement in politics.[35] The slave disturbances during this time were a direct expression of their frustration under Ch'oe House rule. The fact that they revolted underscores their political awareness and their understanding of the power structure. With their hopes of political and economic influence contained and their social advance again blocked, revolt was one of the readiest ways to escape their desperate situation. Slave uprisings signaled not only a breakdown in the social structure but also Ch'oe Ch'unghŏn's success at reordering the entire social scale.[36]

In contrast to his tempered pacification of peasant disturbances, Ch'oe Ch'unghŏn countered the slave revolts with extreme severity. In Manjŏk's rebellion, he interrogated suspects and drowned the accused in a river. After the Chinju slave revolt several years later, he at once sent officials to pacify the area. With another slave disturbance in the capital in 1203, Ch'oe Ch'unghŏn captured, interrogated, and drowned some fifty slaves. To those slaves who were willing to expose such revolts, Ch'oe Ch'unghŏn offered rewards including manumission.[37] Through such policies he effectively countered slave uprisings until well after the Mongol invasions had commenced.

THE STATUS OF SLAVES

Despite the lack of records, slaves probably continued to perform their former economic functions of collecting rents and levies for their masters. Some slaves found positions in the power structure. Furthermore, the Koryŏ histories relate that when northern invaders defeated the dynastic troops in 1217, the kingdom selected public and private slaves to serve as soldiers.[38] Slaves not only went into the dynastic forces but private citizens had these people join their own guards. In 1218, Tae Chipsŏng and others, because they had no private troops of their own, coerced slaves, monks, and others to join their forces.[39]

Ch'oe Ch'unghŏn treated his own personal slaves well, guaranteeing them support and watching after their needs.[40] Consider, for example, his slave Tonghwa and her husband Ch'oe Chunmun:

> Ch'unghŏn had a slave called Tonghwa. She was beautiful and had relations with many local men. Ch'unghŏn too had relations with her. One day, playing, he said: "For whom could you be a suitable wife?" The slave responded: "The recommendee of Honghae, Ch'oe Chunmun." Ch'unghŏn at once summoned Chunmun and retained him at his house, using him as a slave. Later he appointed him a sublieutenant, whence he advanced to become a grand general. Chunmun saw special favor every day. Those who wanted appointments would attach themselves to him.[41]

Ch'oe Ch'unghŏn found a husband for his slave Tonghwa and then placed him in the military and promoted him to top positions. Although Ch'oe Ch'unghŏn reinstated traditional class rigidity, he did not always enforce it and bestowed many benefits on his own cadre and friends. Like many of his other activities, Ch'oe Ch'unghŏn's restoration was tainted with favoritism. To men who worked for the Ch'oe House and were closely tied with its policy, Ch'oe Ch'unghŏn removed customary restraints and promoted them to suit his own will. He viewed all others as a threat and watched them carefully. Even though it carried contradictions, this strategy ultimately enabled Ch'oe Ch'unghŏn to consolidate his power expeditiously and bring stability to Koryŏ.

Many of the patterns observed in the changing fortunes of slaves are evident with others from the lowborn class. Eunuchs, traditionally of humble social status, actively formulated political and social decisions during the early military period. But as Ch'oe Ch'unghŏn consolidated his power, he removed these people from influential and sensitive areas. His steps, however, were incomplete. As in his slave policy, Ch'oe Ch'unghŏn vigorously curtailed lowborns as a group but was generous with individuals who supported his structure and had ties with his house. The net result was a basic tightening of the social order for all but his confidants.

Throughout his rule, Ch'oe Ch'unghŏn restrained eunuchs and regarded them with suspicion.[42] His antipathy toward this group was confirmed when eunuchs played a significant role in Kil In's counterrevolt in 1196 and then in Hŭijong's attempt to assassinate him. Ch'oe Ch'unghŏn's anti-eunuch stance was behind his order to destroy the well at Tarae and his mandate that the court use the well at Kwangmyŏng temple instead. In doing this he pointed to Koryŏ tradition, which claimed that if the king should drink from the Tarae well the eunuchs would gain power.[43] This action revealed Ch'oe Ch'unghŏn's determination to undermine eunuch influence and thereby restrain potential sources of royal authority. For the duration of his rule, eunuchs all but disappeared from the historical records.

Not only did Ch'oe Ch'unghŏn deny eunuchs privileges, he also forced artisans to curtail their activities. In 1199, the histories reported that he forbade artisans to wear headgear. (People with headgear usually worked for the royal household and therefore enjoyed prestige.) By reviving discarded customs, Ch'oe Ch'unghŏn was attempting to ensure greater social stability in the country and reassert the primacy of Koryŏ's social codes. Four years later, another example appears. *Kisaeng*, female entertainers, were classified among the lowborn. Ch'a Yaksŏng had two sons by a *kisaeng*. One had entered the Royal Confucian Academy and the other had reached a position above the sixth *p'um* grade. Ch'oe Ch'unghŏn ordered that they be limited to the seventh *p'um* rank and be removed from the academic roster.[44]

Although there were many social restrictions, enforcement was incomplete. The advancement of certain slaves has been mentioned, and Ch'oe Ch'unghŏn aided other lowborns and people in the *namban* (technical services).[45] The *Koryŏsa* reports that when one U

Kwangyu became provision warder of the Royal Archives (Kwŏnji Hammunjihu), ranking officials commented:

> "Since Kwangyu is in the *namban*, it is not right for him to hold high office." Accordingly, they would not give him clearance. Ch'unghŏn then responded: "Kwangyu formerly was quite able in handling investiture and foreign relations with Chin, so I especially gave him high offices. How can you firmly insist on regulations?"[46]

Ch'oe Ch'unghŏn, who would not allow two sons of a *kisaeng* into the upper ranks, was permitting others of humble background to advance. Although trying to enforce social regulations, the Ch'oe House leader was also politically alert and willing to compromise his own social policy in order to reward the loyal and able. His system, which accented his primacy, was undoubtedly strengthened by this flexible attitude that accepted social limitations as a convention, but not as a binding rule for his followers.

LOWBORNS UNDER CH'OE U, HANG, AND ŬI

Ch'oe U essentially continued Ch'unghŏn's policies. Ch'oe U was an astute man who realized that much of what his father had inaugurated was politically expedient. But he was diligent in removing any of Ch'oe Ch'unghŏn's loyal followers who threatened his structure. One of his first acts after establishing himself on his father's death was to banish people who had been close to Ch'oe Ch'unghŏn. In this group were slaves such as Tonghwa. These slaves surrounded Ch'oe Ch'unghŏn and, much like eunuchs attending a king, served and aided the Ch'oe leader in all his endeavors. They were quite familiar with Ch'oe politics, and now their interference in U's affairs could be fatal to the Ch'oe House.

Loyalty and individual ties were important bonds in the Ch'oe period. Power came to men who could recruit trusted followers and maintain their allegiance. For this reason, Ch'oe Ch'unghŏn went to extremes to provide for the needs of slaves like Tonghwa and his retainers in general. These people, in return, gave uncompromising fidelity to Ch'oe Ch'unghŏn. But as witnessed by their subsequent purge under U, their loyalty was not transferable. One of the weaknesses of the Ch'oe power structure was its inability to translate loyalty toward individual leaders into a sense of allegiance to the whole house. Furthermore, an environment in which each leader is surrounded by his own cadre of followers enhances the potential for power conflicts within the entire structure among subordinate groups jockeying for influence. Ch'oe U seems to have understood this quite well. For he quickly isolated military opponents of his rule and expelled his father's faithful servants, replacing them with his own followers. As Ch'oe U speedily eliminated one group of slaves, he would shower others with favors and positions in an effort to consolidate his own following. An Sŏkchŏng was the son of a private slave. Ch'oe U was generous with him, granting him a position in the Taegak (a censorial body) over the objections of others. As this slave was useful to Ch'oe U and his structure, U protected and promoted him.[47]

Toward other people of lowborn status, Ch'oe U enforced the same policy of upholding social restrictions that could easily be suspended when politically expedient. For example, the *Koryŏsa* reported: "Yu Sŏk's great-grandmother was Yejong's concubine. Because of national codes, he could not get into the censorial bodies or high offices." U also enforced a regulation that limited the advance of one Son Pyŏn because Son's wife was from a branch of the royal family. In these cases, the Ch'oe House resurrected the old social order and restored the dynastic hierarchy. But others, such as chosen eunuchs, found favor. When the civilian Yu Ch'ŏnu wanted to return to the Personnel Authority, he first had to win the support of a eunuch by means of a financial gift. Another eunuch in 1245 gained recognition for passing with the top score in a national examination.[48] The Ch'oe leaders enforced former dynastic regulations for the general administration of the kingdom, yet they applied a different code for their own cadre of close followers. The Ch'oe House essentially sought a restoration that would suit its own needs.

Although Ch'oe U's successors, Ch'oe Hang and Ch'oe Ŭi, relaxed the rigid regulations applied to the lowborn class, they did not institute a massive manumission of slaves. Aside from the fact that both Ch'oe Hang and Ŭi, as offspring of mothers who were concubines, could themselves be classified as lowborn,[49] there was some infiltration of men of humble origins into the top offices of the dynasty during this time. Slaves like Ch'oe Yangbaek became confi-

dants to Hang. In 1258, the dynastic histories relate how Ch'oe Ŭi's
house slave became a junior colonel *(nangjang)* and note that the
appointment of slaves to posts of the sixth *p'um* grade and above
commenced from this time.[50]

Ch'oe Social Policies

Although the Ch'oe leaders might have had some proclivity toward
enlisting men of similar social backgrounds into their administration, one is led to speculate on the possible effect of the Mongol
invasions on social mobility. Slaves played a defensive role against
the invaders. At Ch'ungju, for example, they formed a patrol unit to
withstand the Mongols. This slave unit revolted soon after the Mongols retreated, however, because they became embroiled in a dispute
with the local elite. The slaves were willing to defend their area, but
when local leaders tried to curb their influence, they revolted.
Twenty years later, however, slaves who had been given ranks in the
dynasty as a reward for their merit achieved manumission in the
name of national defense.[51] In 1253, one Kim Yunhu, who was leading a defense against the Mongols in the Ch'ungju area, promised
that every man, regardless of class status, would receive an office. To
demonstrate his sincerity he burned the government slave registers.[52] One can only estimate how many similar incidents may have
occurred and the extent of social emancipation at this stage. But
undoubtedly some slaves were able to escape their humble status
through such action.[53]

It is difficult to offer any conclusions on the economic functions
of slaves at the end of Ch'oe rule. Although there are no records to
indicate that slaves of the elite resumed their former activities—such
as assisting their masters in land acquisitions or participating in tribute exchanges—they most probably performed such duties. Emphasis must be placed rather on their social liberation and political
advances. Undoubtedly this new mobility at the end of the Ch'oe
period may have facilitated slave efforts to achieve economic gains.
And it may have been the basis for further advances when Koryŏ submitted to control by the Mongol Yuan dynasty. Nevertheless, hereditary slavery was still in force and the Koryŏ elite would not tolerate
losing such a valuable economic resource. Moreover, those slaves

who did advance were able to capitalize on their ties with powerful officials to improve their personal situations.[54]

The general easing of social restrictions and the advancement of slaves in the late Ch'oe period were accompanied by a rise in the status of other lowborns, even house servants. When Ch'oe Hang's servants began to wear caps, the sources report, "the former regulations allowed only servants of the royal family to wear caps. . . . The wearing of caps by servants of powerful officials starts here. After this, servants of powerful houses generally all wore them."[55] Eunuchs played a more important role. When ranking officials were discussing strategies to check the Mongols, a eunuch participated in the council.[56] Ch'oe Ch'unghŏn had tried to ostracize eunuchs, but Ch'oe U and Hang looked to them—either in eagerness to broaden their political contacts or in response to the exigencies of the age, which demanded loyalty first.

Many men of humble origin rose to prominence during this late Ch'oe period. The best example is Kim Chun, the man who first served the Ch'oe House as a slave servant but later led troops to defeat his masters and end sixty years of Ch'oe rule. Moreover, the social emancipation that commenced at this time was not cut short with the Ch'oe collapse. When the king rewarded those who participated in the overthrow of the Ch'oe House, he permitted all who were of low status to advance, regardless of social background. Furthermore, eunuchs continued to enjoy mobility: in 1260, two years after the downfall of the Ch'oe House, a eunuch reached the sixth p'um grade.[57]

The attitude of the Ch'oe leaders governed the pace of social mobility. As Ch'oe Ch'unghŏn consolidated his power, he sought to freeze the social structure. Rather than attempt daring new social changes, he met challenges to his regime with traditional methods of stabilization. To Ch'oe Ch'unghŏn, one of the fastest and most expedient means of restoring order to the country was to regulate the social classes, limit social mobility, and restore the effective functioning of the dynastic administration. He also dispatched many officials to various parts of rural Korea and reinvigorated regional administrations. When revolts continued, he used armed might to enforce his will. Ch'oe U accepted and followed this policy. It was a balanced and flexible strategy that allowed room for rewards and advancement for supporters while maintaining the regulations of traditional Koryŏ society. Although there were contradictions and inconsistencies in this structure, it worked quite effectively and demonstrated the ability of the Ch'oe administration to secure order. Even when faced with serious peasant and slave unrest, Ch'oe Ch'unghŏn was able to blend a rigid authoritarianism with opportunities for the social advance of select followers. He tempered his policy with a strategy that showed pragmatism and compromise. After Ch'oe Hang's succession to power, social restrictions started to relax as people of lowborn status played a greater role in the ruling structure. These changes were encouraged by the new tone set through Ch'oe Hang and Ch'oe Ŭi's leadership, but the Mongol invasions were also a force in eroding social barriers since they required that all sectors of society be mobilized. These developments, however, appear to have been short-lived. In subsequent decades the Koryŏ central elite once again, much like Ch'oe Ch'unghŏn, restricted the options that would allow lowborns to advance socially.

7

Buddhism under the Military

Buddhism during the military period remained at the center of Koryŏ's religious, intellectual, and cultural life, much as it did during the entire five centuries of Koryŏ. Not only were Buddhist monks tied to many of the leaders that dominated the dynasty during this age, but clerics assumed a new intellectual role and provided new directions to Buddhist speculative inquiry. This chapter assesses the relationship between Buddhism and the military rulers of Koryŏ.[1] Although we cannot avoid touching upon philosophical developments, our primary focus will be on the institutional and social changes that marked Buddhism's dynamic growth.[2] Many scholars have noted the emergence of Sŏn (Zen) Buddhism as the dominant religious expression of the age, but its links to the military leaders and their reasons for fostering this particular school need to be explored in greater detail. This chapter also assesses the relationship between the military leadership and the other Buddhist schools. Moreover, while benefiting from the patronage of the military leaders, Buddhism also prospered under increased attention from other sectors of society. Buddhism during the military period attracted many of the finest minds of the kingdom to its temples, as scholars and young students studied with the learned clerics of the age. The result was an inevitable commingling of Buddhist and Confucian inquiry. This chapter explores these themes in an effort to evaluate the role of the military leadership and particularly the Ch'oe House in these vibrant changes.

Buddhism in Early Koryŏ

Buddhism permeated Koryŏ culture. From the founding of the dynasty in 918, Buddhist doctrine and Buddhist priests were always present to lend the dynasty's leadership not only philosophical sustenance but also political legitimacy. Wang Kŏn's "Ten Injunctions" vividly demonstrated this function, and the king's frequent reliance on monks like Yiŏm is well known. In the social realm, elites and commoners alike enjoyed Buddhist holidays and celebrations: the Assembly of Eight Prohibitions (P'algwan) and Lantern Festival (Yŏndŭng) were especially popular. The vitality of the faith is evident, too, through the diversity of its expression. Flower Garland (Hwaŏm; Ch. Huayen) and Dharma Characteristics (Pŏpsang), the main sects of Doctrine (Kyo) Buddhism, the dominant school, forwarded a scholastic approach by emphasizing textual study. Sŏn, however, the Meditation school that initially appeared in Korea in late Silla, focused on sudden enlightenment and downplayed the use of scripture. Sŏn developed a devoted following among the regional lords of rural Korea, and in Koryŏ its leadership split into nine lineages.[3]

The monk Ŭich'ŏn (1055–1101) in the late eleventh century introduced new changes to this Buddhist world.[4] Ŭich'ŏn, son of King Munjong (r. 1046–1083), traveled to China and returned committed to bridging the difference between the Doctrine and Meditation schools. He preached the tenets of the Heavenly Terrace (Ch'ŏnt'ae; Ch. T'ien-t'ai) school, attempting to combine the special properties of Doctrine and Meditation into Heavenly Terrace. Respected both for his lineage and for his erudition, Ŭich'ŏn enabled Heavenly Terrace to win widespread acceptance up to his death.

Although Sŏn suffered neglect at the hands of Ŭich'ŏn and his followers, by the start of the twelfth century it was enjoying a revival as both the royal family and a number of prominent scholars showed intense interest.[5] King Yejong (r. 1107–1122) patronized a number of Sŏn Buddhist temples, such as Poje temple and Anhwa temple, and singled out the Sŏn monk Tamjin for special recognition. Scholars such as Yi Chahyŏn and Yun Ŏni also focused on Sŏn teachings. Generally Sŏn of this time was characterized by its isolation from worldly concerns and its emphasis on individual cultivation.[6] Yi

Chahyŏn of the Inju Yi lineage, for example, abandoned the secular world in search of meditation, living in a remote mountain area, and quickly earned such renown that King Yejong sought him out for instruction in Sŏn practices.[7]

The Doctrine (Kyo) school, having forged close ties with the court and ruling elites from the beginnings of the kingdom, remained the dominant force in Buddhism throughout the first half of the twelfth century. Its stress on the reading of scriptures and sutras appealed to the learned aristocrats, who lavishly patronized Doctrine temples. Koryŏ's capital Kaegyŏng, the center of aristocratic life, housed more than seventy temples, many of which were Kyo. Hŭngwang temple, near the palace, received special royal attention, and the court oversaw temple repairs there during Ŭijong's reign (1146–1170).[8] Sons of the eleventh-century monarchs Hyŏnjong, Munjong, and Sukchong became Doctrine monks, and Ŭijong's brother Ch'unghŭi was a Hŭngwang temple monk. The civil aristocrats forged similar ties. Kim Tonjung and his brother, for example, sons of Kim Pusik, built Kwanyŏn temple near Kaegyŏng.[9]

Koryŏ aristocrats supported temples for many reasons. Although genuine piety may have been one impulse, these elites also secured sizable economic gains. By ordaining family members into one of the Buddhist orders, they took advantage of Koryŏ tax codes that exempted clergy from certain responsibilities. Other laws allocating yields from the state land stipend system to monks also benefited these families. Moreover, by generous donations of material wealth and land, families could gain financial and spiritual blessings.

As a beneficiary of lavish donations, the Doctrine order gradually became one of the largest landholders in the kingdom.[10] In addition to landholdings, temples also owned slaves and controlled tenants who cultivated temple property. Moreover, temples managed a large number of handicraft industries, including weaving, porcelain manufacturing, wine making, and tea cultivation. Profits from these enterprises benefited both the temples and their patrons, who gained tax breaks and immunities associated with the temples.[11] Through its social, political, and economic ties, the Kyo Buddhist establishment formed symbiotic links with the dynasty and civil elites as all three parties became mutually dependent for their own well-being.

Buddhism and the 1170 Coup

By forcing King Ŭijong to abdicate and removing a number of key civil aristocrats from the government, the 1170 military revolt posed a threat to the Kyo Buddhist hierarchy. The skillfully fashioned links that bound the Doctrine school to the destiny of the court and central aristocrats were jeopardized by the military's attack on the highest element of dynastic power. After a period of cautious waiting, the main Kyo temples in the Kaegyŏng region rebelled in 1174 in hopes of restoring full authority to the king and the civilian elites.[12] The Kyo temples rebelled out of indignation as well as for political and economic reasons. In the 1170 military coup, many of the aristocratic patrons of the temples had been either killed or removed from power. Conditions deteriorated further in 1173 with the failure of Kim Podang's counterrebellion and then the murder of the former king, Ŭijong. Regarding these attacks as a direct threat to the existence of their temples, the monks chose to resist the new military leaders. But as neither side could destroy the other, the monks and military leaders were obliged to soften their mutual opposition and reevaluate their policies. Although the generals suppressed this revolt, after reasserting their authority they attempted to accommodate Doctrine interests. The success of this policy of combined suppression and conciliation can be seen in the fact that no major Doctrine resistance was registered again until the rise of General Ch'oe Ch'unghŏn at the end of the century.

Although somewhat constrained, Kyo temples continued to function and remained a focus of elite attention. Certainly the royal family did not forsake its interest in Kyo temples; the new king Myŏngjong became a most active patron. A number of his sons by concubines became monks and freely entered and left the palace.[13] Civil elites likewise lent support to the Doctrine establishment. And as the military leadership slowly fell into its own internal quarrels, the Kyo temples took advantage of this neglect to revive themselves.

Sŏn Buddhism, which had experienced renewed interest earlier in the century, also profited from royal, civil, and military support. A Sŏn examination to regulate advancement through the order started in 1170, the year of the military coup.[14] Poje temple, the most prestigious Sŏn temple in the capital, received special attention.[15] A year after his enthronement Myŏngjong visited first Poje temple and then several other unnamed temples.[16] After Yi Ŭibang's murder in 1174, monks rallied at Poje temple to press for further demands and refused to leave until the king dispatched special emissaries.[17] Military officials likewise patronized Sŏn temples. In 1175 the military commander Chŏng Chungbu repaired Poje temple and then held a completion ceremony. He also asked the king to attend despite the objection of an official in the Censorate.[18] Furthermore, many of the civilian elite who assisted the military officers at this time had already forged a close alliance with Sŏn temples.[19]

During these initial decades of military rule, as the governing structure deteriorated, both Sŏn and Kyo Buddhism functioned as important social institutions. Besides visiting Poje temple, the king made excursions to numerous other temples.[20] The court sponsored Buddhist ceremonies and on a number of occasions fed more than ten thousand monks at one seating.[21] Monks reciprocated by helping to stabilize unrest and even considering enlistment into the army.[22] Moreover, in 1181 a number of officials met at Pongun temple to devise new regulations for the kingdom. Clearly the major schools of the Buddhist hierarchy had accommodated themselves to the new power structure.

Because of their stature, and especially their ties to the civil elites, Buddhist temples continued to be repositories of wealth. This affiliation made them the targets of bandits and popular discontent. During the years after the coup, as military leaders engaged in their own bloody feuds, peasants were often left to fend for themselves. Embittered and impoverished by social and political unrest, some looked upon temples as easy prey. When the local bandit Mangi rebelled in 1176, hoping to redress personal grievances against the military lords, he captured a neighboring temple and killed the monks. A year later, bandits attacked Myodŏk temple and Hyangsan temple, capturing the resident monks.[23]

Monks were not always innocent bystanders; on occasion they too perpetrated misdeeds. Even in times of tranquility, clergy who were less than devout strayed far from their chosen calling in a quest for personal aggrandizement. In this age of turmoil and accelerated unrest, devious monks frequently became the center of plots and corruption. In 1177 and then again in 1178, monks at Hŭngwang temple in Kaegyŏng claimed fellow clerics were planning to rebel.

After sorting through the charges, the Council of Generals (Chungbang) arrested those deemed guilty.[24] When Kyŏng Taesŭng seized power, he quickly removed monks who had been affiliated with Chŏng Chungbu and his group.[25]

Besides attempting to manipulate government authority, monks relied on charms and superstition to win over elites and commoners alike. The monk Irŏm, more than any other personage, symbolizes the spiritual degeneration and instability of the age. Hearing claims that the monk could make the blind see and the dead live, King Myŏngjong called Irŏm to court. On the way, people flocked to attend him and even drank his bathwater, considering it holy. Once in the capital, the *Koryŏsa* claims, "high and low, young and old, competed to have an audience."[26] Although he was ultimately discovered to be a fraud, his popularity exposes the degenerate state of Buddhism and society. Officials, civilian and military alike, neglected their responsibilities of governing. During the last years of Myŏngjong's reign, as the tyranny of the newest military ruler, Yi Ŭimin, spread over the land, government leaders pursued individual quests and indulged in frequently meaningless Buddhist ceremonies. Both Myŏngjong and Yi Ŭimin used temples for their own personal gain: Myŏngjong relied on them as residences for his sons; Yi Ŭimin tapped them to enhance his political and economic advantage.[27] Historians, commenting on this corrupt state of affairs, complained that the king failed to act responsibly and charged that officials who should have been watching for omens *(t'aesa)* "only want to serve Buddha and pray in order to confuse the king's mind."[28]

Buddhism and the Rise of the Ch'oe House

The rise of Ch'oe Ch'unghŏn in 1196 saw a dramatic shift in the tenor of the period. If the years after the initial coup in 1170 marked a time of drift and a lack of national direction, Ch'oe Ch'unghŏn's rule imparted a new dynamism to the country's leadership as his military dictatorship charted policies that would stabilize society and government and thereby bring security for his own personal rule. Change is clearly visible in the Ch'oe House's attitude toward Buddhism. If the early military period was initially characterized by a policy of repression followed by an unclear agenda with regard to Buddhism, the Ch'oe period saw definite attempts to quell any political activity on the part of the Buddhist establishment. Philosophically, the Ch'oe rulers appreciated the Sŏn stance of disengagement in worldly affairs. But it was not until late in Ch'oe Ch'unghŏn's rule that they became active patrons of Sŏn monks and temples. During this later stage, the Ch'oe House fostered scholarship in the process of supporting Buddhist endeavors, thereby enabling the temples to become centers for schooling and speculation for Koryŏ's literary masters. Their support of Buddhism also helped Sŏn thought flourish among ordinary people.

Ch'oe Ch'unghŏn, who had witnessed the degeneration that occurred under Yi Ŭimin's rule and was disturbed by the corruption that pervaded the Buddhist hierarchy, immediately set out to check the more flagrant abuses. In the ten injunctions issued shortly after his own coup, Ch'oe Ch'unghŏn attacked both the needless proliferation of temples and the corruption of monks. He noted the problems caused by too many monks taking advantage of royal influence to extract profits from interest on grain loans and by powerful officials building too many temples for their own economic advantage. His message was clear: temples and their monks must remove themselves from political and economic pursuits.

He followed up this attack with definite action. First he demanded that Myŏngjong's sons who had become monks must leave the capital and return to their temples. When Ch'oe Ch'unghŏn forced Myŏngjong to abdicate, he banished these monks to offshore islands.[29] Having watched both Ŭijong and then Myŏngjong fall captive to Buddhist monks and neglect decorum and state affairs to patronize temples and priests, Ch'unghŏn concluded that only an authority free from these unsavory influences could prosper. Ch'oe Ch'unghŏn challenged not only the clergy, but the laity as well, as he attempted to curtail contacts that could be used for economic and political gain. Initially his goals were political. By curbing the Buddhist hierarchy, he could remove a potential as well as real threat to his structure and thus enhance his power.

These new policies prompted resistance from Buddhist monks—especially those affiliated with the Doctrine school. Although their response was not immediate, over the first twenty years of Ch'oe rule monks both inside and outside of Kaegyŏng revolted and once even seriously threatened Ch'oe Ch'unghŏn's life. The records list the following monk revolts during Ch'oe House rule:[30]

1202:	Puin temple; Tonghwa temple in the Taegu area
1203:	Pusŏk temple; Puin temple in Hŭngju; Ssangam temple in Songsaenghyŏn
1209:	Kwibŏp temple in Kaegyŏng
1211:	Monks join plot against Ch'oe Ch'unghŏn
1217:	Hŭngwang temple; Hongwŏn temple; Kyŏngbok temple; Wangnon temple; Anyang temple; Suri temple in Kaegyŏng

All these temples appear to have been affiliated with the Doctrine school. Just as this school revolted against the military leadership in the 1170s, it again registered its opposition to Ch'oe Ch'unghŏn.[31] Besides these overt physical threats, a number of plots were uncovered and false rumors surfaced periodically.[32] Ch'oe policies that threatened the economic and political status of temples sparked much of this unrest. To all of these threats, Ch'oe Ch'unghŏn responded with vigorous determination to be the master of the kingdom. Through force of arms he routed the recalcitrant monks.

Ch'oe Ch'unghŏn tempered his assaults on the Doctrine hierarchy with a measure of compromise. In 1197, aware of strained relations with the school, he proposed a visit to Hŭngwang temple.[33] Ch'oe Ch'unghŏn's son U likewise sought an accommodation with the Doctrine school and in 1223 sent eighteen small stupas made of yellow gold and a flower vase to Hŭngwang temple.[34] Furthermore, at this time there were Doctrine monks like Yoil, Taeho, and Chinŏk who actively propagated tenets of the faith.[35] Aware of the Doctrine school's power and anxious to avoid contests that only sapped the strength of the kingdom, the Ch'oe House hoped that a policy of reconciliation would mollify opposition and bring stability to Ch'oe rule and the dynasty.

The Sŏn Revival

The Ch'oe House pursued ties with the Sŏn school with special vigor. By turning to Sŏn, the Doctrine school's leading rival, Ch'oe Ch'unghŏn may have hoped to weaken or counterbalance Doctrine's dominant position in the Buddhist establishment. According to this reasoning the Doctrine school—too closely affiliated with the royal family, civilian elites, and sources of opposition to Ch'oe—could be checked not only through armed suppression and accommodation but by lending support to a competing school. Furthermore, Sŏn suited Ch'oe philosophical needs. For centuries Sŏn had had links with antiestablishment groups and held special appeal to the soldier. During the late ninth century, both of these elements are evident in Sŏn's ties with the regional strongmen who were undermining the authority of the Silla kingdom.[36] Earlier we noted Sŏn's increased popularity with certain men in Yejong's and Injong's reign who had chosen to shun central politics.

Sŏn suited the interests of the soldier. In the years after the military coup of 1170, Poje temple, the leading Sŏn temple in Kaegyŏng, became the focus of increased attention. With its emphasis on meditation and sudden enlightenment, Sŏn, more than any other Buddhist school, addressed the needs and the minds of all sectors of the army from the unlettered combatant to the sophisticated officer. Although it did not appeal exclusively to warriors, Sŏn's simplicity and its emphasis on meditation as a path to salvation gave this austere philosophy a particular attraction for military personnel.[37] Sŏn's dissociation from secular matters was another attractive feature. During Ch'oe Ch'unghŏn's rule, as this school flourished, Sŏn temples far from Kaegyŏng grew aloof from the centers of power.

Buddhism played a crucial role as a legitimizing force in Koryŏ society. Early leaders turned to Buddhism to show divine sanction for their rule. Monks frequently performed an important function as advisers to those on the throne. T'aejo had Yiŏm; Injong had Myoch'ŏng; later King Kongmin (r. 1351–1374) would have Sin Ton. These clerics-turned-advisers offered alternatives that might not have been supported by entrenched civil aristocrats or officials tied to specific programs.[38] The Sŏn order, offering the new military rulers another avenue of expression, provided a similar outlet. By communicating with Sŏn monks and supporting their endeavors, the Ch'oe leaders hoped to gain both spiritual and political benefits.[39]

The great revival of Sŏn under the Ch'oe House has been studied by many.[40] At the center of this revival was the monk Chinul (1158–1210). He had passed an examination for the Buddhist clergy in 1182 and then, after a time at Poje temple, went to southern Korea, stopping first in the southeast. Then, in 1188, he joined others at Kŏjo temple on Kong Mountain. This community at Kŏjo tem-

ple attracted many followers, and in 1197 Chinul decided to relo-
cate. In 1200, Chinul arrived at what was to be called Susŏn temple.
This area remained the base of his activities until his death in 1210.[41]
Over the course of his life, Chinul invigorated Sŏn thought. From a
philosophy that pursued only individual cultivation he transformed
it to one that sought a collective approach to cultivation and involved
all sectors of society.[42]

Chinul's teachings offered several paths to enlightenment. For
the less intellectually inclined, meditation was an accepted avenue.
For those who sought scholarly insight, Chinul advanced the pro-
fundity of text. Chinul was one of the great harmonizers of Korean
Buddhism. In some respects he was following the tradition of the
Silla monk Wŏnhyo who in the seventh century tried to unify Korea
spiritually. Chinul, maturing during the social and political turmoil
associated with the Myŏngjong period and searching for solutions to
contemporary problems, sought to breach the chasms of society with
Buddhist philosophy. Although Ch'oe Ch'unghŏn probably played
no direct role in Chinul's philosophical growth, he and his son U
certainly welcomed in principle ideas that argued for syncretism and
sought to end exclusiveness. Nevertheless, it is difficult to gauge the
depth of any of the Ch'oe rulers' intellectual understanding of Buddhism. Like most leaders, even today, they went through the public
motions of devotion and adherence to a spiritually acceptable path.

The Ch'oe House fostered Sŏn Buddhism in many ways. Both
Ch'oe Ch'unghŏn and U sent sons to study under Sŏn masters.[43]
The third Ch'oe dictator, Hang, who studied under Hyesim
(1178–1234) as a boy, had always been an ardent advocate of the
faith, even banishing those who belittled Buddhism.[44] The Ch'oe
leaders endowed and constructed Sŏn temples. Ch'oe Ch'unghŏn
took special interest in Ch'angbok temple and Taean temple and U
in Susŏn temple.[45] Other temples, such as Tansok in the Chinju
region of Kyŏngsang, Ssangbong in Chŏlla, and Chongnim temple
and Kangwŏl hermitage in the Namhae area, were centers of Ch'oe
influence. In 1245, at the height of the Mongol invasions, Ch'oe U
erected a Sŏn temple on Kanghwa Island.[46]

The Ch'oe leaders became patrons of key Sŏn monks, starting
with Chinul. Ch'oe Ch'unghŏn, U, and Hang sought to promote
Sŏn masters, and Ch'unghŏn intervened at least once to see that the
monk Chŏnggak became royal tutor *(wangsa)*.[47] Moreover, the

Ch'oe leaders sent their retainers to guard esteemed clerics, asking the monks to instruct them by presenting lectures on Sŏn topics.[48] Ch'oe U corresponded with Chinul's disciple, Hyesim, discussing Buddhist thought and laws. He asked Hyesim to travel to the capital to lecture on Sŏn. And later, when Hyesim became ill, Ch'oe U sent physicians to treat him.[49]

The Heavenly Terrace school (Ch'ŏnt'ae) did not disappear. In fact, it enjoyed a resurgence during the Ch'oe period. In shunning the political world, like Sŏn, it sought a new base in the outlying districts of the country, forming a major center in southwestern Korea not far from Chinul's community. The monk Yose, who had joined Chinul's retreat at Kŏjo temple, established a Heavenly Terrace community at Paengnyŏn temple on Kong (Mandŏk) Mountain. Preaching the Lotus Sutra, Yose also sought to reform Buddhism, making this faith accessible to elite and commoner alike. This community found strong support from local dignitaries and officials with regional ties.[50] The Ch'oe House offered donations and extended to Paengnyŏn temple a modicum of support.[51]

Buddhism Under Ch'oe Rule

The monarchs during the Ch'oe rule, as during much of Koryŏ, continued to be fervent supporters of Buddhist functions.[52] The Ch'oe House, manipulating kingship to promote stability and its own legitimacy, had established a curious relationship with the throne. (See Chapter 9.) The Ch'oe leaders, viewing such activities as beneficial for the kingdom, were content to have the kings patronize the various schools as an expression of their royal functions. They hoped that such public actions would defuse antagonism toward Ch'oe dominance and thereby increase stability and secure their legitimacy. There were dangers, of course. When Hŭijong, supported by a number of monks, joined a plot to kill Ch'oe Ch'unghŏn, the Ch'oe House struck back by exiling Hŭijong and the monks.

Hŭijong's revolt was the exception. Most kings forged close links with the Buddhist establishment in accordance with Ch'oe designs. As in previous reigns, the kings at this time made countless excursions to the country's renowned temples such as Kyo's Wangnyun temple and Sŏn's Poje temple.[53] Some trips were done out of piety, some for pleasure, and some to pray for the nation. The Ch'oe per-

mitted the kings to pursue Buddhist endeavors and even allowed
Kojong to live at Hyŏnsŏng temple in troubled times.⁵⁴ Furthermore, temples often housed dynastic tablets requiring royal attention. The Ch'oe House, to demonstrate its sincerity and its desire to
protect the kingdom, initiated numerous efforts to treat these sym-
bols with reverence, and it supported royal activities that forwarded
this policy. To protect Kangjong's royal portrait, for example, the
court moved it to Wangnyun temple. Later it moved Sŏngjong's portrait to Kaeguk temple.⁵⁵ The Ch'oe House also recruited monks
during Hŭijong's reign to repair royal tombs that had been damaged by robbers.⁵⁶ Through these policies, state interests and Buddhist interests merged, benefiting the Ch'oe authority as well.

During the middle of the Ch'oe regime came first the Khitan and
then the Mongol invasions—attacks that threatened not only the
survival of Ch'oe rule but also the very existence of Koryŏ. If the
Ch'oe House had initially relied on the Buddhist establishment for
legitimacy, it now turned to Buddhist priests, regardless of school, to
invoke divine intervention to protect the kingdom. The court
became an especially active patron of grand Buddhist services
(toryang) that often brought thousands of monks together for
prayers.⁵⁷ The Ch'oe leaders enlisted all Buddhist schools to offer
services. In responding to these appeals, both the Doctrine and the
Heavenly Terrace schools gained stature.⁵⁸ After escaping to Kanghwa Island, the Ch'oe leaders commissioned special services by the
Flower Garland (Hwaŏm) school, which had traditionally been tied
to the dynasty and the royal family. It regularly held such key Buddhist observances as the Assembly of the Eight Prohibitions and the
Lantern Festival.⁵⁹

The most dramatic appeal to divine intervention was the inscription of the Tripitaka onto 81,000 woodblocks. The Ch'oe House was
an active champion of this endeavor, expending large sums to complete the project and establishing a special directorate general to
collect additional funds. In carrying out this massive, sixteen-year
project, the Ch'oe House drew on many resources and looked to all
schools to lend support. Both Doctrine and Sŏn assisted. That the
Doctrine monk Sugi, who resided at Kaet'ae temple, took charge of
editing the Tripitaka reveals once again the improved stature of this
school.⁶⁰

Monks not only defended the nation through prayer. They even
took up arms to preserve the kingdom. When the Khitan incursions

worsened in 1215, the authorities recruited monks into the army. And when temples faced Khitan attacks, monks showed little reluctance to take up arms in defense of their monastery.[61] Later, as the Mongol invasions grew especially severe, bold monks risked their lives to resist the invaders.[62] Out of their common concern for the nation's destiny, the interests of monks and the Ch'oe leaders eventually became closely intertwined, causing them to work in concert.

Apart from the many functions just enumerated, the Buddhist establishment came to play an important economic role under Ch'oe rule. In his ten injunctions, Ch'oe Ch'unghŏn registered alarm at the proliferation of privately endowed temples and sought to limit their number and size in the kingdom. Although the records do not indicate to what extent the Ch'oe House confiscated temple lands, the Ch'oe leaders took an aggressive interest in tapping all resources of wealth. We have no figures showing the commercial enterprises and landholdings of temples during this period, but both Ch'oe Hang and his brother Manjong made considerable economic gains when they were monks.[63] By affiliating with temples, the Ch'oe House, like other leading families, was able to acquire not only spiritual blessings but also tax benefits and economic resources. They could merge their land with temple land, taking advantage of tax exemptions, and tap the commercial enterprises of temples. But in marked contrast to a century earlier, when both the court and civil officials corrupted their links with temples, the Ch'oe leaders were diligent in preventing other officials from drawing on similar sources for their own economic benefit.

In this way the Ch'oe House recast earlier court and Buddhist interests to enhance Ch'oe legitimacy and harness the resources of the temples into Koryŏ's efforts to resist the Mongols. During its later years, the Ch'oe House also depended on key temples to gather additional resources from various areas of the country to support its private endeavors. (See Chapter 8.)

Buddhism and Scholarship

Buddhist temples, especially those adhering to Sŏn practice, became the intellectual centers of the kingdom under Ch'oe rule. At the time of the military coup in 1170, scholars fearing disfavor fled to the countryside to avoid further political complications. Some, witnessing the turmoil caused by the early military leaders, found solace in a creed more removed from social concerns and turned to Buddhism for spiritual answers. Over a century later, Yi Chehyŏn (1287–1367) responded to a question about why scholars study under Buddhist monks. After the military coup, he noted,

> those escaping death fled deep into the mountains where, shed-
> ding their rank and putting on Buddhist garments, they spent
> their remaining years. . . . The state has gradually restored civilian
> rule, but those who desire to study have no place to go. There-
> fore, they have all followed Buddhists to study. This is why I said
> that the idea of students learning from monks started at this
> time.[64]

These developments, coupled with active Ch'oe patronage of temples like Susŏn, made temples an attractive environment for learning and study. Out of this merger of scholar and monk, of Confucian
principle and Buddhist speculation, would appear a commingling of
these beliefs that would pave the way for the Neo-Confucian speculation that developed during the rise of the Chosŏn kingdom.[65]

During the Ch'oe House's rule, a number of great literary figures
flourished. Nearly all of them forged close ties with monks and spent
considerable time at temples. Yi Kyubo (1168–1241), perhaps the
dynasty's most renowned writer, wrote about his many excursions to
temples and became especially attached to Sŏn. Later in life he
wrote a number of epithets to monks that have been preserved on
memorial steles.[66] Yi Illo (1152–1220), a contemporary of Yi Kyubo
and an author of near-equal status, journeyed to a mountain temple
and became a monk when confronted with the military coup. Later
he returned to active civil life and passed the state examination, but
he never disavowed his Buddhist links.[67] Scholars throughout the
dynasty had always had close affiliations with temples, but during
this period their ties were especially pronounced and long-lasting as
they wrote, discussed, and shared their lives with monks.[68] Other
government officials had formerly been monks, too, but for political
reasons returned to lay life.[69]

Not only did scholars actively engage in Buddhist speculation, but
there are numerous examples of monks who excelled in Confucian
scholarship. Hyesim, Chinul's successor at the helm of Susŏn temple, is the most prominent example. Following his mother's wishes,
he studied Confucianism and passed a lower-level examination that
enabled him to enter a state school. He was well on his way toward a

civil career when his mother died, freeing him of a vow to her and thus enabling him to become a monk.[70] Ch'ŏnin, a later follower of Yose, passed the *chinsa* examination at the age of seventeen and entered the Royal Confucian Academy, where he excelled in his studies. At twenty-three he gave up secular life and, together with a friend, became a monk.[71] Ch'ŏnch'aek, another monk who studied under Yose, is another example of a man who passed the state examination but chose the spiritual over the secular.[72] Other men chose to spend most of their lives in government service, but with the approach of old age abandoned themselves to temples and Buddhist studies.[73]

Monks and scholars were at ease as they studied and learned together. The military period saw a new fluidity in relationships that enabled the Confucians and Buddhists to share their traditions. Like the literati, monks during this time responded to these exchanges by producing some of the most exciting Buddhist treatises of the age. Temples became intellectual centers. Chinul, from his community in southwestern Korea, drafted and published numerous writings on Sŏn thought.[74] His disciple Hyesim and a number of other national masters continued this tradition.[75] The Heavenly Terrace monk Yose likewise drafted works. Monks became historians, as well, writing several texts crucial for understanding this period. Kakhun, a Kyo cleric, wrote his masterpiece, the *Haedong kosǔng chŏn*.[76] Iryŏn, a Sŏn monk who matured during the military period, wrote one of Korea's most renowned works, the *Samguk yusa* (Memorabilia of the Three Kingdoms), several decades after the fall of the Ch'oe House. Technological developments, both in the production of woodblocks and in the use of movable metallic type, furthered the publication and dissemination of these works.

Temples replaced schools as centers of learning. As Yi Chehyŏn noted, young scholars flocked to temples to study under monks. And through their mutual investigations, the differences between Buddhism and Confucianism diminished. Hyesim, writing a letter to the scholar Ch'oe Honggyun, stated:

> In the past I worked in the magistracy, but the magistrates have now entered my religious society. The magistrates are Buddhist Confucians, but I am a Confucian Buddhist. We have become the guests and hosts of one another, call each other masters or disciples. This has been the case for a long time; it is not something

that has only just begun. If one acknowledges simply their names, Buddhism and Confucianism are dramatically different. But if one knows their core, Confucianism and Buddhism are without distinction.[77]

Much of the intellectual dynamism that began during this period and continued into the subsequent years of Koryŏ flows largely from these developments.[78] For Neo-Confucian thought to flourish, Confucian thinkers had to understand Buddhism, especially Sŏn speculation. By its patronage of Confucian scholars and Sŏn activities, the Ch'oe House fostered this encounter and thereby helped prepare the way for Korean acceptance of Neo-Confucianism in the late thirteenth century.

Buddhism Ascendant

Buddhism remained at the center of Koryŏ life during the military period. But in marked contrast to its earlier role, the political force the clergy had exerted through the great temples of Kaegyŏng had been drastically curtailed—not so much with the 1170 military coup but rather with the rise of Ch'oe Ch'unghŏn. Monks who had once acted as political advisers and frequently visited the court were now displaced and encouraged to settle on secluded mountains, far from centers of power. As the Buddhist establishment, particularly the great Doctrine temples, endured a dramatic loss in financial resources, Sŏn temples became centers of intellectual rigor.

The Ch'oe House—by its active patronage of Buddhism and its determination to keep monks out of politics—presided over a dramatic transformation in Buddhism and in Koryŏ intellectual life. Turning away from the aristocrat-supported Doctrine school, the Ch'oe leaders discovered spiritual nourishment in the less politically oriented Sŏn. Both Sŏn and Ch'ŏnt'ae (Heavenly Terrace), which also regained vigor at this time, located their centers far from the capital in an environment secluded from the busy secular world. There they shaped a philosophy that met the needs of both commoners and elites. Under Ch'oe Ch'unghŏn and his successors, Sŏn became the great assimilator, denouncing exclusivism and supporting a syncretic stance that merged the principles of both sudden enlightenment and gradual cultivation, both meditation and schol-

arship. Through this philosophical transformation, Buddhism
became a more popular belief that addressed the needs of all levels
of society.

The new leaders of the day, both military and civilian, became
active patrons of these temples. Just as military and civilian interests
merged in other sectors of Koryŏ life, they now merged in Buddhism. Military officers and civilian leaders jointly endowed temples
and paid for services by leading clerics. Military and civilian officials
together studied Sŏn philosophy. Moreover, as the Ch'oe House had
presided over a merger of military and civilian interests, it also fostered a commingling of Buddhist and Confucian beliefs. Monks and
scholars studied together and taught each other. Out of this dia-
logue emerged a greater understanding of Buddhist and Confucian
principles. This discourse, by raising a metaphysical consciousness
intrinsic to Sŏn Buddhism, laid the foundation for the deeper investigations into Neo-Confucian principles that characterized philosophical inquiry in the Chosŏn kingdom.

8

Land and Other
Economic Issues

When Ch'oe Ch'unghŏn came to power in 1196, he inherited an unstable economic structure. The court was almost without funds. Eleven years earlier, in 1185, the *Koryŏsa* indicated that the royal granary was nearly empty even though it was receiving all the tribute presented from foreign exchanges. In the next year, with the dynastic granary again drained, the kingdom borrowed gold and cloth to cover salaries. With the deterioration of state finances, people began expanding their private landholdings through a number of ploys, such as dispatching their slaves, acquiring dynastic patronage, or merely expropriating property.[1] As we have seen, Ch'oe Ch'unghŏn launched reforms in many areas of government administration. Fiscal restraint was an important part of his approach. Unless he restored fiscal solvency, his entire program would collapse along with his authority, relegating him to the same fate that beset his predecessors. Sound policies focusing on the land would alleviate some of the burdens confronting the peasants and win their support. Decisive fiscal action would also assure Ch'oe Ch'unghŏn adequate funds to support the dynasty and his own private structure, thus solidifying the loyalty of his followers.

Above all, Ch'oe Ch'unghŏn needed funds to pay the officials in the government. To cover these demands he could rely on the land stipend law *(chŏnsikwa)*, inheritable private lands *(sajŏn)*, and the salary system *(nokpong)*.[2] He also needed ample finances to cover the costs of public administration—and could again look to the stipend land system, other public land allotments *(kongjŏn)*, and revenue

148

from taxation. But Ch'oe Ch'unghŏn also needed funds to cover his own personal expenses. He required wealth to pay his loyal followers, his retainers *(mun'gaek)*, and other personal attendants. He also had his own administrative costs and expenses to bolster his autonomy and authority. Here Ch'oe Ch'unghŏn turned to the land stipend system, using both public *(kongjŏn)* and private *(sajŏn)* holdings for his personal advantage. By occupying dynastic offices, he received a fixed grant under the salary system and prebends under the land stipend system. Since these incomes were regulated according to one's government rank and in any case were insufficient to cover the myriad costs of the Ch'oe House, Ch'oe Ch'unghŏn had to turn to other sources of income. By gaining control over large tracts of inheritable land and organizing estates, he acquired dependable sources of income. The *sigŭp*—a prebendal system that based allocations on the number of households instead of land area—offered another source of income. Other means of augmenting personal finances included investments in temple projects, the ownership of slaves, and trade. But to utilize these various sources of income, Ch'oe Ch'unghŏn needed to bring stability to the country and revitalize both the land system and the tax structure. We have already noted his endeavors to pacify slave and peasant discontent and thus ensure tranquility in the kingdom. Here we will look at the role of finances in guaranteeing the success of his rule.

Ch'oe Fiscal Policy: Land

The key to Koryŏ finances was land. During the tumultuous period that marked Myŏngjong's reign, not only were many peasants forced off the land because of excessive land levies but powerful figures took land—removing it from the tax registers and encroaching on the land stipend system. In theory, enforcing earlier land system designations and resettling the uprooted would allow peasants to till fields and pay taxes. This accomplished, revenues could be remitted to the government to cover salaries and expenses, and prebends could be made to officials holding collection rights under the land stipend system. Ch'oe Ch'unghŏn started to adopt this order, but there was a flaw in this scheme: the Ch'oe House had very specific needs distinct from those of the dynasty. Ch'oe Ch'unghŏn needed to revitalize the land stipend system to support officials, but he also needed to expand his own private holdings to cover his burgeoning expenses. The net result was that the Ch'oe House pursued a diverse and somewhat conflicting policy that can best be understood from the vantage of the Ch'oe leadership.

One of the first moves that Ch'oe Ch'unghŏn initiated after he assassinated Yi Ŭimin was to call for the reordering of landholdings. In Proposal 3 of his ten-point reform he declared:

> Under the system set up by the former king ... those in office have become very greedy, snatching both "public" and "private" land and holding it indiscriminately. A single family's holdings of fertile land may extend across districts, causing the nation's taxes to decline. . . . Your Majesty should instruct the agencies concerned to check official records and see that all illegally seized property is returned to its original owners.[3]

The reference to public and private land may mean land owned by the state and by private individuals. Or it could refer to the operation of the land stipend law: in this system, private land referred to "prebends granting tax collection rights to a designated recipient" and public land was "land on which the state collected taxes."[4] Ch'oe Ch'unghŏn realized that the kingdom's finances rested on a stable land order. From land he could acquire the funds to support the dynastic bureaucracy. And with the officialdom well paid, he could hope for their support and goodwill. Furthermore, by restoring order to landholdings, he could curtail large estates and return peasants to the land, thus moderating their resistance. Finally, by breaking up large estates he would be eliminating the economic power of potential opponents to his regime. Through a sound land policy, therefore, Ch'oe Ch'unghŏn could guarantee his authority.[5]

Ch'oe Ch'unghŏn supplemented his call for a redrawing of landholdings by confiscating the estates of his opponents. On coming to power, he purged a number of people from the government and curtailed the authority of unreliable officials. Upon the execution of Yi Ŭimin, for example, Ch'oe Ch'unghŏn dismantled Yi's land and power structure in Kyŏngju. Undoubtedly much of this land reverted to the state or to Ch'oe Ch'unghŏn. Neither the total amount of land confiscated from purged officials nor its dispersal are recorded, but it is quite conceivable that part of it went to the state to help replenish its tax base.

There were limits to Ch'oe Ch'unghŏn's questionable altruism, however. For in conjunction with the reordering of the landhold- ings, he also sought to assure his own fiscal security. Although, from the offices he held, he received prebends under the land stipend sys- tem, he could personally profit much more if he were able to acquire inheritable private land *(sajŏn)* where onerous levies to the state could be avoided and general landholdings *(minjŏn)* on which a tax yield of about 25 percent was collected. Through control of private landholdings in particular, a strong official could acquire financial power from the accumulation of rents and yet remain independent of the court and the dynastic tax system. By carefully using the land as one of the financial foundations of his structure, Ch'oe Ch'ung- hŏn was able to erect an autonomous economic system.[6] He also tried to expand his control over other types of land. The court unknowingly aided Ch'oe Ch'unghŏn in this effort when, for exam- ple, it granted 100 *kyŏl* of royal estate land to him in 1215. Royal estate land was public land, and Ch'oe Ch'unghŏn was thus able to acquire profits from transactions.[7] While 100 *kyŏl* is a rather small allotment, if Ch'oe Ch'unghŏn were to receive similar grants in the future, as he no doubt did, the opportunity for gain would be immense. Ch'oe Ch'unghŏn enlarged his holdings by other means as well. He took advantage of the merit and protected farmland *(kongŭmjŏn)* privilege and, like many other powerful figures of the twelfth century, seized land at will. After his death the histories noted: "Because his father Ch'unghŏn seized public and private land and tenants, in each case Ch'oe U returned the land and tenants."[8]

Ch'oe Ch'unghŏn's descendants inherited this order, but they made modifications. Ch'oe supporters received public offices and the accompanying prebendal rights under the land stipend system and the regular salary system. Yet there are clear signs that the land system was in trouble as Ch'oe U, like his father before, made a pub- lic display of trying to stabilize landholdings at the outset of his rule by returning seized land and people (possibly meaning slaves) to their original owners. The Ch'oe House had an ongoing need for funds with which to reward loyal followers and men who had not received government posts. In 1228, for example, Ch'oe U distrib- uted some 200 *kyŏl* of his private fields to various military officers.[9] By judiciously distributing small allotments like 200 *kyŏl* of land, he won the allegiance of his followers. By freely releasing land like this when it was politically expedient, Ch'oe U demonstrated confidence in his own authority. Clearly he had sufficient land to support his own needs and was secure enough to give away private land. No exact accounting of his holdings is recorded. But judging from the offices he held and the expenses he incurred to maintain retainers and sizable private forces—and to act as de facto ruler—he must have controlled extensive property. His descendants, Ch'oe Hang and Ch'oe Ŭi, continued to amass large holdings as well. When the Ch'oe House was confronted with incessant Mongol invasions, it even sought to place land on Kanghwa Island under its direct control. In 1257, for example, 3,000 *kyŏl* of Kanghwa land was granted to Ch'oe Ŭi.[10]

The Ch'oe family was not alone in enlarging its estates and land parcels through grants from the court and forceful seizures. The dynastic sources report that the magistrate Chŏn Sŭngu resented Supreme General Kim Hyŏnbo for enlarging his fields through extortion. Chŏn therefore confiscated Kim's land taxes *(cho)* and put them in the government treasury.[11] This passage is significant: it reveals that men such as Kim Hyŏnbo were using irregular methods to increase their landholdings. In response to such acts, other officials ostensibly tried to maintain the integrity of the land system. Although Ch'oe U later overruled the action, Chŏn intended to restrain the activities of men like Kim. The magistrate *(hyŏllyong)* seems to have been commissioned to oversee the entire land tax system in the region under his jurisdiction, for it was his office that collected taxes and sent them to the Ministry of Revenue. The state then delivered them to their proper recipients. The Ch'oe House generally had an interest in checking the landholdings of other military men lest they gain an economic independence that could free them from Ch'oe control.

It is difficult to analyze the role of the court in these proceedings. The royal family was traditionally the biggest landholder in the country. Although there are records indicating that the court gave land to the Ch'oe House and probably to other powerful figures,[12] it also retained holdings for its own use. The royal estate *(naejang)* was one source of supplemental funds for the court. Royal estate land *(ch'ŏ)* is first mentioned in 1226.[13] Although these sources of wealth might have bolstered royal finances, the court did not have the upper hand in finances in its relations with the Ch'oe House. In

1257, for example, when Ch'oe Ŭi received 3,000 *kyŏl* of Kanghwa land, the state granary received the smaller allotment of 2,000 *kyŏl*. The royal clansmen and leading ministers took the remaining land along the rivers and sea.[14] The court played a very minor role in this land division. Even more obvious is the fact that the court, whose functions were curtailed, now needed fewer funds and resources while the Ch'oe House, as the de facto government, required much more land to govern the kingdom.

How significant were the changes in the land system at this time? The land stipend system did not disappear, and the public granary was still important enough to be granted 2,000 *kyŏl*, even at the end of Kojong's reign. Ch'oe Ch'unghŏn reformed the land system at the start of his rule to provide his officials with a fixed emolument from a dynastic institution. (They were later to serve concurrent positions in both the dynastic system and his own private house organization.) By maintaining the semblance of a dynastic land system whereby prebends were allotted under the land stipend law and other land served as a tax base for the state, Ch'oe Ch'unghŏn could cover the expenses of his own administration as well. This system remained under constant attack, however, as private land and especially large estates expanded, allowing men to establish an economic base separate from the court and independent of the throne. It was the Ch'oe leaders who led this assault to meet their own personal needs. Fiscally free of the court, they could recruit their own followers, such as retainers, and support them not only through government offices but also with profits from private holdings. The trends toward expansion of private land and the employment of retainers, which emerged before the Ch'oe House assumed power, gained momentum under its rule.[15]

Ch'oe Fiscal Policy: The *Sigŭp*

Ch'oe Ch'unghŏn also used the *sigŭp* to strengthen his fiscal resources. The *sigŭp*, as noted, was a prebendal system that based allocations on the number of households instead of land area. The term *"sigŭp"* has been translated as fief, but such a rendering fails to convey the essentially prebendal nature of the grant and also suggests, incorrectly, that there may be feudal ties to the *sigŭp*. The *sigŭp* comprised a designated number of households in a fixed territory that paid taxes and labor service to the holder of the *sigŭp* instead of the state. The *sigŭp* holder did not, however, possess full autonomy over the households or the land. Generally payments from the households went to the state treasury and were then remitted to the holder of the *sigŭp*.

Dating back to the Silla period, the *sigŭp* reappeared during Injong's reign as a source of support for powerful figures but was not used again until the rise of the Ch'oe House, which resurrected the *sigŭp* to extend its economic base and thereby further secure its independence from dynastic finances. When the state granted the *sigŭp* merely as an honor, apparently the accompanying enfeoffment was not automatically heritable. If a piece of land was included, however, it seems to have been transferred to the heirs of the recipients. The king granted the same *sigŭp* to three of the four Ch'oe leaders, Ch'oe Ch'unghŏn, U, and Hang.[16] Although it is unclear exactly when the latter two men received their *sigŭp*, Ch'oe Ch'unghŏn received his in 1205—some nine years after he came to power. That these Ch'oe *sigŭp* were only technically heritable was demonstrated both by the king's command that Ch'oe Hang receive his father's *sigŭp* and by the lack of direct evidence that Ch'oe Ŭi then inherited Hang's *sigŭp*.[17] Even though there was no fixed succession right to the *sigŭp*, it appears that Ch'oe U did succeed to his father's *sigŭp*, which was in turn passed on to Ch'oe Hang.

Shortly after each of these men received his *sigŭp*, each was also granted a title along with an administrative office *(pu)*. The king decreed, for example, that Ch'oe Ch'unghŏn be given the title of Chinganghu (Duke of Chingang) with an administrative office in the first month of 1206, just a month after he received his *sigŭp* at the end of 1205. The following month, the *Koryŏsa* reports that Ch'oe Ch'unghŏn was enfeoffed as Chinganggong (Marquis of Chingang) and that an administration called the Hŭngnyŏngbu was established.[18] Although the date Ch'oe U received his *sigŭp* is unclear, he was invested Chinyanghu (Duke of Chinyang) in 1234, shortly after the capital was moved to Kanghwa. Once Ch'oe Hang was in power and his *sigŭp* was established, the king invested him with the title of duke *(hu)* and created an administration for him. Ch'oe Hang demurred for two years. Then in 1253 the king issued another decree to the same effect enfeoffing Hang.[19] The title and the administration in each case seem to have been little more than honorary grants given after the *sigŭp* had already been extended.

In theory the king granted the *sigŭp* to the Ch'oe leaders because of the merit they had earned by supporting the throne. Although no one can dispute the fact that the *sigŭp* had traditionally been given to meritorious subjects, the heads of the Ch'oe House, like other leaders earlier in the dynasty, sought the *sigŭp* not only to demonstrate that they had been protectors of the throne but also for the economic benefits that accrued therefrom. As his *sigŭp*, Ch'oe Ch'unghŏn received the area around Chinju (in modern Kyŏngsang *namdo*). It is interesting to speculate on Chinju's role in the Ch'oe power structure. Although Ch'oe Ch'unghŏn once served in the area as a government official, the records do not detail his relation with this territory.[20] Undoubtedly the entire region, including parts of Chŏlla and Kyŏngsang, formed a base for his power, since he developed close marriage ties with the Chŏngs of neighboring Hadong and the Ims of Chŏngan in Chŏlla. Furthermore, his mother's family, the Yu clan of Chinju, had a base of power here.[21] The size of Ch'oe Ch'unghŏn's original *sigŭp* was some three thousand households; the real grant was three hundred households.[22] It is difficult to ascertain whether this grant changed in subsequent years, but in 1242 a request was made to increase Ch'oe U's *sigŭp* and the same was done for Hang's *sigŭp*.[23]

Under the dynastic system, *sigŭp* payments went directly to the state granaries. But during both Ch'oe U and Hang's rule this method was challenged. For when an official in error sent the produce from Ch'oe U's Chinyang *sigŭp* to the public granary, the king protested that payments should be sent directly to U. The king often acted as a spokesman for Ch'oe wishes. Here the king's protest may have reflected his desire to anticipate Ch'oe wishes or confirm changes that had already commenced. Ch'oe U diplomatically responded that in this one instance the customary system should be used.[24] Seven years later, the court again decreed that all Chinyang produce should be sent directly to Ch'oe Hang's house, but Hang politely declined this honor.[25] The word "directly" *(chik)* in the original text indicates that even under the former system, the holder of the *sigŭp* would ultimately receive its produce although it usually went to the dynastic granary before subsequent redistribution. This same scheme was used in the payment of rents under the land stipend system. The Ch'oe House might have detoured from this tradition, however, as evidenced by the king's protest when the produce was not sent directly to Ch'oe U. By this logic, under Ch'oe rule the *sigŭp* revenues might have bypassed dynastic agencies and gone straight to the Ch'oe House. In this case the *sigŭp,* which initially had been prebendal in nature, would have changed dramatically in its operation under Ch'oe control.

This question whether the *sigŭp* by 1250 retained its prebendal character or not affords added insight into the Ch'oe relation with dynastic institutions. If the prebendal quality continued, it certainly demonstrated the effectiveness of central government operations as being essential in the redistribution of prebendal allotments. But if the Ch'oe House started to bypass the central granaries and collect allotments directly, this new system would point to the deterioration of the old order. Such a change would streamline the administration of *sigŭp* payments and, more important, put the whole operation of the *sigŭp* under the Ch'oe House and free from court interference. If the dynasty was bypassed and lost its jurisdiction over *sigŭp* finances, this change would ultimately leave the dynasty devoid of any control over stipend lands as well. In retrospect it appears that the Ch'oe House attempted a little of both.

The Ch'oe House wanted institutions to serve dual purposes. Publicly it called for the maintenance of the traditional order whether in social relations or landholdings. Privately it often pursued the opposite aim as it sought to build and sustain itself through personal means. In this same way it started a process to change the nature of the *sigŭp.* Given the two incidents of 1243 and 1250, there was ambiguity in how *sigŭp* allotments should be remitted. On the one hand, the Ch'oe leaders struggled to maintain dynastic institutions; on the other, they wanted to assure the primacy of their personal privileges.

The *sigŭp,* then, is a microcosm of the entire Ch'oe structure and an excellent example of how the Ch'oe House used legal dynastic institutions to establish its own system. Initially the Ch'oe structure depended on grants from the king. In this respect one might claim that the Ch'oe House was part of the dynastic structure. But once these institutions were established, the Ch'oe House used them to secure its independence from the court. The Kyojŏng Togam was established by royal command, for example, but it soon became the center for all Ch'oe administration and above reproach from the court. Likewise, the king granted a *sigŭp* and the Ch'oe House used this grant to increase its resources and provide funds so it could operate free from dynastic restraints. In theory, the king was at the apex of the entire Ch'oe system. In reality, he merely came to acknowledge Ch'oe will and provide the necessary setting to cloak Ch'oe actions with legitimacy.

The Chinju *sigŭp* provided the Ch'oe family with textiles, corvée labor, and local tribute taxes. In affording the Ch'oe House access to households, the *sigŭp* was much more lucrative than private land grants that provided links only to the produce of the land. Chinju is a rich agricultural area even today and must have been a choice site in the thirteenth century. During the early Chosŏn kingdom, Chinju had a population of 5,906 people situated in 1,628 households. A local gazetteer described it as having rich lands with warm weather and light breezes. In Chinju there was 12,730 *kyŏl* of arable land that grew grain, fruit, cotton, and hemp. Honey, mushrooms, fish, tea, lacquer, bamboo, medicine, and skins were all produced locally. Salt was available, too, as well as low-grade, locally manufactured porcelain.[26] With Chinju as its *sigŭp*, the Ch'oe House claimed most of these products, giving it a solid economic base that became increasingly important as its needs kept expanding.

The *sigŭp* came to have an entirely different significance from its original intention. Initially the court families were the chief benefactors of the *sigŭp* in the Koryŏ dynasty. The Ch'oe House severed this relation, however, as the royal family no longer received *sigŭp*. Moreover, cut off from *sigŭp* profits, the court had to search for new means to build its economic base and began to rely on the royal estate *(ch'ŏ)* and the royal estate residence *(naejang)* for funds.[27] After the fall of the Ch'oe House, those who supplanted Ch'oe Ŭi, such as Kim Chun, continued to use the *sigŭp* to support their authority.[28]

Ch'oe Fiscal Policy: Temples, Slaves, and Trade

Temples provided an additional source of income for the Ch'oe House. No doubt Ch'oe Ch'unghŏn and his descendants used their links with temples to accrue funds. When Ch'oe Hang was a monk on Chindo, for example, he recruited unscrupulous clerics to assist him in extracting levies from the neighboring peasants. The dynastic record recounts:

> Ch'oe U's sons by a concubine, the monks Manjong and Manjŏn, assembled hoodlum monks, making them their disciples. They made the pursuit of wealth their profession, devising ten thousand schemes to get gold, silver, grain, and silk. Their disciples divided

and occupied famous temples. Relying on their power, they
became arrogant and their tyranny spread all over. Their saddles,
horses, and dress all followed Tartar customs, and they called each
other "government men." Their actions were improper, as some
forcefully defiled women, some arbitrarily took station horses, and
some insulted officials. There was nowhere they did not venture.
Other monks, riding well-fed horses and wearing good clothes,
falsely claimed to be their disciples. Wherever they invaded and
disturbed, the districts [chu and hyŏn] recoiled in fear. There was
no one who dared ask who or why. Everyone hated them. In
Kyŏngsang, from the rice and grain that had been stored, they
loaned out more than 500,000 sŏk, collecting interest from the
people. As soon as the autumn harvest was ripe, they divided up
and sent disciples, pressing severely and collecting from the peasants. The people carried everything they had and several times
missed their tax payments. . . . As head monk of a Chindo temple,
Manjŏn once was very despotic with his followers.[29]

This passage reveals the importance of temples in the Ch'oe scheme,
as well as the brazen use of monks to win financial gain for the Ch'oe
family. Both Kyŏngsang and Chŏlla, where Chindo temple was
located, were vital geographic centers for Ch'oe prosperity.

Through affiliations with temples there were many ways in which
the Ch'oe House increased its revenues. Ch'oe U's son Manjong, for
example, remained in the clergy, and when the Ch'oe House was
overthrown he controlled large estates. Although specific evidence
is lacking, the Ch'oe House undoubtedly attempted to use its capital to offer loans, perhaps through temples, and to acquire profits
from interest. They might also have taken advantage of the income
that temples reaped through the handicraft industry, tea and spirit
production, and the storage of goods and grains. During the
eleventh and twelfth centuries, temples maintained steady incomes
that were available to the Ch'oe House throughout its years in power.
The Ch'oe House patronized Changbok temple, Sŏpot'ong temple,
and Taean temple in the capital, Susŏn temple in Kanghwa, and Tansok temple, Ssangbong temple, and Kangwŏl temple in the south. It
was able to use these religious centers to tap the economic resources
of these regions.[30]

The Ch'oe House likewise controlled slaves to work its fields and
manage minor affairs. Although Ch'oe Ch'unghŏn and U generally
curbed slave activities in the upper echelons, as we have seen, they

did not object to the use of slaves at lower levels. Slaves provided a cheap and ready labor force to help bolster Ch'oe resources.

Profits from trade were another source of Ch'oe income. Trade along the northern border did not halt with the internal upheaval that followed the 1170 military takeover. The border towns continued to be bustling centers of commerce, and men who accompanied missions to Chin usually accumulated substantial profits. This trade continued unabated after Ch'oe Ch'unghŏn assumed power. Indeed, the search for trade intensified after the onset of the Khitan problem in 1216. The Koryŏ histories report: "Merchants compete to amass profits. Although [government officials] strictly regulate and confiscate goods, there is no limit to the greed of those who secretly continue to conduct trade."[31] Thus, despite official attempts to curtail such commerce, trade continued. Merchants came from Sung and Chin China, for example, in 1201, 1205, and 1211. In 1205, when one of the Chinese merchants was unjustly imprisoned and flogged, Ch'oe Ch'unghŏn dismissed the responsible official at once. On another occasion, in 1231, a Sung merchant presented Ch'oe U with a water buffalo. In return, Ch'oe U granted the merchant ginseng and silk, giving the water buffalo to the king.[32] Contacts with Japan were less frequent but nevertheless presented opportunities for profit. To stabilize relations, Ch'oe U sent a man to Japan with a letter calling for peace. When the envoy returned, Ch'oe U rewarded him with lavish gifts. Exchanges continued. In 1244, a Japanese vessel loaded with silk and silver washed ashore at Cheju Island, but by then the increasing ferocity of Mongol attacks by land and Wako pirate raids by sea from Japan made such ventures dangerous and less profitable.[33]

It is hard to estimate the extent to which the Ch'oe House was able to profit from this form of commercial activity. Even though there are no records to demonstrate that Ch'oe Ch'unghŏn was able to use either official or unofficial exchanges to bolster his income, he must have tapped these sources whenever feasible. Furthermore, as in every other sector of his society, Ch'oe Ch'unghŏn sought to check any possible autonomous movement. Since people who could establish their independence through trade might threaten his structure, it was necessary to curb such competition. Foreign trade, moreover, offered a potential avenue for spies to infiltrate into the country. This might explain why in 1216 the state strictly regulated trade. It may also indicate that Ch'oe Ch'unghŏn sought to acquire profits from both official and unofficial exchanges.

Once the Mongol invasions grew severe, there are few records of official tribute missions or accounts of covert international trade. Merchants rarely came from China or Japan. Rather than benefiting from exchanges, the Mongols burdened the Ch'oe House and Koryŏ at this time with exorbitant demands for all sorts of local tribute products. If the Ch'oe House had once been able to accrue profits from international exchanges, the Mongol invasions put an end to it.

Ch'oe Fiscal Policy: Tax Structure

The tax structure was closely tied to the land system. By controlling the tax structure and using it as they did the land system, Ch'oe Ch'unghŏn and his descendants could acquire not only economic assets but also political leverage. One aim of Ch'oe Ch'unghŏn's initial ten-point proposal for reform was to restore the integrity of the tax system. In Proposals 4 and 5, he admonished that people in poverty could not pay taxes. Furthermore, unjust clerks only transgressed and injured the weak, making the situation still more intolerable. The solution, according to Ch'oe Ch'unghŏn, was to dispatch honest officials to inspect the provinces and forbid the presentation of gifts. From Ch'oe Ch'unghŏn's call for reform, it is apparent that in the years following the military assumption of power in 1170 the tax structure had deteriorated considerably. With its collapse, the kingdom could not operate efficiently. This is evident too in the fiscal bankruptcy of Myŏngjong's court. Ch'oe Ch'unghŏn had sought to correct this situation and had succeeded.

Despite the chaos caused by the Mongol invasions and the court's flight to Kanghwa Island, the reinvigorated tax structure was still operating toward the end of Kojong's reign. At that time, the Koryŏ histories report that one Yi Hyŏn betrayed the kingdom by offering a suggestion to the Mongols: "My country's capital lies on a sea island. Tribute taxes all come out from the rural districts [*chu* and *kun*]. If your army secretly crosses the border before autumn, the people of the capital will be faced with an emergency."[34] Yi Hyŏn acknowledged the operation of Koryŏ's tax system some twenty years after the capital had moved to Kanghwa and noted the rulers' dependence on tax income. It was the effective administration of this system, particularly the Ch'oe House's ability to maintain its links with the agriculturally rich south, that allowed the Koryŏ military leaders to withstand the Mongol onslaught for so long.

Both the Ch'oe House and the court administered the tax structure. The court in theory had ultimate control over the operation of the tax system. On at least one occasion, it requested a reduction in corvée levies to alleviate the burdens on the agricultural sector of the economy. In 1250, Ch'oe Hang made a similar demand to reduce taxes all over the country. As Ch'oe Hang had just come to power after his father's death, it made good political sense to reduce taxes at this time in order to gain the support of the people. Ch'oe Ch'unghŏn undoubtedly was connected with levies as well. In 1202, for example, a soldier, falsely claiming that Ch'oe Ch'unghŏn had dispatched him, led troops to Pongju to collect silver and silk.[35] From this it can be inferred that although Ch'oe Ch'unghŏn had not approved of this particular incident, he had directed men to collect levies in the past.

Even as the king's authority waned, the tax system continued to operate in the traditional manner during the Ch'oe period with only minor changes. Local officials or men dispatched by the central government still handled the collection of taxes.[36] Once levies were gathered, usually in the autumn after the harvest, they went to the Ministry of Revenue in the capital. Tax revenue would be used for administration. And since the Ch'oe House in effect controlled the dynasty, both it and the bureaucracy benefited. Enforcement of the tax system was well planned and timely. The Ch'oe House realized that tax revenues could be used for sensible political, economic, and defensive purposes. Thus after Kwangju's stalwart self-defense against foreign invaders in 1235, the Ch'oe House rewarded the area with an exemption from the usual corvée and local products taxes.[37] Using Kwangju as an example, the leadership hoped to encourage other areas to offer equally valiant resistance against the Mongols. Such tactics have been soundly employed by dynasties throughout history to fortify and support ravaged peasants. The Ch'oe leaders offered similar exemptions to people who left their homelands and went to mountain fortresses or coastal areas. In times of peace, peasants who returned to their land received other tax incentives. Tax exemptions went also to areas that suffered from foreign invasion and faced subsequent starvation.[38] Through such actions, the Ch'oe

House won the endorsement of hard-pressed peasants and enlisted them in their efforts to resist the Mongols. The Ch'oe House gained not only monetary benefits, therefore, but also political support from these tax policies.

If the Ch'oe House's administration of the tax structure was enlightened and flexible, it was also expansive. The Ch'oe leadership looked continually for new ways to enlarge the system to include previously exempt people. Until Ch'oe Ch'unghŏn's rule, the high-ranking officials (commonly referred to as *yangban*) had usually been spared from most forms of taxation. In 1208, when the state repaired the promenades in the capital, it assessed the *yangban* of the five capital districts to pay the expenses. The histories relate that *yangban* corvée labor began here.[39] The weavers *(yangsuch'ŏk)*, a special class with low social status, were also exempt from the corvée and other duties throughout the early part of the dynasty. Ch'oe Ch'unghŏn's immediate predecessor, Yi Ŭimin, apparently removed this exemption. It is reported that Yi Ŭimin's son collected onerous tribute from the weavers, and Ch'oe Ch'unghŏn, calculating the number of weavers, taxed them even more heavily.[40] It can only be guessed how many other people Ch'oe Ch'unghŏn's initiatives brought into the tax structure, but it is certain that Ch'unghŏn and his descendants used taxes to gain economic and political support. By enforcing and expanding the tax system, the Ch'oe House gained more funds for its own operations as well as financial backing for policies it enforced in the name of the dynasty.

The salary system, which was supported by tax revenues, was also maintained for the duration of Ch'oe rule. So long as revenues were available, dynastic officials received their salaries without incident. These payments served as an adequate supplement to land-yield allotments. Once the Mongol invasions reduced the dynasty's control over the peninsula, however, the tax revenues and prebendal income from the land stipend system were cut—forcing the Ch'oe House to seek new sources to pay the stipends. In 1257, after discussing the possibility of dividing fields and using land to replace stipends, officials established a Directorate General for Land Grants (Kŭpchŏn Togam) to implement this design.[41] Three months later, the Ch'oe House divided Kanghwa Island: most of the land went to Ch'oe Ŭi and the dynasty; the rest went to royal clansmen and officials according to rank.[42] Conscious that its authority depended on the allegiance of officialdom, the Ch'oe House took numerous precautions to guarantee their remuneration.

A Time of Fiscal Transition

The Ch'oe House was not only politically the strongest family in the kingdom but also economically the richest. Through deliberate, cautious policy, Ch'oe Ch'unghŏn and his descendants were able to amass huge landholdings using grants from the court and more covert means such as forceful land seizures. The Ch'oe leadership acquired wealth from prebendal allotments under the land stipend system, as well, and tapped other revenue through the *sigŭp*. The Ch'oe House was also able to control the tax structure and benefit from profits realized through local tribute and corvée taxes. International trade was another source for income, but it was an uncertain supply that depended on foreign relations and international stability. Slaves and temple holdings were additional economic resources.

Although it relied on well-tested means, the Ch'oe House was dynamic and flexible in its pursuit of income. It enlarged its assets slowly and remained willing to forgo immediate profits in pursuit of long-term gains. Where opportunities permitted, it also found innovative new sources to be tapped. Its vast administration and accompanying personnel were a huge burden to support. Although the Ch'oe House relied on its own private sources to fund part of this system, it also attempted to maintain the land stipend system and tax structure to provide officials with prebendal salaries. There are no precise records showing the extent of Ch'oe wealth. But taking into account its estates in Kyŏngsangdo and Chŏllado, its *sigŭp*, and its scattered holdings granted under state-initiated allotments, its property appears to have been vast.[43] Besides land, the Ch'oe House had additional stores of wealth. When the Ch'oe House collapsed near the end of Kojong's reign, one of Ch'oe Ŭi's minor granaries held over 15,000 *sŏk* of rice. He also had special areas for breeding and raising horses.[44] Once the Ch'oe House was destroyed, the state sent officials to both Chŏllado and Kyŏngsangdo to list and confiscate the slaves, cloth, and grain on the estates of Ch'oe Ŭi and his uncle Manjong.[45] One can only surmise how many other granaries—and what additional financial operations—the Ch'oe House maintained.

There were other men in the kingdom who had money and wealth. But like the court, they depended on the support of the Ch'oe House.

During the Ch'oe rule, there was a gradual shift from dependence on revenue from dynastic sources, such as the land stipend system, to dependence on private landholdings, the *sigŭp*, and tax revenue. Although the land stipend system provided prebends to officials, it interfered with the personal Ch'oe needs for income from other holdings. As dynastic access to land revenue gradually withered, the Ch'oe House filled the vacuum by privately covering salaries and general administrative expenses. The Ch'oe House had no alternative but to accept this expanded responsibility since it had removed large tracts of land from state control and placed them under its own supervision. The Ch'oe House did retain the tax structure, however, as it was a ready source of income from lands throughout the country regardless of classification or ownership.

The Ch'oe family was presiding over a period of transition. The land order and tax system had started to deteriorate many years before Ch'oe Ch'unghŏn came to power. He strengthened the dynastic structure to meet his needs. While on the one hand he restored the decaying dynastic structure, on the other he continued the trends that would ultimately leave the dynasty's access to land revenue and the court itself much weaker by supporting the expansion of Ch'oe private lands and income at the expense of the dynasty. He also initiated action, as seen in the *sigŭp*, that would impair the dynasty's authority to redistribute land and household levies, instead allowing individuals to assume this responsibility. The extent to which this process was exacerbated by the Mongol invasions is unclear. But after Koryŏ capitulated to Mongol demands, the land stipend system and the dynastic tax structure were practically useless. In their place arose large estates controlled by powerful politicians, rich families, and temples as Korea entered a new phase in its economic transformation.[46]

9

The Ch'oe Dilemma

The Ch'oe House was founded on two inherently competing systems: dynastic and private institutions. Pressed with crises from the start of his rule in 1196, Ch'oe Ch'unghŏn had to react quickly and decisively to the challenges posed by domestic unrest, poverty, Buddhist opposition, and a powerful military class. The most expedient solution was to restore the dynastic structure, which already maintained offices and agencies to resolve the country's problems and govern it effectively. Through the dynastic organization, individuals could be mobilized and decisions could be made to effect the changes and reforms Ch'oe Ch'unghŏn needed to secure his authority. Once assured of his command, however, Ch'oe Ch'unghŏn began to fashion his own agencies, superimposing them upon the dynastic structure. From this scheme of dual offices, dynastic and private, set up to administer state affairs, grew competing agendas that would lead to the eventual undoing of the Ch'oe House. Private offices were the locus of Ch'oe administration and power. But by retaining and even relying on dynastic institutions, Ch'oe Ch'unghŏn acknowledged the importance of a dynastic order that could later be used by others as the basis for a challenge to the Ch'oe hegemony and the restoration of authority to the king.

This was the basic dilemma confronting the Ch'oe House, but out of it sprang many more. This chapter assesses the role of the king, Confucian ideology, and civilian precepts in the Ch'oe system, as well as the problems deriving from reliance on these institutions. We will also explore other issues facing the Ch'oe House, such as the contradictions caused by the retainer system and the social and economic chaos of the age. The Ch'oe House collapsed as much from its inability to resolve these dilemmas as from its inability to halt the Mongol invasions.

The Monarch

Although the king was at the apex of the entire dynastic structure, the relations between the Ch'oe House and the royal family were unique. (For a list of the Koryŏ kings, see Figure 1 in the Introduction.) During Ch'oe Ch'unghŏn's twenty-year rule, five separate kings held the throne. He forced the removal of two of them (Myŏngjong and Hŭijong), two died in office (Sinjong and Kangjong), and one (Kojong) survived him. Pak Chinjae, Ch'oe Ch'unghŏn's nephew, led the first attack against the monarchy in 1197 when, pointing to the king's ineffectiveness, he called for Myŏngjong to be ejected from office:

> The king has ruled for twenty-eight years. He is old and weary; he has lost his diligence. The various princes use favors and royal authority to disturb the country's affairs. The king also gives favors to the petty, and many receive gold and silk. The treasury is empty. How can we not have him abdicate?[1]

To Ch'oe Ch'unghŏn and his followers, Myŏngjong's dismissal was imperative if stability and good administration were to be achieved. The military leaders enthroned Myŏngjong's brother, who reigned as Sinjong with little incident for seven years until he died of illness. Sinjong's son Hŭijong succeeded him. After seven years on the throne, however, Hŭijong became impatient with his subservience to the Ch'oe House and, abetted by various anti-Ch'oe forces, tried to assassinate Ch'oe Ch'unghŏn in 1211. Ch'oe Ch'unghŏn exiled him for his participation in this plot and enthroned Myŏngjong's son as Kangjong. When Kangjong suddenly died in office two years later, at the age of sixty-two, his son became the new monarch Kojong. Kojong, whose reign would prove to be the longest in the history of the dynasty, was monarch for forty-six years. He died one year after the Ch'oe House collapsed.

By restoring the dynastic structure and retaining the monarch as an integral part of this scheme, Ch'oe Ch'unghŏn reasserted the royal prerogative in theory but not in fact. He went to the court immediately after the assassination of Yi Ŭimin to obtain royal sanction. In front of the palace he explained:

> The bandit official [Yi] Ŭimin was once responsible for the crime of rebellion. He was cruel, he caused trouble for the people, and he eyed the throne. For a long time we were sick at seeing this. Now, for the sake of the country, we have punished him. We only feared this affair would be [prematurely] revealed so we did not dare request your official command. His is a crime of death, a crime of death.[2]

Ch'oe Ch'unghŏn declared that he had to kill Yi Ŭimin in order to avenge Yi's criminal acts and protect the king. He also explained why he had had to keep his plans secret from the king and now came to inform him and gain his consent. The king was important to Ch'oe Ch'unghŏn, for he hoped to link his own designs to royal needs, thereby facilitating the consolidation of his own power. By obtaining royal approval of his coup, he was able to inaugurate his policies as an officer of the king acting on behalf of the royal will. By acknowledging the royal position and uniting his cause with that of the king, Ch'oe Ch'unghŏn elevated his stature to that of protector of the court.[3]

Once he had won the support of the monarch, Ch'oe Ch'unghŏn gradually manipulated the court into a defensive posture. This was a subtle policy, well calculated and effective, that commenced with Ch'oe Ch'unghŏn's ten proposals for reform, which were issued a month after the assassination of Yi Ŭimin. In his last proposal, Ch'oe Ch'unghŏn turned to the court and remonstrated with it for harboring sycophants and extortionists and disregarding ministerial advice. When the king's behavior did not improve significantly, he forced Myŏngjong to abdicate. The prestige of the royal family continued to decline during Sinjong's reign. At Myŏngjong's death in 1202, rather than inter him with the rites befitting a king, Ch'oe Ch'unghŏn ordered him buried with the ceremony fit for a queen. The court and royal family wore black mourning hats for only three days. Two years later, when Sinjong died, Ch'oe Ch'unghŏn reduced the official mourning period from the customary twenty-six days to fourteen.[4] The royal household's gradual loss of dignity and prestige was matched by a corresponding decline in power.[5]

During much of Kojong's reign, the king had little real authority, as the Ch'oe leaders fashioned most of the decisions. Kojong sadly acknowledged his plight in 1255 when he repeatedly summoned an official who each time failed to appear. Although the angry Kojong wanted to seize the administration and fire the disobedient official, he lamented: "Even though I should take over the government today, tomorrow I would definitely return it. What type of punishment could I give?"[6] Many years earlier, Chŏng Sukch'ŏm had declared that the monarch was indeed powerless and the consequences would be disastrous for the country.[7] It had taken Ch'oe Ch'unghŏn nearly twenty years and five monarchs before he found a pliable king. Part of his dilemma stemmed from his attempt to establish a facade of royal power to mask his own independence. Such a system was not easy to administer. To succeed in circumventing the king's authority, the Ch'oe House depended not on its military might alone but on many other institutional mechanisms.

Ch'oe Ch'unghŏn looked to family ties as one means to influence the court. In 1219, near the end of his rule, he took the royal surname Wang, demonstrating his loyalty to the throne and his merit in defending it.[8] The granting of the royal surname was reserved only for loyal subjects who protected the dynasty. Ch'oe Ch'unghŏn also turned to marital unions—a common tactic employed by aristocrats to control monarchs. During the early Koryŏ period, kings often had several wives, since many of the royal consort families, such as the Kyŏngwŏn Yi lineage and Ansan Kim family, sought to influence royal prerogatives through intermarriage with the court. The Chŏngan Im lineage, as the maternal family to Myŏngjong and Sinjong, and the Kangnŭng Kim lineage, as the maternal line of Hŭijong and Kangjong, had this potential during the military period. These marriage ties had been formed before the Ch'oe House came to power. The prominence of the Im lineage has already been discussed in some detail. Presumably through their close ties with the Ch'oe House as well, the Ch'oe leaders would be able to have some say in the affairs of the court. The Kangnŭng Kim lineage's role during this period is less conspicuous. This family had a long history and was highly esteemed during the early years of the Koryŏ dynasty, but in the military period its influence was less obvious. In addition to these ties, Hŭijong married a member of the Chŏngan Im lineage and Kangjong married the daughter of Yu family member Song, Marquis of Sinhan.[9]

Ch'oe Ch'unghŏn had Kojong, the final king, marry Hŭijong's daughter (the king's own second cousin). Marriage among siblings and cousins was openly practiced during the Koryŏ period. In the tenth century, for example, Kwangjong married his half-sister, hoping through such a union to curtail the influence of consort families. The Ch'oe House had the court pursue this same policy—perhaps for the same reasons. Moreover, in 1197 Ch'oe Ch'unghŏn went to battle to prevent his brother from marrying into the royal family. He felt such a grave act at that time would destroy the structure he was so carefully erecting. But if Ch'oe Ch'unghŏn was to deny his own family access to the king through marriage ties, he was also anxious to block others from doing the same. By having Kojong marry his own second cousin, Ch'oe Ch'unghŏn would be achieving this policy. Furthermore, by restricting the king to only one wife, Ch'oe Ch'unghŏn, like the earlier military leaders, was curtailing the political influence of aristocratic families in court and state affairs.

Ch'oe Ch'unghŏn was not in a sufficiently secure position to establish direct marriage ties with claimants to the throne. His son U, however, was able to achieve this goal and see that his descendants would rule the kingdom as monarchs. Ch'oe marriage ties with the royal household began during Ch'oe Ch'unghŏn's rule when he selected royal princesses as spouses for his sons and grandsons (Chapter 2). Ch'oe U perpetuated this policy. Then, at a strategic time, Ch'oe U arranged for his own granddaughter, the daughter of Kim Yaksŏn, a Kyŏngju Kim, to marry Kojong's son, the crown prince and future King Wŏnjong. The son of this union eventually ascended the throne as King Ch'ungnyŏl in 1274. Ch'oe U was able to plot this move—a maneuver his father had not dared to consider—because now that the Ch'oe House was firmly established he was in a much more secure position politically and socially. The prestige of the Ch'oe House was already obvious because of strategic marriages with many of the prominent military and civilian households of the kingdom. Furthermore, Ch'oe U's granddaughter, a member of the Kyŏngju Kim lineage, belonged to one of the most prestigious Koryŏ families, a lineage that already had long ties with the court. Having this girl marry the crown prince offered little affront to royal prestige. It was a wise maneuver. For it cemented the relationship of the Ch'oe House to the ranking lineages of the day and the royal family.

The Ch'oe House was able to dominate the court through economic means as well. Its land policy provided the court with needed property and guaranteed the integrity of royal estates. Ch'oe Ch'ung-hŏn presented the court with gifts to help it meet expenses. Ch'oe U gave lavish gifts—such as a double coffin decorated in silver and gold when the queen dowager died in 1232.[10] Ch'oe Ŭi, coming to power in the closing days of the Ch'oe House, demonstrated his generosity by presenting the court with land, 2,570 *sŏk* of rice, cloth, oil, and honey.[11] These deeds were in part impelled by the plight of the court and in part caused by the Ch'oe House's eagerness to exercise control over the court by obligating it through gifts. The Ch'oe House also used the court to obtain *sigŭp*—grants of land commonly reserved for royal clansmen.[12]

The Ch'oe House's adroit use of institutions further solidified its dominant position over the court. By controlling the military forces, it was able to circumvent any ploy the monarch might have devised to strengthen his own position by military means. The Ch'oe House gradually dominated the administration of the dynasty, as well, leaving the king virtually powerless. Palace attendants had once been court attendants who sided with the king. Under Ch'oe Ch'unghŏn, however, they became favorites of the military lords, frequently acquiring appointments through Ch'oe patronage. Kojong's lament that he was unable to summon even a petty official dramatically reveals the dependent position into which the court had fallen.

With so much power accumulating under Ch'oe Ch'unghŏn, it is possible he contemplated becoming king. In fact, his nephew Pak Chinjae spread a rumor: "My uncle plans to do away with the king."[13] Besides marking the rupture in relations between Pak Chinjae and Ch'oe Ch'unghŏn, this incident must have forced Ch'unghŏn to abandon any plans he might have had of usurpation. Nevertheless, the dream lived on. Under the rule of Ch'oe U, the Ch'oe House achieved immense security and power. In fact, Ch'oe U was so well ensconced that he did consider the possibility of becoming king. A diviner named Yŏnji secretly discussed this matter with Ch'oe U, saying: "Now the king has lost the appearance of a ruler, while you have the presence of a monarch. Destiny rests with you. How can you avoid it?" Ch'oe U talked it over with a confidant, but when the confidant questioned Yŏnji, the diviner became alarmed and the discussion ended.[14] Ch'oe U considered the possibility of becoming king but decided against it. Ch'oe Ch'unghŏn may have considered the same option and reached a similar decision. These leaders, with nearly total authority in their grasp, refrained from the last step of ascending the throne themselves and proclaiming a new dynasty.

Ch'oe Legitimacy

The court filled many roles during the Ch'oe period, but its most important function was to provide a legal setting for Ch'oe House designs. When Ch'oe Ch'unghŏn decided to sustain the dynastic structure, he also guaranteed the position of the royal family. For the monarch was indispensable to the Ch'oe House's operations. The king had propaganda value. He could mouth the words of the Ch'oe leaders and bolster their authority. He could sanction the rule of each of the Ch'oe leaders, offering them a cloak of legitimacy. Ch'oe Hang's rule was especially honored with a number of royal decrees.

The monarchs played an important role in administering dynastic ceremonies and fulfilling the functions of a Confucian king. One of the first steps Sinjong took after becoming king in 1197 was to issue pardons and grant awards to officials throughout the kingdom. In 1208, King Hŭijong personally presented wine and food to the aged, to the filial, to chaste widows, and to other exemplary individuals. At the same time, he also aided the sick and orphaned. The king prayed for the reduction of banditry on a number of occasions. Once, when bandits raided and insects plagued the northern area of the kingdom, Kojong dispatched palace attendants (naesi) to pray at shrines in the capital and provinces to end these scourges.[15] Besides these ceremonial functions, the king also took charge of the royal tombs and maintained the rites and proprieties demanded for these sepulchers. When ghouls disturbed one tomb, Hŭijong demanded that the Ministry of Rites establish a patrol to protect it. These duties were not novel. Throughout the earlier years of the dynasty, besides sustaining the customs of the kingdom, kings protected the people and their royal ancestors. But in fulfilling their duties, the kings of the Ch'oe period were characterized as "figureheads without power" and as rulers "so weak while officials were so strong."[16] Though the kings performed ceremonial functions, they had little power. They were important basically as a source of Ch'oe legitimacy and an expression of government compassion.

The preservation of the monarchy fostered Confucian ideology.[17]

By guaranteeing the primacy of the state examinations and other means such as recruiting scholars into the government, Ch'oe Ch'unghŏn and his son U went to great lengths to promote the Confucian system. Through such measures the Ch'oe House preserved an order that civilian officials believed was above reproach. This system—the body of ideas expressed in Confucian thought—provided the perfect rationale for the maintenance of the monarchy and the entire dynastic system. When Ch'oe Ch'unghŏn chose to revive the dynastic structure, he unavoidably had to foster its ideology, Confucianism. Furthermore, there was no other readily accessible political ideology to take the place of Confucian theory.

But there were serious implications for Ch'oe Ch'unghŏn in taking this step. Although Confucian thought justified the dynastic order, it provided no raison d'être for the other half of the Ch'oe structure: the private Ch'oe organization. In supporting Confucianism, as in supporting the dynastic structural framework that included the king and civil officials, Ch'oe Ch'unghŏn undermined the foundations of his regime over the long run. The lack of any type of ideological support for his innovations was a crucial weakness in his system. Often at the start of a new regime, a new philosophy arises as the rationale for the emerging structure. When Wang Kŏn rose to the throne at the start of Koryŏ, he sought to combine support from geomantic precepts, Buddhist power, and Confucian theory as the basic ideology for his kingdom. This scheme was embellished during Sŏngjong's reign when Ch'oe Sŭngno did much to expand Koryŏ Confucian thought.[18] The foundation of Chosŏn was also based in part on the growth of a new ideology: Neo-Confucianism.

Ch'oe Ch'unghŏn was unable to devise any rationale that could justify the operation of two competing organizations. Rather, by maintaining the Confucian system he held his structure accountable to Confucian norms. The men who worked for him would be loyal to him as a leader. But their ultimate allegiance, if they believed at all in Confucian theory, would be to the ruler, their king. By this necessary compromise the Ch'oe House was able to bring temporary stability to the age, but it sowed the seeds of its own vulnerability. In less auspicious times, or under a less adept Ch'oe ruler, Confucian theory would be used to justify the expulsion of the Ch'oe House and the restoration of full authority to the king.

There were other reasons why the royal family had to be retained.

Certainly fear of Chinese intervention prevented the Ch'oe leaders from establishing a new dynasty. This is reflected in a discussion between Ch'oe Ch'unghŏn and his confidants when they were confronted with the necessity of removing Myŏngjong. One man proposed Marquis Chin, an obscure member of the extended royal family, as a possible heir. Ch'oe Ch'unghŏn, however, countered this suggestion: "Min, Duke of P'yŏngnyang, is the king's brother by the same mother. He is expansive and has a sovereign's magnanimity. Moreover, his son Yŏn is wise and likes learning. He would be a fitting heir apparent." Pak Chinjae replied: "Either Marquis Chin or Min could become king. The Chin emperor, however, does not know Marquis Chin. If we enthrone him, the emperor will consider this a usurpation. It is not as sound as enthroning Min. As in Ŭijong's abdication, because they are brothers we can announce this without anxiety.[19]

This episode demonstrates Ch'oe Ch'unghŏn's caution when contemplating changes in the royal position. He claimed to be concerned about the legitimacy of the royal house and securing a wise monarch. But he was even more anxious about the response of the Chinese emperors, who at this time were represented by the Jurchen Chin dynasty. Any unusual succession had to be carefully explained to the Chinese court.[20] When Ch'oe Ch'unghŏn forced Myŏngjong off the throne, he informed Chin that Myŏngjong was ill and then announced his death in 1198—years before he actually died in 1202.[21] When Hŭijong's attempted assassination failed, Ch'oe Ch'unghŏn again explained to Chin that since the king was ill, he would have to vacate the throne. The Chin histories even report that Hŭijong died in 1212—he actually lived on until 1237—and furthermore the Chinese histories completely pass over Kangjong's accession.[22] Without Chinese approval, the legitimacy of the Koryŏ dynasty and the Ch'oe House would be threatened. If the Ch'oe House was hesitant about having to explain to the Chinese their choice of successors within the royal Wang family, the idea of overthrowing the royal family and founding a new dynasty led by the Ch'oe family must have been inconceivable.

Upheaval in China's political world spilled over into Korea. Compared to China, where dynasties rose and fell, Korea experienced only three major dynastic eras—and the latter two, Koryŏ and Chosŏn, were extremely long periods. Korean dynastic changes occurred only when the Chinese court was divided and challenged by various elements within China. The Koryŏ dynasty arose during the disruptive Five Dynasties period of Chinese history. Although Wang Kŏn went to the major dynasties for their tacit approval of his new Korean dynasty, the early Koryŏ kings did not worry over a Chinese ally rushing to the aid of the deposed Silla monarch. The Silla king relinquished his throne for reasons that were basically domestic. But the fact that he could not rely on the backing of a Chinese emperor to support his prerogatives made it that much easier for Wang Kŏn to establish his Koryŏ line. The same situation occurred when Yi Sŏnggye founded his dynasty. In China, the Mongol Yuan and the Chinese Ming dynasties were vying for control. Yi Sŏnggye was able to take advantage of this dispute to overthrow the last vestiges of Koryŏ rule and establish Chosŏn.

Ch'oe Ch'unghŏn was not in such a position. For when he came to power the Chin dynasty was still at its peak. Chin acknowledged the authority of the royal Wang clan and, when Ŭijong abdicated in 1170, Chin reluctantly approved Myŏngjong's succession.[23] Chin's commitment to the Wang lineage did not falter. If Ch'oe Ch'unghŏn had assumed power when the dynasty in China was on a downswing, perhaps the Ch'oe House could have ushered in a new era and a new dynasty. But this avenue was not available at the end of the twelfth century. The Ch'oe leaders had to be mindful of a latent Chinese threat of invasion if rebels imperiled the dynasty.

Still another consideration for Ch'oe Ch'unghŏn was the loyalty of the Koryŏ bureaucracy to the Wang line. If Ch'oe Ch'unghŏn had tried to depose the royal family, there would have been moral indignation around the country. Rather than bringing the stability he sought, he would have further inflamed passions and incurred the opposition of the civil bureaucrats. Such an act might also have prompted intervention by the Chin dynasty, for Koryŏ officials could have cried foul play and pleaded for Chin aid. Chin would then have had a legitimate excuse to initiate an expedition against Ch'oe Ch'unghŏn. In fact, this almost happened in 1175 when Cho Wich'ong revolted against the early military leaders and sought Chin aid to restore power to the rightful rulers.[24]

Ch'oe Ch'unghŏn opted for the more secure alternative of maintaining the royal family. This scheme enabled him to carry on with his work and gain the support of both the Chin dynasty and the civil-

ian structure of the Koryŏ kingdom. He could retain the monarchy
while still selecting kings who were amenable to his direction. This
situation, as noted earlier, was similar to the Japanese institutional
use of the emperor at historically the same time. But there was a key
difference between Korea and Japan: the Ch'oe authority cloaked
itself much more completely with the royal mantle. Even physically
the Ch'oe head and the monarch shared the same capital. In Japan
the Kamakura shogunate was more autonomous and geographically
removed. Of the earlier Koryŏ kings, some were quite aggressive in
fulfilling their responsibilities while others relegated their power to
officials and merely assumed ceremonial functions.[25] Ch'oe Ch'unghŏn cultivated the latter type of monarch, thus assuring the Ch'oe
House of nearly all responsibility for the affairs of the kingdom, leaving the king as a passive participant in the government.

This was an expedient move, forced by necessity, but in the end it
paved the way for the collapse of the Ch'oe House. Ch'oe Ch'unghŏn and his descendants had to acknowledge a power higher than
theirs. Behind every act was the sanction of the throne. Ch'oe
Ch'unghŏn and U could work in this system, and they were strong
enough to control this relationship with the king to their own advantage. But planted in this fictive maintenance of royal power were the
seeds for later opposition. Someday the royal position would serve as
a rallying point to throw off the Ch'oe rule. This was the path that
Japan followed in bringing an end to the Tokugawa *bakufu* in 1868.
It remained a very real threat to the Ch'oe House, as well, which
would always be vulnerable to the potential revival of full royal power.
The concept of legitimacy, tied to the authority of the monarch, was
central to Koryŏ society and to the Ch'oe House.

Civilians

To operate the dynastic structure that he had chosen to revive,
Ch'oe Ch'unghŏn had to depend on civilian cooperation. The role
of civilian power in the military period follows a noteworthy pattern.
Of all identifiable officeholders during Ŭijong's reign, civilians held
approximately 90 percent of the offices in the civil dynastic structure. This proportion dropped to 77 percent at the start of Myŏngjong's reign and then to 54 percent by the end of his reign.
Although civilians gradually declined in power during this period,

they were still a force to contend with. When Ch'oe Ch'unghŏn restored the dynastic system, he tried to win the support of the civilian leaders and the proportion of civilian officeholders began once more to increase. These same trends are also reflected in the number of successful examination candidates who served in the dynastic structure. (See Table 8.)

Civilians, then, were essential to the Ch'oe House. Ch'oe Ch'unghŏn needed armed might to rule, but he would not be effective if he ruled by the sword alone. By winning civilian approval, the Ch'oe House secured their support and aid in governing. By bringing respect and esteem to the Ch'oe House, civilians aided in pacifying resistance and creating tranquility. They were invaluable, too, in handling administrative matters and managing the kingdom. Through the appointment of able officials, Ch'oe Ch'unghŏn could rule the country more efficiently and justly. The fact that the Ch'oe House looked so readily to civilian solutions suggests that Korean society had reached a level of administrative sophistication at which it could best be governed not by military alliances but by restored civil institutions. Furthermore, civilians would be an important counterweight to military power. It was the discontent of the civilians during the end of Myŏngjong's rule that helped Ch'oe Ch'unghŏn eliminate Yi Ŭimin. By supporting Ch'oe Ch'unghŏn, they continued to be invaluable in inhibiting the success of potential Ch'oe opponents.

As the Ch'oe period progressed, the distinctions between military and civilian leaders gradually blurred. As it matured, the Ch'oe rule became less military in its outlook. Civilians once again assumed greater responsibility. Although there were fewer active military officers in the dynastic structure, there seems to have been a general mixing of the branches as military leaders assumed all types of dynastic positions. Military officers passed the state examination, as well, heralding a new era in which officers received training in Confucian learning and were well read in the classics. Civilians became less rigid, too, and less reluctant to assume military posts. The Chamber of Scholarly Advisers (Sŏbang), which planned military tactics and strategy, comprised civilian officials. This same blurring of distinctions can be seen in the makeup of lineages. During the early years of the Koryŏ dynasty, certain lineages had separate military lines. Now, however, differences were visible even within generations. T'aesŏ of the Kyŏngju Kims was a civilian who had a number

Table 8. Composition of the Civil Dynastic Structure, 1146–1257

Background	Üijong	Myŏngjong (1170–1175)	Myŏngjong (1175–1196)	Ch'unghŏn	U	Hang
Total	96	44	76	80	96	35
Civilian	90 (93%)	34 (77%)	46 (61%)	43 (54%)	69 (71%)	26 (74%)
Military	6 (6%)	9 (20%)	26 (34%)	16 (20%)	24 (25%)	7 (20%)
Unclear		1	4	21	3	2
Exam	41 (42%)	22 (50%)	34 (45%)	20 (25%)	43 (45%)	22 (63%)
A	39 (40%)	21 (48%)	31 (41%)	32 (40%)	46 (48%)	18 (51%)
AA	21 (22%)	12 (27%)	19 (25%)	13 (16%)	28 (29%)	11 (31%)
Functionary			1			1
Lowborn			4	1	1	

Note: Exam: passed examination; A: one ancestor fifth grade or higher; AA: two or more ancestors fifth grade or higher.

of sons. One became a civilian official and two became military officers. One of the sons of the noted General Chŏng Sukch'ŏm of the Hadong Chŏng clan passed the state examination and became a civilian official. The conflicts and antagonisms that had erupted between military and civilian elements in Ŭijong's and Myŏngjong's reigns were changing into a relationship of mutual trust and cooperation. One's service background was no longer a barrier to holding office. But the reduced emphasis on military traditions and increased stress on civilian norms would also bring attempts to reassert the full powers of the dynasty and its structure.

Retainers

Sources of dysfunction in the Ch'oe scheme are visible in the retainer system that Ch'oe Ch'unghŏn and his descendants constructed. Retainers in theory reserved their ultimate loyalty for their masters. The Ch'oe House operated through retainers who usually held a position in the Ch'oe offices along with a simultaneous post in the dynastic order. By giving them dual appointments, Ch'oe Ch'unghŏn never doubted that his retainers would remain loyal supporters of his leadership. But the same dualism posed a serious problem to the thoughtful retainer. A retainer who received a position from Ch'oe Ch'unghŏn owed loyalty to him as his master, but his dynastic office also called for allegiance to the king. This was not too great a dilemma for most men during the early Ch'oe period, because Ch'oe Ch'unghŏn and U were too powerful to challenge. Yet the potential remained. Ideology and office could be used to topple the Ch'oe House.

Weaknesses in the Ch'oe retainer system were apparent whenever a Ch'oe leader died. The succession of each new Ch'oe ruler was always accompanied by extensive purges of men who were not trusted or who were considered a threat to individual Ch'oe leaders. In forcing the dishonest and the sycophants to leave, Ch'oe U executed many of his father's confidants and replaced them with people he could trust. We can see, then, that the loyalty of Ch'oe Ch'unghŏn's retainers did not transfer automatically to his son. The retainers of the Ch'oe House seem to have been loyal to the individual leaders but not to the house itself. When Ch'oe Hang succeeded U, a similar situation evolved as he exiled many of his father's faithful supporters. There was no ideological basis for justifying their loyalty to the Ch'oe House. Although they could support individuals for reasons of fidelity or expediency, there was no established theory to rationalize support for the organization. In the system that the Ch'oe House fostered, moreover, ultimate loyalty would always be directed to the dynasty. By fostering the dynastic order beside its own structure, the Ch'oe House was permitting a competing institution and a competing source of power. The dynastic hierarchy was always there: a dormant order that could be used as a base to challenge Ch'oe authority.

Social and Economic Contradictions

During the politically turbulent years before Ch'oe Ch'unghŏn rose to power, there were definite changes emerging in the social structure. Men of humble *(ch'ŏn)* status began to receive appointments to dynastic offices, and a number of them even entered the coveted State Council. Slaves with talent began to play a more prominent role in society by aiding their masters in land acquisitions or economic endeavors. Social legislation at this time was relaxed, but this very slackening was accompanied by peasant revolts and domestic unrest. As a member of a military officer's family, Ch'oe Ch'unghŏn witnessed these events and was impelled to establish his own rule. His solution was simple. He immediately sought to reconstruct the old hierarchy by curtailing the role of slaves and eunuchs and assuring positions for the socially prominent. Ch'oe Ch'unghŏn had accepted the Confucian scheme, which acknowledged an established social order and a dependence on men of learning. By curbing the activities of people like slaves and utilizing talented officials, domestic unrest could be pacified and the system stabilized.

The lineage of the men who served in the Ch'oe structure reflects this renewed interest in status. Of the individuals found in officialdom during the late Myŏngjong period, four men of humble origin reached ranking positions while only one such man was found in the structure during Ch'oe Ch'unghŏn's rule. Thirty-one of the men (41 percent) holding office in Myŏngjong's civil structure had fathers of the fifth *p'um* rank or above, moreover, compared to thirty-two (40 percent) discovered in Ch'oe Ch'unghŏn's rule. Ch'oe U and Hang continued the patterns begun at this time. The Ch'oe House effectively excluded men of humble status from prestigious rank or influence until Ch'oe Hang's period. Even in Ch'oe Hang's time, such people did not get high government offices but rather assumed informal appointments in the Ch'oe structure, acting as aides and confidants for the Ch'oe leader.

One must not get the impression that the Ch'oe House rigidly restricted the lower classes on all levels. Indeed much of its policy sought to alleviate the discontent of the peasants, and each leader paid considerable attention to his own favorites and personal slaves. Although Ch'oe Ch'unghŏn and U imposed certain restrictions on social mobility and restored influence to prominent military and civilian families, developments under Ch'oe Hang and Ŭi opened the door for further social emancipation. From the days of Silla rule there had been a gradual expansion of prerogatives and the granting of political privileges to more and more people. The Silla kingdom restricted political authority to the ranking Silla nobles. From the start of the Koryŏ period, access to power extended to a still larger group, including those who had not been among the elite in Silla times. Under the military rule, military leaders also assumed prominent roles in decision making. For part of the time, even slaves were reaching high-ranking offices. Although Ch'oe Ch'unghŏn subsequently restricted slaves, the door had been opened. During the years immediately after Ch'oe rule, a small number of slaves again rose to prominence. At the end of the Ch'oe period, social limitations relaxed momentarily.

Turning his attention to economics, Ch'oe Ch'unghŏn also tried to rehabilitate the dynastic fiscal structure. The government required funds as much as Ch'oe Ch'unghŏn did. The dynastic system was already in place and merely needed to be implemented. Ch'oe Ch'unghŏn made this his task. By revitalizing the land stipend system (chŏnsikwa) and forcing people to return land they had seized, Ch'oe Ch'unghŏn curtailed the power of the large landholders, strengthened the dynasty, and obtained new tax revenues. By clarifying and regulating the land and tax system, this plan also resolved many peasant grievances and restored order to the dynasty. It prevented military leaders from developing close ties with the land, as well, keeping them as bureaucratic retainers rather than as vassals with fiefs. In rejuvenating the dynastic land system, Ch'oe Ch'unghŏn sought to guarantee his own preeminence. But his restoration of the land system was incomplete. For while he curtailed the large holdings of other men, he permitted himself the luxury of expanding his own property, thus perpetuating the very practice he was trying to abolish. Seeds of dysfunction sprouted in his dual dynastic/private system, too, for he could not expand one order without undermining the other.

The Ch'oe Position

Under the guise of restoration, the Ch'oe House established itself as the highest agency in the kingdom. It sought to achieve this goal by dissolving or weakening competing institutions. It accepted no intervening power between itself at the top and society below. Since its strongest competitor for prominence was the royal family, the Ch'oe House sought to subdue the court through marriage ties, economic tactics, and other institutional mechanisms, such as control over the military establishment. The Ch'oe House even tried to merge itself with the court and assume the respect and authority traditionally directed to the royal house. The Ch'oe House might have succeeded in this endeavor had it not at the same time perpetuated the Confucian order that placed the royal house at the apex of the state, no matter how great Ch'oe power came to be.

The Buddhist establishment was a second major force that posed a threat to the Ch'oe hierarchy. Through memorials, brute force, and sponsorship of a competing sect, Ch'oe Ch'unghŏn tried to break the strength of the great Kyo Buddhist order. At this he succeeded. In its place he fostered a sect that was philosophically more suited to his own purposes and politically less likely to challenge his authority. Sŏn Buddhism, through the patronage of the Ch'oe House, became the most prominent religious force in the kingdom. For the duration of Ch'oe rule, Buddhist institutions and clerics did not interfere in the political life of the state. The Ch'oe House had successfully restrained one of the major forces in the kingdom.

Challenges to the Ch'oe House were latent, too, in slave and peasant unrest and in individual attempts to establish economic independence. Ch'oe Ch'unghŏn pursued a deliberate attack and by numerous ploys was able to quell local revolts. To subdue the powerful, Ch'oe Ch'unghŏn enforced the dynastic land system, thereby preventing extensive landholdings from falling to potential rivals.

Trade was another ready source of wealth that could be used by an innovative person to bolster his power and independence from the ruling structure. Through maritime trade, Chang Pogo and others had been able to accumulate huge resources and enough strength to challenge the Silla kingdom. This potential was undoubtedly alive in the Ch'oe period. But Ch'oe Ch'unghŏn checked this possibility, too, taking an active personal interest in commerce and its profits. Strict regulations prevented individuals from gaining too much wealth and establishing an order that could compete with his own power structure.

The military establishment was a final source of potential competition—and perhaps the most formidable domestic opponent. Each of the Ch'oe leaders tried to curtail military opposition, but the problem was most acute for Ch'oe Ch'unghŏn. Ch'oe Ch'unghŏn purged a number of men who were potential threats and thereby neutralized much of the military opposition. Many of the policies he pursued were also tailored to curb the renascence of any military revolt. By building his own military structure, Ch'oe Ch'unghŏn constructed a system that would be powerful enough to guarantee his military preeminence and assure the subservience of others. Furthermore, in supporting civilian and Confucian ideology he sought to emulate civil models of rule and give his system a much more civilian, and less military, orientation. He was attempting to defuse the military time bomb. So long as recourse to arms was the basis for power—and so long as there was no philosophical or institutional means to secure support for a ruler—politics would be decided by military might. This was a very unstable way to administer a kingdom. Ch'oe Ch'unghŏn was presiding over a transitional stage in which the excesses of the earlier military period were being countered and civilian authority reasserted. Ch'oe U and Hang inherited and continued these basic patterns. Many competing institutions were neutralized as the Ch'oe House's position of leadership endured for some sixty years.

Ultimately Ch'oe power rested on its military might. Because the Ch'oe House was able to summon force to institute its programs, it was able to maintain its position in the kingdom. Force alone was evidently not enough, however, for the Ch'oe family had to bolster its position by employing civilian scholars, by restoring the revered dynastic structure, and by appealing to Confucian legitimacy. The

Ch'oe House then had the necessary means to enact its policies. Without the dual support of military and civilian forces, it would have been next to impossible to administer the kingdom and restore stability to the age.

Collapse of the Ch'oe House

One of the most obvious reasons for the collapse of the Ch'oe House is the disruption caused by the Mongol invasions. Since its beginnings, the Koryŏ dynasty had often been confronted with serious threats from the north. Then, in 1225, several years after Ch'oe Ch'unghŏn had died, the first difficulties with the Mongols developed. By this time the Mongols had expanded their power in northern China and were already threatening the Chin dynasty. Over the next forty years the Mongols repeatedly invaded the Korean peninsula, but the Ch'oe House refused to surrender. When the first major invasion commenced in the fall of 1231, Koryŏ marshaled a stalwart defense. When a second invasion commenced in the following year, Koryŏ again resisted. The Ch'oe leaders and the court, refusing to be subdued, decided to move the capital to nearby Kanghwa Island and resist offshore. When subsequent invasions followed, the leaders urged endangered peasants to evacuate to offshore islands and mountain fortresses.

During the years between 1231 and 1359, the Mongol invasions unfolded in six massive waves.[26] Not all parts of the country were ravaged during the repeated invasions, however, and between the storms of attack peasants were able to return to their lands and tend their fields. The southern part of the peninsula along the coast escaped many of the invasions, and this area continued to be the Ch'oe breadbasket. The island of Kanghwa enjoyed a boom as massive construction of palaces, government buildings, and private mansions was undertaken to house the Ch'oe leaders and the court, which sought shelter there.[27] From this island the Ch'oe leaders directed the defense and also sought to govern the land.[28] When confronted with mounting devastation, the Ch'oe leaders exempted certain areas from taxation. In the middle of the fifth invasion in the mid-1250s, the state treasury was nearly exhausted, yet revenue still found its way to Kanghwa Island. By the time Ch'oe Ŭi came to power, starvation must have reached alarming proportions for twice in 1257, the year before he was assassinated, state and private granaries gave out food.[29] Although the upheaval wrought by the Mongols caused many to yearn for peace, the Ch'oe House to its end resisted surrender. That it was able to withstand these invasions for so long testifies to its basic strength.

Koryŏ developed a creative foreign policy in responding to Mongol demands for surrender. In the 1250s, a crisis arose over whether the king should go to the mainland to meet with Mongol envoys. Ch'oe Hang, in a display of bravado, declared his opposition to any member of the royal family making such a journey but left the final decision to the king. By having two policymakers (the king and Ch'oe Hang) emerge at this time, Koryŏ skillfully obfuscated any decision. The Mongols quickly perceived the tactic and declared that if Ch'oe Hang did not offer to surrender along with the king, no truce could be called. Realizing the impasse, Ch'oe Hang reverted to traditional Ch'oe tactics and called for a scorched earth policy as the most effective means to counter Mongol attacks.[30] The repeated invasions took their toll, however, and the government drifted toward bankruptcy as peasants abandoned their farms to escape the invaders. Surrender to the Mongols came after the demise of the Ch'oe House, but even capitulation met resistance when military leaders carried out a final stand in the Sambyŏlch'o revolt.

Flaws in the Ch'oe system itself must also be examined as additional causes for its collapse. The power of the Ch'oe House rested with its leaders. In the retainer system that the Ch'oe House nurtured, the Ch'oe leader himself was the fulcrum of all loyalties. If he were removed, there was no institutional guarantee that the structure would stand. Ch'oe Ch'unghŏn and U, under whom the Ch'oe House rapidly expanded and matured, were capable men who understood the politics of the age and were able to balance the competing forces to assure their own survival. The last two Ch'oe leaders, Hang and Ŭi, were products of a different environment and could not match the acumen of their ancestors. As the Ch'oe House developed, it brought stability to the kingdom. Civilian institutions were openly praised. A search for literary accomplishment and Confucian ideals replaced the military atmosphere of the early Ch'oe years. Ch'oe Hang, who spent youthful years in Chŏlla province training in Sŏn thought, was unfamiliar with martial pursuits and court life. It is no wonder, then, he had so little skill in handling political problems, comprehending civilian sensibilities, and commanding the Ch'oe House. Ch'oe Hang's son Ŭi, equally ill prepared for the responsibilities of his position, delegated most of his powers to his confidants. Weaknesses in the Ch'oe system had always been present. Whereas Ch'oe Ch'unghŏn and U were able to master them, Hang and Ŭi were gradually overwhelmed by them. The institutions of the Ch'oe leadership as well as the later Ch'oe leaders themselves contributed to the collapse of the Ch'oe House.

The last years of the Ch'oe House, holding out on Kanghwa Island, are pictured in rather desperate terms. With the collapse of the kingdom's economic foundations and the constant Mongol attacks, the imminent death of the entire Ch'oe system must have become obvious to the men around the Ch'oe leaders. Ch'oe policy toward the Mongols was part of the issue. The Ch'oe leaders' refusal to surrender might have stemmed from fear of the consequences. The Mongols lived on a reputation of immense cruelty toward those who chose to resist—and Koryŏ under Ch'oe leadership had resisted for more than twenty-five years. To the Ch'oe supporters, surrender meant the end in all senses of the word. Beyond fear for themselves, hatred for the Mongols remained intense. And as invasion followed invasion, this feeling that Koryŏ must not be ruled by Mongols grew stronger. Even after the surrender, the military rebelled and refused to accept peace. When the Ch'oe leaders could not establish policy, it was the Ch'oe confidants and ranking civil officials who brought an end to Ch'oe rule. They realized that the Ch'oe House, cut off from supplies and limited in options, had become vulnerable. And when they saw the corpulent youth Ch'oe Ŭi advised by an uncle, they deemed the Ch'oe House no longer competent to rule.

The potential collapse of the Ch'oe House was of course always present. Seeds of decay are inherent in many systems, and the contradictions besetting the Ch'oe economic and social structure have already been noted. The Ch'oe House was especially vulnerable since, as we have seen, it was fostering two competing sets of institutions. The Ch'oe leaders maintained the traditional dynastic structure with the king and civilian personnel, but within this order they formed the Ch'oe House machinery. The fatal flaws in the Ch'oe structure were its cultivation of civilian officials and Confucian ideals and its failure to devise a new ideological basis for its system. The civilian leadership gradually reasserted control over the structure and neglected military ideals. Their Confucian beliefs—including the concept that legitimacy resides in the monarch—fed into what became an irreversible torrent of antipathy toward continued Ch'oe rule. With or without the Mongols, the Ch'oe House and military rule would not have survived Koryŏ's civil tradition.

The Ch'oe House's Legacy

The period of Ch'oe hegemony was a major watershed in Korean history. The Ch'oe House formed novel political and military systems and superimposed them on the dynastic agencies. They were novel in that they bypassed the established dynastic order and put ultimate power into the hands of the Ch'oe leaders and their closest allies. The king was actually peripheral to this system, but the military had a significant role. Ch'oe institutions such as the Personnel Authority and the Yabyŏlch'o continued to play key roles well after the Ch'oe House vanished.

Even in these new structures, however, legacies of the past were retained. The paramount Ch'oe organization—the Directorate General for Policy Formulation (Kyojŏng Togam)—operated on a consensus basis, much as had the earlier oligarchy under the state councillors. Furthermore, people within this structure came from many formerly powerful families, and it incorporated much of the previous social order. That the Ch'oe House did not break completely with the past was both its greatest strength and its most ominous flaw. By adapting its new order onto the old, established system, the Ch'oe House gained the time needed to devise its structure. But acceptance of the norms of a previous era meant it would never be able to free itself completely from the restrictions of that time. The Ch'oe House was not able to advance philosophically beyond the days of Korea before the military coup. And although it turned to Sŏn Buddhism as a rationale for its new order, Sŏn tenets made poor political theory. In the end, the Ch'oe House could only depend on Confucian concepts of legitimacy to rationalize its command. In its call for Confucian ideals, however, it suffered the embarrassment of having to acknowledge the supremacy of the dynastic ruling house.

Military officers assumed the positions of supreme power in twelfth-century Korea. Although power slipped from their grasp within a century, the impact of military rule in general, and the

Ch'oe House in particular, was profound. It set much of the political and social tone for the remainder of the Koryŏ dynasty. Most prominent of the many institutional innovations introduced during the six decades that the Ch'oe House controlled the kingdom was the evolution of private armies and private systems of authority. Under Ch'oe initiatives, the security of the kingdom became the responsibility of the Ch'oe House and the Ch'oe-directed Tobang and Yabyŏlch'o became its military arms. To staff these organizations, the Ch'oe leaders used retainers who gained their positions from allegiance to the individual Ch'oes, not through regular dynastic channels.

Changes in the Koryŏ social structure were mixed. Some aristocratic families declined in importance, while others sustained their eminence. In the lower orders of society, the Ch'oe House suppressed peasant revolts that marred the years following the military coup of 1170. It also restructured the social order, denying privileges to many people of lowborn status. Here too, however, its policy was contradictory. It permitted supporters of the Ch'oe House to advance to positions of prominence regardless of their status. In doing this, it was cautiously permitting the erosion, already set in motion after 1170, of the rigid social distinctions that marked much of the earlier Koryŏ period.

Ch'oe economic policies engendered equally significant developments. The Ch'oe House sought to bypass the dynastic administration wherever feasible. In the administration of the *sigŭp*, for example, ambiguity emerged in the ultimate jurisdiction over the collection and deposition of *sigŭp* yields. By eliminating the dynastic government's traditional power in such matters, the Ch'oe House could place individuals in direct control of their own lands and free from the dynastic middlemen. More significant than the operation of the *sigŭp* was the rapid expansion of private estates that seriously encroached on the dynasty's ability to collect revenue from the land. Although this trend did not culminate in the Ch'oe period, the dynasty did eventually lose control over state finances. Land was increasingly seen as the private property of individuals, not as a possession of the dynasty.

The Ch'oe House not only sought to expand its control over revenues but also looked for new sources of wealth. During the Ch'oe rule both *yangban* and *yangsuch'ŏk*, for example, assumed certain tax-paying responsibilities. The Ch'oe House, even while it was expanding its own private holdings, also employed the central administration to ensure that revenue from the countryside would be more expeditiously collected and transported to state granaries for state needs. Under Ch'oe authority, the central government at the start of the thirteenth century reasserted its influence over the provinces as well as the capital city.

Apart from these social and economic changes, new patterns emerged in the Buddhist hierarchy at this time. The Kyo sect, with its elaborate doctrine, gradually lost primacy to Sŏn, which emphasized meditation and rejected a slavish dependence on scripture. The stage was set for a type of Buddhist thought that would have much more significance for the average person. Buddhism had the potential to become a popular religion with deep appeal to the masses as well as the capital elite.

Ch'oe Ch'unghŏn and his descendants also reinvigorated the dynastic civil structure, which had suffered setbacks in the years immediately following the 1170 coup. The Directorate General and the Personnel Authority—agencies of the Ch'oe House—actually managed all government operations. Under the auspices of these organs and through such traditional means as the civil service examination, the Ch'oe House recruited many civilian scholars into the formal government and into its own structure as retainers. Indeed, the Ch'oe leaders expanded the scope of the state examinations by holding them more frequently and passing a greater number of candidates. In this atmosphere, Confucian learning recovered its former esteem. Partly because of Ch'oe patronage, a vigorous intellectual life, coupled with major literary developments, ensued. The Ch'oe age was crucial for the development of civilian ideals.

Early Koryŏ society was continually disrupted by attempts to resolve the rivalry between military and civilian forces. It was indeed the tensions between these elements that set the stage for the coup that ushered in military rule. Tensions between military and civilian were not resolved until the rise of the Ch'oe House. And even then the resolution was unexpected. The establishment of the Ch'oe House led to a new period of accommodation. It is an ironic twist of history that it was during this phase of military rule that the Koryŏ kingdom was able to bring some resolution to centuries of military/civilian rivalries. To advance politically, a service background no longer represented a barrier and academic merit became an important criterion. It took a general in the position of greatest power in the country to realize that his authority could not be secured without cooperation between military and civilian elements and their participation in government. Because the Ch'oe House became so dependent upon civilian cooperation, it was in this military period that the foundation was firmly set for Korea's lasting civilian legacy.

APPENDIXES

Appendix 1. Palace Attendants in Ŭijong's Reign (1146–1170)

Name	Origin	Information
Ch'in Hyŏngwang		B
Chin Tŭngmun		L
Ch'oe Hyŏn	Haeju	A/B
Ch'oe Kwanggyun	Hannam	A
Ch'oe Yunsŏ	Haeju	A/B
Chŏng Ham		H
Chŏng Sŏ	Tongnae	A/G
Ham Yuil	Hanyang	L/G
Han Yugong		
Hwang Munjang		A/E
Kim Ch'ŏn	Kyŏngju	A/G
Kim Chonjung		E
Kim Hŏngwang		
Kim Kŏgong	Pugwŏn	L
Kim Kŏsil		B
Kim Kwang		B
Kim Kwangjung		A/E/B
Kim Tonjung	Kyŏngju	A/E/B
Kim Yu	Kwangju	L
No Yŏngsun	Kigye	G

(continued)

Name	Origin	Information
Pae Yŏn	Kigye	A/B
Pae Yunjae		G
Pak Hŭijun		
Pak Tonjung		L
Pak Yungong		B
Yi Hongsŭng		E
Yi Pokki		B
Yi Sŏngyun		
Yi Tangju		A/B
Yi Yangyun		
Yŏng Ŭi		H/B
Yu Chang		
Yun Chiwŏn		
Yun Ŏnmun	P'ap'yŏng	A
Yu Pangŭi		B
Yu Unggyu		A

Note: The lineage origin is indicated where known.
Key:
A: father or close relative in fifth *p'um* rank or above
B: removed from office in 1170 coup
E: examination
G: advanced after 1170 coup
H: histories claim humble *(ch'ŏn)* background
L: histories claim functionary background

Total	36
A	12
B	13
E	5
G	6
H	1
L	5

Appendix 2. Men Removed from Power in 1170 Coup

Name	Office	Miscellaneous
Chin Hyŏngwang	Palace attendant	
Chin Yunsŭng	Military Affairs	
Ch'oe Ch'i	Ministry	
Ch'oe Chun	Dep. Dir. Sacrificial Ceremonies	
Ch'oe Hyŏn	Palace attendant	
Ch'oe On	Security Council	Origin Chiksan; Father Hangjae; partied with king; military commissioner
Ch'oe Tonsik	Censorate	
Ch'oe Yuch'ing	Executive	Partied with king
Ch'oe Yunsŏ	Taebu Dep. Dir.; palace attendant	Origin Haeju
Cho Mungwi	Office of Regalia	
Cho Munjin	Executive	Exam
Cho Tonghŭi	Military Affairs	
Chŏn Ch'iyu	Pongŏ	
Han Nŏe	Recording Editor	
Hŏ Chadan	Taesasŏng	
Hŏ Hongjae	Personnel; Military commissioner	Exam; examiner
Im Chongsik	Security Council	Partied with king
Kang Ch'ŏgyung	Ministry	
Kang Ch'ŏyak	Military Affairs	
Kim Chagi	Astrology	Diviner
Kim Kisin	Censorate	
Kim Kŏsil	Haenggung Pyŏlgam; palace attendant	
Kim Kwang	Palace attendant	
Kim Kwangjung	Royal Archives; palace attendant; military commissioner	Origin Kwangyang; exam; examiner
Kim Sujang	Special Comm.	

(continued)

Name	Office	Miscellaneous
Kim Tonjung	Security Council	Origin Kyŏngju; exam/palace attendant; father Pusik
Kim Tonsi	Ministry	Origin Kyŏngju; exam; father Pusik
Pae Chin	Chihu	Father Kyŏngsŏng
Pae Yŏn	Palace attendant	Father Kyŏngsŏng
Paek Chadan		Eunuch
Pak Pogyun	Taebu Dep. Dir.	
Pak Yungong	Censorate	Palace attendant
Sŏ Sun	Security Council; Examiner	Military Commissioner
Um Chungin	Astrology	
Wang Kwangch'wi		Eunuch
Yang Sunjŏng	Security Council	
Yi Chisim	National University	Exam; examiner
Yi Inbo	Ministry	
Yi Pokki	Censorate	Partied with king Palace attendant?
Yi Set'ong	Security Council	
Yi Tangju	Palace attendant	
Yi Yunsu		Son: Yi Kyubo
Yŏng Ŭi	Palace attendant	Father banished; mother's ancestor a traitor
Yu Ikkyŏm	Chihu	
Yu Pangŭi	Palace attendant	
Yun Chongak	Taebu Chubu	Origin P'ap'yŏng; exam; father Inch'ŏm
Yun Sunsin	Personnel	Origin P'ap'yŏng; exam; father Ŏni; alias Tosin

Total removed	47
Palace attendant	13
Security Council	6
Minister of military affairs	3
Censor	4
Astrologer	3
Military commissioner	4
Examiner	8

Appendix 3. Civil Dynastic Structure in Myŏngjong's Reign
(1170–1175)

Name	Service	Path	Background	Office
Ch'oe Tang	C	E	AA	Lower Royal S–C
Ch'oe Uch'ŏng	C	E		Lower Royal S–C
Ch'oe Yŏhae	C	E		Lower Royal S–C
Ch'oe Yuch'ŏng	C	E	A	State Council; Personnel/Rites
Ch'oe Kyun	C	E		Rites
Ch'oe Ch'ŏkgyŏng	C	E		Censorate
Chang Ch'ungŭi	C	E	A	Unclear
Chang Ingmyŏng	C			Rites
Chin Chun	M		AA	State Council
Chin Kwangin	C	E		Censorate
Cho Wich'ong	C			Military Affairs
Chŏng Chungbu	M		A	State Council
Ham Yuil	C			Military Affairs
Han Ch'wi	C	E		State Council; Exam
Han Onguk	C	E		Lower Royal S–C; Exam
Im Kŭkch'ung	C	E	A	State Council
Im Minbi	C	E	A	Lower Royal S–C
Ki T'aksŏng	M			Lower Security Council; Censorate
Kim Ch'ŏn	C	E	AA	State Council; Lower Security Council; Exam
Kim Hwayun	C	E		Lower Royal S–C; Exam
Kim Podang	C		AA	Lower Royal S–C; Public Works
Kim Sŏngmi	?			Dept. of Ministries
Kwak Yangsŏn	C	E		Lower Royal S–C; Exam
Kyŏng Chin	M			State Council
Min Yŏngmo	C	E	AA	Lower Security Council; Punishments; Exam
Mun Kŭkkyŏm	C	E	AA	Lower Security Council; Rites; Exam
No Yŏngsun	C		A	State Council

(continued)

Name	Service	Path	Background	Office
Sŏ Kong	C		AA	State Council
Song Sungbu	C			Unclear
Song Yuin	M			Lower Security Council
Wang Segyŏng	C	E	A	Lower Royal S–C
Yang Suk	M			State Council
Yi Chimyŏng	C	E		Dept. of Ministries
Yi Chunŭi	M			Lower Security Council
Yi Kongsŭng	C	E	A	State Council
Yi Kwangjin	C		AA	State Council
Yi Kwangjŏng	M			Lower Security Council; Censorate
Yi Munjŏ	C		AA	Dept. of Ministries; Personnel
Yi Soung	C			Lower Royal S–C
Yi Ŭibang	M			Lower Security Council; Military Affairs
Yi Ungch'o	C	E	AA	Rites
Yi Ungjang	C		AA	Censorate
Yu Unggyu	C		A	Public Works
Yun Inch'ŏm	C	E	AA	State Council; Exam

Total	44
Civilian (C)	34 (77%)
Military (M)	9 (20%)
Unclear (?)	1
Examination (E)	22 (65% of all civilians)
One ancestor (A)	21 (48%)
Two or more (AA)	12 (27%)

Appendix 4. Civil Dynastic Structure in Myŏngjong's Reign
(1175–1196)

Name	Service	Path	Background	Office
Ch'ae Sunhŭi	M			Lower Security Council
Chang Ch'ungŭi	C	E	A	Dept. of Ministries
Chin Kwangin	C	E		Works/Censorate
Chin Saryong	M?			Military
Ch'oe Ch'ŏk	C	E		Lower Royal S–C
Ch'oe Ch'ŏkkyŏng	C	E		Military/Rites
Ch'oe Chŏng	C	E	A	Rites/Exam
Ch'oe Ch'ungnyŏl				State Council; Punishments
Ch'oe Hyojŏ	C	E		Exam
Ch'oe Munjun?	C	E	AA	State Council; Lower Security Council/ Military
Ch'oe Sebo	M		H	State Council; Personnel
Ch'oe Sŏn	C	E	AA	Exam
Ch'oe Tang	C	E	AA	Dept. of Ministries; Personnel
Ch'oe Uch'ŏng	C	E		State Council; Lower Royal S–C
Ch'oe Yŏhae	C	E		State Council
Ch'oe Yŏn	M			State Council/Rites
Ch'oe Yuga	C	E		State Council/Exam
Cho Wŏnjŏng	M		H	Lower Security Council/ Works
Cho Yŏngin	C	E	A	State Council/Exam
Chŏng Kukkŏm	C			Censorate
Chŏng Seyu	M			Punishments
Ham Yuil	C			Dept. of Ministries/Works
Han Ch'wi	C	E		State Council
Hong Chungbang	M			Dept. of Ministries
Hwangbo T'ak	C	E		Lower Royal S–C/Exam
Hyŏn Tŏksu	C			Military
Im Hang	C	E	A	Rites

(continued)

Name	Service	Path	Background	Office
Im Minbi	C	E	A	State Council; Lower Security Council/ Censorate
Im Pu	C	E	A	Personnel
Im Yu	C	E	A	Lower Security Council/ Rites/Exam
Ki Hongsu	M			Lower Security Council
Ki T'aksŏng	M			State Council; Personnel
Kim Pu	M		A	Rites
Kim Sun	M		AA	State Council
Kwŏn Chŏlp'yŏng				State Council/Rites
Kyŏng Chin	M			State Council
Min Yŏngmo	C	E	AA	State Council; Personnel
Mun Changp'il	M		AA	State Council; Lower Security Council/ Censorate
Mun Chŏk	C			Lower Royal S–C/Lower Security Council
Mun Kŭkkyŏm	C	E	AA	State Council; Personnel
No T'agyu	M		AA	Punishment
O Kwangch'ŏk	M			Personnel
Paek Imji	M			State Council; Punishments
Pak So	C	E		Revenue
Pak Sunp'il	M		H	State Council; Military
Sin Poji	M			Dept. of Ministries/ Censorate
Son Ungsi	C			Rites
Song Chŏ	C	E		Lower Royal S–C
Song Ch'ŏng	M			Lower Security Council
Song Yuin	M			State Council/Military
Tu Kyŏngsŭng	M		A	State Council; Lower Security Council/ Censorate
U Hagyu	M		A	State Council
U Suryu	C?			Punishment
Wang Segyŏng	C	E	A	Lower Royal S–C/ Personnel

(continued)

Name	Service	Path	Background	Office
Yi Chimyŏng	C	E		State Council; Lower Royal S–C/Exam
Yi Chunch'ang	C			State Council; Punishments
Yi Hyogyu	C	E	A	State Council
Yi Insŏng	?			State Council
Yi Kongjŏng	C			State Council/Military
Yi Kwangjin	C		AA	State Council
Yi Kwangjŏng	M			State Council
Yi Munjŏ	C		AA	Lower Security Council
Yi Sangno	C			Personnel
Yi Soŭng	?			State Council
Yi Sunu	C	E		Lower Royal S–C
Yi Ŭimin	M		H	State Council; Military/ Punishments; Dept. of Ministries
Yi Ungch'o	C	E	AA	State Council; Lower Royal S–C
Yi Ungjang	C		AA	Rites/Censorate
Yi Yŏngjin	M			Military/Punishments
Yŏm Sinyak	C	E	AA	State Council/Lower Security Council/ Personnel/Rites
Yu Kongwŏn	C	E	AA	State Council/Lower Royal S–C/Military/ Exam
Yu T'aek	C	E	AA	Censorate
Yun Chonghae	C		AA	Ministry?
Yun Chongham	C	E	AA	Exam
Yun Chongyang	C	E	AA	Punishments
Yun Inch'ŏm	C	E	AA	State Council

Total	76
Civilian (C)	46 (61%)
Military (M)	26 (34%)
Unclear (?)	4
Examination (E)	34 (74% of all civilians)
One ancestor (A)	31 (41%)
Two or more (AA)	19 (25%)
Humble (H)	4

Appendix 5. Civil Dynastic Structure in Ch'oe Ch'unghŏn's Regime
(1196–1219)

Name	Service	Path	Background
An Wan	?		
An Yubu	C?	E?	
Ch'a Ch'ŏk	C?		
Ch'ae Chŏng	C	E	clerk
Ch'ae Sunhŭi	?		
Chang Yunmun	C/M	ŭm/E	A
Ch'a Yaksong	M		A
Chin Hwa	C/M	E	AA
Cho Ch'ung	C	E	A
Cho Chun[a]	C	E	AA
Ch'oe Tang	C	E	AA
Ch'oe Kwangu	C		
Ch'oe Ch'unghŏn	M		A
Ch'oe Chŏngbun	C	E	
Ch'oe Hongyun	C	E	A
Ch'oe Posun	C	E	A
Ch'oe Pu	C?		
Ch'oe Sŏn	C	E	AA
Ch'oe Wŏnse	M		
Chŏng Chin[a]	M		A
Chŏng Kongsun	?		
Chŏng Kukkŏm	C		
Chŏng Kukon	M		A
Chŏng Kwangsŏ	?		
Chŏng Onjin	M		
Chŏng Pangbo	M		
Chŏng Sech'ung	C?		
Chŏng Sukch'ŏm[a]	M		A
Chŏn Wŏngyun	C	ŭm	A
Cho T'ong	C	E	
Cho Yŏngin	C	E	A
Hyŏn Tŏksu	C		
Im Yŏngsik	?		

(continued)

Name	Service	Path	Background
Im Yu	C	E	AA
Ki Hongsu	C/M		
Kim Ch'ŏkhu	M		
Kim Chujŏng	C		A
Kim Chun	?		
Kim Chunggwi	M		A
Kim Kunyu	C	E	AA
Kim Onju	?		
Kim P'yŏng	C	E	
Kim Pongmo	C	*ŭm*	AA
Kim Wŏnŭi	M		A
Kum Kukŭi	C	E	AA
Min Sik	C	E	AA
Mun Yup'il	C		AA
No Kwan[a]	?	low	
Paek Chonyu	M		
Paek Kwangsin	C	E?	A
Paek Sujŏng	?		
Paek Yŏju	C?		
Pak Chinjae[a]	M		
Pak Hyŏngyu	C	E	
Pak Insŏk	C	*ŭm*	AA
Pak Siyun	C?		
Pak Tukmun	?		
Pang Unggyo	C?		
Sa Hongjik	?		
Song Hongryŏl[a]	?		
Song Hyosŏng	C?		
Tae Sujŏng	?		
U Sulyu	C		
U Sunggyŏng	M		
Wang Kyŏngŭi	C?		
Wang Kyu	C		AA
Wang Ŭi	C		
Yi Chajŏng	?		

(continued)

Name	Service	Path	Background
Yi Ch'unro	C		A
Yi I	C?		
Yi Kuksŏ	?		
Yi Kye	?		
Yi Munjung	M		
Yi Silch'un	C?		A
Yi Ŭi	?		
Yi Yŏnsu	C	*ŭm*	A
Yi Yusŏng	M		A
Yu Kongsun	C?		
Yun Seyu	C		AA

a Ch'oe relative.

Total	80
Civilian (C)	43 (54%)
Military (M)	16 (20%)
Mixed (C/M)	3
Unclear (?)	18
Examination (E)	20 (47% of civilians)
Protective (*ŭm*)	5 (6%)
One ancestor (A)	32 (40%)
Two or more (AA)	13 (16%)
Ch'oe relative	6

Appendix 6. Civil Dynastic Structure in Ch'oe U's Regime (1219–1249)

Name	Service	Path	Background	Office
An Sŏkchŏng	?		H	Censorate
Ch'a Ch'ok	M			State Council/Lower Security Council/ Censorate
Ch'ae Songnyŏn	M			Lower Security Council
Chin Sik	C	E	AA	Lower Security Council/Censorate
Ch'oe Cha	C	E		Lower Royal S–C
Ch'oe Chongbŏn	C	E	AA	Lower Security Council
Ch'oe Chŏngbun	C	E	A	State Council/Exam
Ch'oe Chŏnghwa	C			State Council; Revenue
Ch'oe Chongjae	C	E	AA	Lower Royal S–C; Dept. of Ministries/Exam
Ch'oe Chongjun	C	E	AA	State Council; Lower Security Council/ Personnel
Ch'oe Ch'unmyŏng	C		A	Lower Security Council
Ch'oe Hang	M		AA	Lower Security Council/Revenue
Ch'oe Imsu	?			Lower Royal S–C
Ch'oe In	C	E	AA	State Council/Exam
Ch'oe On	C	E	AA	Exam
Ch'oe Posun	C	E	A	State Council/Exam; Personnel
Ch'oe Poyŏn	C		A	Punishments
Ch'oe Pak	C	E		Exam
Ch'oe U	M		AA	State Council; Lower Security Council/ Personnel; Military/Censor
Cho Ch'ung	C	E	AA	State Council
Cho Paekki	C	E	AA	Lower Security Council
Cho Su	C	E		Lower Royal S–C
Cho Yŏmgyŏng	M			Rites
Chŏng Pangbo	M			State Council

(continued)

Name	Service	Path	Background	Office
Chŏng T'ongbo	C			State Council; Personnel/Rites
Chu Suk	M			Lower Security Council
Han Kwangyŏn	C	E	AA	State Council; Works/ Revenue/Exam
Hong Kyun	C	E		State Council; Military/Exam
Im Kyŏnggyŏm	C		AA	Lower Security Council
Im Kyŏngsuk	C	E	AA	Lower Security Council/ Dept. of Ministries/ Punishments; Exam
Ki Chŏ	C			State Council/Lower Security Council
Kim Ch'ang	C	E	A	Lower Security Council/Exam
Kim Chŏng	M		AA	Rites
Kim Chunggwi	M			State Council/Lower Security Council/ Military
Kim Ch'wiryŏ	M		AA	State Council/Military
Kim Hyoin	C	E	A	Censor
Kim Kyŏm	C			Lower Royal S–C
Kim Kyŏngson	M		AA	Lower Security Council/Censor
Kim Sujŏng	C			Lower Royal S–C
Kim Sungnyong	M			Lower Security Council/ Personnel/Works
Kim T'aesŏ	C	E	AA	State Council/Exam
Kim Ŭiwŏn	M			State Council/Military
Kim Yaksŏn	M		AA	Lower Security Council
Kim Yanggyŏng	C	E	A	State Council/Lower Security Council/ Punishments/Exam
Kim Yŏnsŏng	C	E	AA	Dept. of Ministries
Kong Ch'ŏnwŏn	M			State Council/Lower Security Council/ Personnel/Rites

(continued)

Name	Service	Path	Background	Office
Kwŏn Kyŏngjung	C	E		Rites
Kwŏn Wi	M			Censorate
Min Hŭi	M			State Council/Censorate
Min Ingyun	C	E		Exam
Mun Hangyŏng	M			State Council/Works
Mun Yup'il	C		AA	State Council/Lower Royal S–C/Dept. of Ministries/Rites
No Yŏn	C			Lower Royal S–C
O Ch'an	C			Censorate
O Sugi	M			Lower Security Council
O Ungbu	M			State Council
Paek Punhwa	C	E	A	Rites
Paek Tongwi	C			Lower Royal S–C
Pak Chonggyu	C	E		Rites/Exam
Pak Hwŏn	C	E	A	Punishments/Exam
Pak Munsŏng	C			State Council/Lower Royal S–C
Pak Sŏ	C		AA	State Council
Pak Sŏngyu	C	E		Rites/Exam
Sa Honggi	C			State Council/Lower Royal S–C/ Personnel/Works
Sa Kwangbo	C			Lower Royal S–C/Security Council/Military
Sŏl Sin	C	E		Censorate/Exam
Son Pyŏn	C	E	A	State Council/Rites
Song Kukch'ŏm	C	E		Punishments/Censorate
Song Kyŏngin	C		AA	Lower Security Council/ Dept. of Ministries
Song Ŏngi	C	E	A	Military/Censorate
Song Singyŏng	M			State Council/Personnel
Song Sun	C	E		State Council/Exam
Song Yun	C			Dept. of Ministries
Tae Chipsŏng	M			Censorate
Wang Hae	C	E		Censorate
Wang Kyu	C		A	State Council

(continued)

Name	Service	Path	Background	Office
Wang Yu	M			Censorate
Yi Ch'ŏgyu	M			State Council/Lower Royal S–C
Yi Chŏk	C		A	Lower Security Council/ Dept. of Ministries
Yi Hang	C		A	State Council
Yi Illo	C	E	A	Lower Royal S–C
Yi Kongno	C	E	A	Lower Security Council
Yi Kŭksŏ	?			Lower Security Council
Yi Kyubo	C	E	A	State Council; Lower Security Council/Exam
Yi Paeksun	C	E		Exam
Yi Sehwa	C	E	A	Lower Royal S–C
Yi Yŏnsu	C			State Council; Personnel/Lower Security Council
Yu Charyang	C		AA	Dept. of Ministries
Yu Chŏnu	C	E		Personnel
Yu Chunggi	C	E		Lower Royal S–C/Exam
Yu Hong	C		AA	Lower Security Council
Yu Inch'ŏm	C		AA	State Council
Yu Kyŏnghyŏn	C	E	AA	Lower Royal S–C/Security Council/Censorate
Yu Ŏnch'im	C		AA	Rites/Punishments
Yu Sŭngdan	C	E		State Council/Lower Royal S–C/Security Council/Exam
Yu T'aek	C	E	AA	Dept. of Ministries/Exam

Total	96
Civilian (C)	69 (71%)
Military (M)	24 (25%)
Unclear (?)	3
Examination (E)	43 (62% of civilians)
One ancestor (A)	46 (48%)
Two or more (AA)	28 (29%)
Humble (H)	1

Appendix 7. Civil Dynastic Structure in Ch'oe Hang's Regime
(1249–1257)

Name	Service	Path	Background	Office
Ch'oe Cha	C	E	A	State Council/Lower Security Council/Exam
Ch'oe Hang	M		AA	Lower Security Council/Personnel; Military/Censorate
Ch'oe In	C	E	AA	State Council
Ch'oe On	C	E	AA	Lower Security Council/Exam
Ch'oe P'yŏng	C	E	AA	Lower Security Council
Cho Kyesun	C		AA	Lower Security Council
Cho Su	C	E		State Council/Exam
Chŏng An	C	E	AA	State Council
Chŏng Chun	?			Lower Security Council
Hong Chin	C	E		Lower Royal S–C
Hwangbo Ki	C	E		Dept. of Ministries/Exam
Im Kyŏngsuk	C	E	AA	State Council/Exam
Ki Yunsuk	M			State Council; Dept. of Ministries
Kim Ch'ang	C	E	A	State Council; Personnel
Kim Chidae	C		F	State Council/Exam
Kim Hyoin	C	E	A	Lower Security Council/Military; Exam
Kim Kison	C		AA	State Council; Dept. of Ministries
Kim Pojŏng	M			State Council
Kim Sugang	C	E		Censorate
Kim T'aesŏ	C	E	AA	State Council
Sŏl Sin	C	E		Lower Security Council
Son Pyŏn	C	E	A	Dept. of Ministries
Song Kukch'ŏm	C	E		Lower Royal S–C
Song Kŭkhyŏn	?			Censorate
Song Sun	C	E	A	State Council
Yi Changyong	C	E	AA	Lower Security Council

(continued)

Name	Service	Path	Background	Office
Yi Chasŏng	M		A	State Council
Yi Chu	C	E		Lower Royal S–C
Yi Hyŏn	M			Lower Security Council
Yi Po	M			Lower Security Council
Yi Sejae	M			Lower Security Council/Censorate
Yu Ch'ŏnu	C	E		Military
Yu So	C		AA	Lower Security Council
Yu Sŏk	C	E	A	Punishments
Yun Kŭngmin	C	E		Lower Security Council/Exam

Total	35
Civilian (C)	26 (74%)
Military (M)	7 (20%)
Unclear (?)	2
Examination (E)	22 (63% of total; 85% of civilians)
One ancestor (A)	18 (51%)
Two or more (AA)	11 (31%)
Functionary (F)	1

NOTES

ABBREVIATIONS

CK   *Chōsen kinseki sōran* [Compilation of Korean epigraphy]. Vols. 1 and 2.
      Seoul: Governor General's Office, 1933.
HK   Yi Nanyŏng. *Hanguk kŭmsŏngmun ch'ubo* [Additions to Korean epigra-
      phy]. Seoul: Chungang University Press, 1968.
KMC   Hong Sŭnggi. *Koryŏ muin chŏnggwŏn yŏngu* [A study of Koryŏ military
      rule], ed. Hong Sŭnggi. Seoul: Sŏgang University Press, 1995.
KS   *Koryŏsa* [History of Koryŏ]. Yŏnse edition. Seoul: Kyŏngin munhwasa,
      1972.
KSC   *Koryŏsa chŏryo* [Essentials of Koryŏ history]. Hosa Bunko edition. Tokyo:
      Gakushuin, 1969.
KT   Hsu Ch'ing. *Kao-li tu-ching* [Report on Koryŏ]. Seoul: Asea Munhwasa,
      1981.
PH   Yi Illo. *P'ahan chip* [Jottings to break up idleness]. *Koryŏ myŏnghyŏnjip.*
      Seoul: Kyŏngin munhwasa, 1972.
POH   Ch'oe Cha. *Pohan chip* [Supplementary jottings in idleness]. *Koryŏ myŏng-
      hyŏnjip.* Seoul: Kyŏngin munhwasa, 1972.
TMS   *Tong munsŏn* [Selected writing from the East]. Seoul: Taehan kongnonsa,
      1970.
TYS   No Sasin et al. *Tongguk yŏji sŭngnam* [Geographical survey of Korea].
      Seoul: Kojŏn kugyŏk, 1964.
YP   Yi Chehyŏn. *Yŏgong p'aesŏl* [Scribblings of Old Man Oak]. *Koryŏ myŏng-
      hyŏnjip.* Seoul: Kyŏngin munhwasa, 1972.
YS   Yi Kyubo. *Tongguk Yi sangguk chip* [Collected works of Minister Yi of
      Korea]. *Koryŏ myŏnghyŏnjip.* Seoul: Kyŏngin munhwasa, 1972.

PREFACE

1. See, for example, *Koryŏsa chŏryo* [Essentials of Koryŏ history], Hosa Bunko
ed. (Tokyo: Gakushuin, 1969), 13:46a–47a, 14:8b. Historians often made com-
ments in the annals. See also *Koryŏsa* [History of Koryŏ], Yŏnse edition (Seoul:

Kyŏngin munhwasa, 1972). For a brief critique of Koryŏ sources see also Martina Deuchler, *The Confucian Transformation of Korea* (Cambridge, Mass.: Council on East Asian Studies, Harvard University, 1992), pp. 29–32.

2. See Clarence N. Weems, ed., *Hulbert's History of Korea* (New York: Hillary House, 1962), pp. 184–185 and 191, and Richard Rutt, ed., *James Scarth Gale and His History of the Korean People* (Seoul: Taewon, 1972), p. 201. Gale, like Hulbert, relied heavily on the fifteenth-century *Tongguk t'onggam* [Comprehensive mirror of the Eastern Kingdom].

3. Hatada Takashi, *History of Korea,* trans. and ed. Warren W. Smith and Benjamin H. Hazard (Santa Barbara: ABC Clio, 1969), p. 51.

4. See Kim Sanggi, *Koryŏ sidaesa* [History of the Koryŏ period] (Seoul: Tongguk munhwasa, 1961); Yi Pyŏngdo, *Hanguksa: Chungsep'yŏn* [Korean history: Middle ages] (Seoul: Uryu munhwasa, 1961); and Yi Kibaek, *Kuksa sillon* [New history of Korea] (Seoul: T'aesŏngsa, 1961).

5. Pyŏn T'aesŏp, *Koryŏ chŏngch'i chedosa yŏngu* [A study of Koryŏ political institutional history] (Seoul: Ilchokak, 1971); Kim Tangt'aek, *Koryŏ muin chŏnggwŏn yŏngu* [A study of Koryŏ military rule] (Seoul: Saemunsa, 1987); Min Pyŏngha, *Koryŏ musin chŏnggwŏn yŏngu* [A study of Koryŏ military officers' rule] (Seoul: Sŏnggyungwan University Press, 1990); Kim Kwangsik, *Koryŏ muin chŏnggwŏn kwa pulgyogye* [Koryŏ military rule and Buddhism] (Seoul: Minjoksa, 1995); Hong Sŭnggi [Hong Seung-ki], *Koryŏ kwijok sahoe wa nobi* [Aristocratic society of Koryŏ and slavery] (Seoul: Ilchokak, 1983), which is a revision of his *Koryŏ sidae nobi yŏngu* [A study of slavery in the Koryŏ period] (Seoul: Hanguk yŏngu ch'ongsŏ, 1981); and Hong Sŭnggi, ed., *Koryŏ muin chŏnggwŏn yŏngu* [A study of Koryŏ military rule] (Seoul: Sŏgang University Press, 1995).

INTRODUCTION

1. This analysis is based largely on the conclusions offered by James B. Palais in his review essay, "Land Tenure in Korea: Tenth to Twelfth Century," *Journal of Korean Studies* 4 (1982–1983):73–206. See also Palais' recent publication *Confucian Statecraft and Korean Institutions: Yu Hyŏngwŏn and the Late Chosŏn Dynasty* (Seattle: University of Washington Press, 1996). Palais based his analysis on many of the primary and secondary sources cited in this work.

2. See Hugh Kang, "The Development of the Korean Ruling Class from Late Silla to Early Koryŏ" (Ph.D. dissertation, University of Washington, 1964), pp. 177–178. If all positions were filled, these divisions would contain about 45,000 men. See also Yi Kibaek, "Koryŏ kyŏnggun ko" [A study of the Koryŏ central armies], in *Koryŏ pyŏngjesa yŏngu* [A study of the history of Koryŏ military institutions] (Seoul: Ilchokak, 1968), and *Koryŏsa pyŏngji yŏkchu* [Translation of the military treatise section of the *Koryŏsa*] (Seoul: Kyŏngin munhwasa, 1969), p. 81.

3. Yi Kibaek, *Yŏkchu,* pp. 6–8.

4. Yi Kibaek, "Koryŏ chuhyŏngun ko" [A study of the provincial armies], in *Pyŏngjesa,* pp. 202–229, and "Korea—The Military Tradition," in *The Traditional Culture and Society of Korea: Thought and Institutions,* ed. Hugh H. W. Kang (Honolulu: Center for Korean Studies, 1975), pp. 19–20.

5. Yi Kibaek, "Military Tradition," pp. 16–18, and "Koryŏ kunin ko" [A study of the Koryŏ soldier], in *Pyŏngjesa*, pp. 82–130. Kang Chinch'ŏl, a noted land historian, offered a slightly different interpretation stating that Koryŏ's military system followed the Tang *fu-ping* and accordingly was based on a farmer/soldier militia. See Kang Chinch'ŏl, "Koryŏ ch'ogi ŭi kuninjŏn" [Military land in early Koryŏ], *Sukmyŏngdae nonmunjip* 3 (1963):145–167. Yi Kibaek argues convincingly that the Koryŏ system relied on professional soldiers. See "Koryŏ pubyŏng chesol ŭi p'ip'an" [Critique of the Koryŏ *fu-ping* theory], in *Pyŏngjesa*, pp. 270–282. See also Palais, "Land Tenure," pp. 95–102.

6. See Kim Yongsŏn, *Koryŏ ŭmsŏ chedo yŏngu* [A study of the Koryŏ protective appointment system] (Seoul: Ilchokak, 1991), and Pak Yongun, *Koryŏ sidae ŭmsŏje wa kwagŏje yŏngu* [A study of the Koryŏ protective appointment system and state civil service examination system] (Seoul: Ilchisa, 1990), for a detailed examination of this system.

7. Hŏ Hŭngsik, *Koryŏ kwagŏ chedosa yŏngu* [A study of the institutional history of the Koryŏ state civil service examination] (Seoul: Ilchokak, 1981), p. 252.

CHAPTER 1: THE MILITARY COUP

1. For details on these incidents see Kang, "Ruling Class," pp. 267–278.

2. Ibid., p. 291.

3. Ibid., p. 235.

4. Some historians have argued that the military class experienced a slow rise in economic, social, and political prominence in the century prior to the coup. This advance in status brought a corresponding increase in aspirations, causing the military to revolt in order to enhance its position in the kingdom. See Pyŏn T'aesŏp, "Koryŏ muban yŏngu" [A study of Koryŏ military officials], in *Chedosa*, pp. 342–398.

5. In "Military Tradition," p. 21, Kibaik Lee (Yi Kibaek) suggests that military officers and soldiers received land of inferior quality. See also Palais, "Land Tenure," pp. 95–114. A *kyŏl* is a fixed crop yield harvested from approximately two acres.

6. Pyŏn, *Chedosa*, p. 347. These men exhibited merit in battles against the Khitans. Although their earlier exclusion may have been a result of the fifteenth-century bias of the compilers, it is also possible that the initial Koryŏ recorders did not give important information about generals until this time.

7. Ibid. See also biographies of No Yŏngsun in *KS* 100:6b–7a; Yŏngsun's son T'agyu in *Chōsen kinseki sōran* [Compilation of Korean epigraphy] (Seoul: Governor General's Office, 1933), 1:415; and Yang Wŏnjun in Yi Nanyŏng, *Hanguk kŭmsŏngmun ch'ubo* [Additions to Korean epigraphy] (Seoul: Chungang University Press, 1968), pp. 145–146. Lineages are identified by ancestral sites called *pongwan:* "Kigye No," for example, means that Kigye is the ancestral site where the clan registry of the No lineage is located. Ancestral sites distinguish lineage groups that share the same surname such as Kim or Yi. See Deuchler, *Transformation*, p. 8.

8. Pyŏn, "Muban," pp. 366–367.

9. Yi Kibaek, "Koryŏ kunbanje haŭi kunin" [The soldier under the Koryŏ *kunban* system], in *Pyŏngjesa*, p. 289 and n. 9.

10. I am grateful to James B. Palais for this insight.

11. Michael C. Rogers, "National Consciousness in Medieval Korea: The Impact of Liao and Chin on Koryŏ," in *China Among Equals: The Middle Kingdom and Its Neighbors, 10th to 14th Centuries,* ed. Morris Rossabi (Berkeley: University of California Press, 1983), p. 162.

12. *KS* 98:23a; *KSC* 11:8a.

13. Ha Hyŏngang, "Koryŏ Ŭijongdae ŭi sŏngyŏk" [The character of Koryŏ king Ŭijong's reign], *Tongbang hakchi* 26 (1981), has studied Ŭijong. In reviewing the causes of the 1170 military coup in "Musin chŏngbyŏnun wae irŏnannun ka?" [Why did the military officers revolt?], in *Hanguksa simin kangchwa* 8 (1991):1–20, he points to Ŭijong's misrule, the grievances of the military, and the discontent of the commoner soldiers. Volume 8 of *Kangchwa* focused on the military period. In 1994, the journal *Yŏksa wa hyŏnsil* presented a bibliographic review of current research on the period.

14. *KSC* 11:17b.

15. Im Kŭkchŏng was Prince Kyŏng's maternal uncle. Im's sister was married to Chŏng Sŏ. Chŏng Sŏ was a key man in extending these relations, for his sisters were in turn married to Ch'oe Yuch'ŏng and Yi Chaksŭng.

16. See Edward Shultz, "Military Revolt in Koryŏ: The 1170 Coup d'Etat," *Korean Studies* 3 (1979):28–29.

17. *KS* 90:28a–b; *KSC* 11:9b–11a.

18. *HK* 100.

19. See Edward Shultz, "Twelfth Century Koryŏ Politics: The Rise of Han Anin and His Partisans," *Journal of Korean Studies* 6 (1988–1989):3–38.

20. *KSC* 11:21b–22a.

21. *KSC* 11:22a.

22. *KS* 128:10a. Chungbu's son Kyun married Kim Iyŏng's daughter. Mun Kŭkkyŏm's daughter married the younger brother of Yi Ŭibang, giving further evidence of this military/civil link. See Kim Nakchin, "Kyŏllyonggun kwa musin nan" [The Kyŏllyong army and the military officers' revolt], in *KMC,* p. 42.

23. *HK,* p. 159.

24. Sado On's father was To, the Duke of Chosŏn, the son of King Munjong. See *KS* 90:18b; *KSC* 10:44a. See also Shultz, "Han Anin," pp. 28–29.

25. *KS* 88:31a. In marrying the daughter of Ch'oe Tan, Ŭijong continued the practice of former kings of having more than one wife. See also Deuchler, *Transformation,* p. 31.

26. See Park Yongwoon (Pak Yongun), "Koryŏjo ŭi tacgan chedo" [The censorial institutions of the Koryŏ dynasty], *Yŏksa hakpo* 52 (December 1971):1–51, and *Koryŏ sidae taegan chedo yŏngu* [A study of the censorial institutions of the Koryŏ period] (Seoul: Ilchisa, 1980). There were two quasi-deliberative bodies emerging at this time, the Chaech'u (State Council) and the Topyŏngmasa, forerunner to the Topyŏngŭisasa, which became the Todang (Privy Council). See Pyŏn, *Chedosa,* pp. 84–89.

27. During Ŭijong's twenty-four-year reign, the Censorate launched more

than thirty-six major protests. At least twenty-five of these occurred in the first seven years of the reign. See Kim Tangt'aek, "Koryŏ Ŭijongdae ŭi chŏngch'ijŏk sanghwang kwa musin nan" [The political circumstances of Koryŏ Ŭijong's reign and the military officers' revolt], *Chindan hakpo* 75 (June 1993):39–40. Many of Professor Kim's ideas are also found in his chapters in *Hanguksa*, vol. 18 (Seoul: T'amgudang, 1993).

28. For criticism of state affairs see, for example, *KS* 99:13a, 17:29a, 18:1b; *KSC* 11:5a, 11:5b, 11:16b. For the attacks on polo see *KS* 17:21a–b, 17:37b–38a; *KSC* 11:1a–b, 11:14a. Other kings had enjoyed this sport, but none was criticized as severely as Ŭijong for watching it. Kim Tangt'aek, "Ŭijongdae," p. 46, suggests that the civil officials attacked the king's enjoyment of polo as a means to undermine the ties that were developing between the king and military officials who had mastered this game.

29. See, for example, *KS* 17:24a–b, 122:11a–12a, 122:14a, 96:33a; *KSC* 11:2b–3a, 11:9b–10a, 11:30b, 11:31b–32a. Other protests occurred in 1152 and 1157. In 1158 the Censorate made a dramatic stand against permitting Chŏng Ham to hold high government positions by saying: "Chŏng Ham's ancestor was un-subject-like and rebellious in T'aejo's reign and thus punished and made into a slave to keep him out of court. Now Ham advances and descendants of T'aejo's merit subjects will be forced to heed a traitorous person. We request that Ham's position be abolished and all those who conspire with him be made commoners." See *KS* 99:13b–14b, 122:13a–b; *KSC* 11:26a–b.

30. *KS* 17:23a, 18:25a; *KSC* 11:2b, 11:37a. In 1151, when the Censorate refused to recant, Ŭijong ignored it and went to watch polo. See *KS* 17:35b; *KSC* 11:12a–b.

31. In 1151, he demoted one Yun Onmun and four men who refused to recant. See *KS* 99:13a–b; *KSC* 11:13b–14a. And in 1157, when an official refused to approve Chŏng Ham's appointment, Ŭijong exclaimed: "Nobles, you do not listen to my wishes. I eat but have no taste; I sleep but have no peace." On hearing this the censors had no choice but to comply with his demands. See *KS* 122:12b; *KSC* 11:24b–25a. Although he won this round, the historians claim that as the eunuch's "power grew, wisdom was blocked. The state councillors and censors were threatened and afraid. The officials closed their eyes and did not speak. In the end came Chŏng Chungbu's revolt. Alas!" See *KSC* 11:25a.

32. In 1163 the Censorate, under the leadership of Mun Kŭkkyŏm, chided the king for supporting the eunuchs and confidants who damaged the throne. When Mun referred to scandals in the palace, an enraged Ŭijong ignited the petition and banished Mun. See *KS* 99:16a–b; *KSC* 11:34a–b.

33. See, for example, *KS* 18:5b–6a, 19:7a–b; *KSC* 11:19a–b, 11:49b. In 1169 and 1170, Ŭijong hosted more than twenty parties, banquets, and cruises for the leading officials of the kingdom, including members of the censorial organs.

34. *KS* 18:20b–21a; *KSC* 11:32b–33a.

35. See, for example, Ch'oe Yunŭi, CK 1:388–390, *KS* 99:25a–b; Kim Tongjun, the son of Kim Pusik, *KS* 98:19b–21b; and Hŏ Hungjae, *KS* 19:3b–4a, *KSC* 11:47a.

36. Men bribed eunuchs to aid their advance; *KSC* 11:44a. Eunuchs also con-

spired with monks who enjoyed royal patronage and engaged in the construction of temples, harassing the peasants and interfering with farming; *KS* 18:18a, 18:11a, *KSC* 11:30b. People of the period openly acknowledged that "power rested with the eunuchs"; *KSC* 11:28b.

37. Yi Uch'ŏl suggests that many palace attendants were eunuchs in his "Koryŏ sidae ŭi hwangwan e tae hayŏ" [Eunuchs of the Koryŏ period], *Sahak yŏngu* 1 (1958):35. See also Kim Nakchin, "Kyŏllyonggun," pp. 10–53. See Appendix 1 for a list of palace attendants during Ŭijong's reign.

38. *KS* 18:26a–b; *KSC* 11:38b. See also Peter Lee, ed., *Sourcebook of Korean Civilization* (New York: Columbia, 1993), vol. 1, p. 313. The *KSC* version, terser than the *KS* entry, describes the right unit as comprised of men of power but says nothing about the composition of the left unit. John Duncan (pers. comm.) suspects the aristocratic/Confucian dichotomy presented in the *KS* version might reflect more the bias of the fifteenth-century compilers than twelfth-century rivalries.

39. *KS* 17:38b; *KSC* 11:14b, 11:30b.

40. *KS* 18:33b–34a; *KSC* 11:43a–b.

41. *KSC* 11:13b.

42. For a similar interpretation of Ŭijong see Ha Hyŏngang, "Ŭijong."

43. In 1156 Ŭijong and his queen vowed that if a son were born to them they would make four sets of the Hwaŏm scriptures in gold and silver characters. When a son was born, they paid to have the walls of Hŭngwang temple repaired and stored two copies of the promised scriptures there. See *KS* 18:5a–b; *KSC* 11:18a–b.

44. *KS* 18:14b, *KSC* 11:29a; *KS* 18:15b, *KSC* 11:29b.

45. IIa, "Wae," pp. 8–11, presents a generally positive interpretation of Ŭijong, arguing he was trying to restore royal power and seriously concerned himself with ruling as a virtuous monarch. Ha also suggests in "Ŭijong" that the king showed acute interest in non-Confucian spiritual activities associated with Buddhism, Taoism, and Korean folk beliefs.

46. *KS* 18:18b, 18:24a, 19:4a–5a; *KSC* 11:31a–b, 11:36a, 11:47a–b.

47. Kim, "Kyŏllyonggun," pp. 15–18, points out that the first mention of the Kyŏllyong army is in the late eleventh century. It was not uncommon for a king to turn to his royal guards to bolster his power. Ha, "Wae," p. 9, discusses the construction of Chunghŭng temple. Chunghŭng conveys the idea of rejuvenation. Ŭijong also bestowed the name on a minor palace. For discussion of the *Sangjŏng kogŭm yemun* see Kim Tangt'aek, "Ŭijongdae," p. 42, and "Sangjŏng kogŭm yemun ŭi p'yŏnch'an sigi wa kŭ ŭido" [The period of publication and the goals of the *Sangjŏng kogŭm yemun*], *Honam munhwa yŏngu* 21 (1992):1–12.

48. Michael Rogers, "P'yŏnnyŏn t'ongnok: The Foundation Legend of the Koryŏ State," *Journal of Korean Studies* 4 (1982–1983):3–72.

49. Kim Tonjung, son of Kim Pusik, held a candle to the beard; *KS* 128:1b, *KSC* 11:49a. The reader is cautioned to recall that the writers of these histories are attempting to establish explicit reasons for the military revolt and this "beard burning incident" accomplishes that goal in dramatic fashion.

50. *KS* 122:12a; *KSC* 11:19b.

51. *KS* 100:6a–b; *KSC* 12:41b.

52. Kim Nakchin, "Kyŏllyonggun," p. 19.

53. Kim Tangt'aek, "Ŭijongdae," pp. 35 and 45.

54. *KS* 128:2a; *KSC* 11:35a–b.

55. *KSC* 11:40a–41a.

56. *KS* 128:2a; *KSC* 11:49a.

57. *HK*, p. 118; *KS* 98:3b. Kim Nakchin, "Kyŏllyonggun," p. 30, disagrees with this assessment: he thinks Chŏng Chungbu came from an obscure background and not from a hereditary military household.

58. Kim Tangt'aek, *Muin*, pp. 14–30, sees within the military both participants and nonparticipants in the coup. Among the participants he discerns moderates such as Chŏng Chungbu and activists such as Yi Ŭibang and Yi Ko.

59. Yi Ŭibang was from the Chŏnju Yi lineage and his brother Chunŭi is a direct ancestor of the future Yi Sŏnggye, founder of the Chosŏn kingdom; *KS* 128:15b. His other brother In married Mun Kŭkkyŏm's daughter; *KS* 99:17b.

60. *KS* 128:2a–3b; see also Lee, *Sourcebook*, pp. 333–334.

61. *KSC* 11:55a. See Appendix 2 for a list of purged officials.

62. Suematsu Yasukazu, in "Kōrai heibashi kō" [A study of the Koryŏ *pyŏngmasa*], *Toyo gakuhō* 39 (1) (1956), and *Seikyū shisō* (1968):207, suggests that civilians who were military commissioners possessed considerable military power.

63. Pak Yongun and others argue that in late Koryŏ the Security Council focused its energies on military affairs. See Pyŏn T'aesŏp, "Chungang ŭi chŏngch'i chojik" [Central political structure], in *Hanguksa* (Seoul: Kuksa p'yŏnchang wiwŏnhoe, 1993), 13:55.

64. Kim Nakchin, "Kyŏllyonggun," pp. 47–51.

65. *KSC* 12:41b.

66. See Appendix 3. For comparative purposes, this same listing of service origins, examination record, and ancestry will be used in subsequent tables. The appendix lists the men who held offices of the seventh rank and above in the Royal Secretariat–Chancellery (Chungsŏ Munhasŏng) and in the Security Council (Ch'umirwŏn), the six ministries *(yuk pu)*, the Censorate (Ŏsadae), and those who served as examiners *(chigonggŏ)*. The sources cite only a fraction of the men who held these offices. There were approximately 150 positions available annually in these agencies. The tables presented here often span years and even decades.

67. See Shultz, "Han Anin," pp. 30–31.

68. *KS* 101:1a–2a, 101:7a–8a; *KSC* 13:32a–b, 13:11b–12a.

CHAPTER 2: MYŎNGJONG'S REIGN

1. Because Sŏ Kong had long resented the arrogance of his civil colleagues, for example, the council ordered that guards be placed around his house to protect him; *KS* 94:7b–8a, *KSC* 12:4a.

2. The council even called for the standardization of weights and measures and the widening of roads in the capital. See *KS* 20:8b–9a, 85:12a; *KSC* 12:51b–52a.

3. *KS* 75:41b, 101:10a; *KSC* 12:56b–57a, 13:15b. The Council of Generals rec-

ommended that palace attendant and *tabang* positions be concurrent. The *tabang* was a civilian rank associated with royal attendants. See Yi Kibaek, *Yŏkchu* 1:96. John Duncan's research substantiates this excess in offices. See John B. Duncan, "The Formation of the Central Aristocracy in Early Koryŏ," *Korean Studies* 12 (1988):53–54.

4. For appointments see *KS* 19:32b; *KSC* 12:30b. For dispatching patrols see *KS* 20:3b, 9a, 82:2a; *KSC* 12:46a, 51b.

5. The following figures are based on Appendix 3.

6. Cho Wŏnjŏng was the son of a jade artisan and government slave; *KS* 128:26b–27a, *KSC* 12:60b–61a. Yi Ŭimin had a similar background; *KS* 128:19a. Ch'oe Sebo's lineage is listed as humble *(pi); KS* 100:21b; *KSC* 13:31a. Pak Sunp'il is also recorded as having humble origins; *KS* 100:22b.

7. The State Council and Council of Generals met jointly on a number of occasions to legislate and perform ceremonies. See, for example, *KSC* 12:51b–52a; *KS* 20:8b–9a, 85:12a.

8. Kim, *Muin,* pp. 14 and 26–27.

9. *KS* 128:16b; *KSC* 12:1a–2a. For Ch'ae see also *KS* 128:16b.

10. Kim Tangt'aek in a recent publication, *Koryŏ muin chŏnggwŏn* [A study of Koryŏ military rule] (Seoul: Kukhak charyowŏn, 1999), pp. 69–93, devotes an entire chapter to examining Kyŏng Taesŭng's short rule, which he portrays as a conservative reaction to the events set in train by the 1170 coup.

11. Kim Tangt'aek reminds us that without acquiescence from the Council of Generals, Kyŏng Taesŭng would not have been successful in his overthrow. See "Chŏng Chungbu, Yi Ŭimin, Ch'oe Ch'unghŏn," in *Kangchwa* 8:27.

12. *KS* 100:18a; *KSC* 12:45b.

13. Kim, *Muin,* pp. 38–39.

14. Ibid., pp. 42–43. Kim notes that both Yi Ŭimin and Myŏngjong gained power as a result of the 1170 coup.

15. Suematsu Yasukazu, "Heibashi."

16. *KSC* 12:2a, 12:26b; *KS* 128:18b.

17. *KS* 128:27b; *KSC* 13:17b–18b.

18. *KS* 100:18a.

19. *KS* 100:18b–20a, *KSC* 12:57b–58b. Kim Chagyŏk's allegation may have been provoked by a feud within the Tobang or a selfish wish to secure favor with the new power holders.

20. *KS* 19:21b–22a, 128:7a–b; *KSC* 12:7b–9a.

21. *KS* 100:7b–11a.

22. Kim Tangt'aek, "Koryŏ muin chipkwŏn ch'ogi millan ŭi sŏnggyŏk" [The character of popular revolts at the start of Koryŏ military rule], *Kuksagwan nonch'ong* 20 (1990):119–139.

23. The ten injunctions are found in *KS* 129:4b–6b; *KSC* 13:40b–42b. See also Lee, *Sources,* pp. 336–339. When Wang Kŏn founded Koryŏ, he too presented a list of ten admonishments. Perhaps Ch'oe Ch'unghŏn was attempting a similar ploy at state building through this statement. Ch'oe Chinhwan, "Ch'oe Ch'unghŏn ŭi pongsa sipcho" [Ch'oe Ch'unghŏn's ten injunctions], in *KMC,*

pp. 54–78, notes that the ten injunctions were used to justify Ch'oe Ch'unghŏn's centralization of power and the overthrow of Yi Ŭimin.

24. See Edward Shultz, "Ch'oe Ch'unghŏn: His Rise to Power," *Korean Studies* 8 (1984):58–82, for a thorough discussion of these issues.

25. *KS* 20:24b–25a; *KSC* 13:20b–21a. A *tongjŏng* appointment was an honorary post given to local elites (John Duncan, pers. comm., August 1998).

26. *KS* 99:29a; *KSC* 12:32a–b.

27. *KS* 128:13a; *KSC* 12:34b–35a. In another case, Wang Kong would send his house slave to bargain for goods and the slave refused to offer a fair price; *KSC* 12:55b–56a.

28. *KS* 128:25a; *KSC* 13:38a–b.

29. See Yi Uch'ŏl, "Hwangwan"; *KS* 20:19a–b; *KSC* 13:8b.

30. *KS* 100:26a; *KSC* 13:10b–11a.

31. *KS* 18:31a–b; *KSC* 11:41a–b.

32. See Pyŏn T'aesŏp, "Nongmin-ch'ŏnmin ŭi ran" [Revolts by peasants and lowborns], in *Hanguksa* 7:204–254; Hatada Takashi, "Kōrai no Meisō Shinsō jidai ni okeru nōmin ikki" [Peasant revolts in the age of Koryŏ kings Myŏngjong and Sinjong], *Rekishigaku kenkyū* 2(4) (August 1934):2–15 and 2(5) (September 1934):2–14. For a monograph on this topic see Yi Chŏngsin, *Koryŏ musin chŏnggwŏngi nongmin-ch'ŏnmin hangjaeng yŏngu* [A study of peasant-lowborn resistance during Koryŏ military rule] (Seoul: Koryŏ University Press, 1991). Pak Chonggi too has examined peasant discontent. Kim Tangt'aek, in *Muin 1999*, p. 95, has studied peasant unrest in the Myŏngjong and Sinjong periods and cites grievances among common soldiers as another cause for these disturbances.

33. *KS* 19:19b; *KSC* 12:6a. By scanning the *Tongguk yŏji sŭngnam* [Geographical survey of Korea], Kojŏn kugyŏk ed. (Seoul, 1964), one can immediately see that a number of localities first obtained district offices *(kammu)* in either 1172 or 1175. For the Western Capital see *KSC* 12:35a. Yi Sanghun, in his study "Koryŏ chunggi hyangni chedo ŭi p'yŏnhwae taehan ilgoch'al" [A study of the changes in the local functionary system during mid-Koryŏ], in *KMC*, p. 255, notes that during Yejong's reign the central government actively sought to extend its authority into rural Korea. The events in Myŏngjong's reign are a logical continuation of this move.

34. *KS* 20:9a–b, 75:17b–18a; *KSC* 12:52a–b.

35. Kim Tangt'aek, "Millan."

36. See, for example, the monk Honggi; *KS* 129:7a, *KSC* 13:42b. These princes were detested by some scholars. See *KS* 101:2a–3a; *KSC* 14:10a.

37. See Min Hyŏngu, "Wŏllamsaji chingak kuksabi ŭi ungi e taehan ilgoch'al" [A study of the tomb inscription to Chingak at Wŏllam temple site], *Chindan hakpo* 36 (October 1973):29–31; and Kim Chongguk, "Kōrai bushin seiken no tokushitsu ni kansuru ichi kōsatsu" [An examination of the special characteristics of Koryŏ military rule], *Chōsen gakuhō* 17 (October 1960):587.

38. When a fire broke out in the palace, monks helped to extinguish it. In 1176 and then again in 1182, monks assisted dynastic forces in suppressing a revolt. See *KS* 19:16a–b, *KSC* 12:5a; *KS* 19:29a, *KSC* 12:25a.

39. When Myŏngjong became king, the new leaders went to considerable lengths explaining Ŭijong's abdication to the Chin rulers. See Michael Rogers, "Koryŏ's Military Dictatorship and Its Relations with Chin," *T'oung Pao* 47(2) (1959):43–62.

40. Or so the sources would have us believe. Myŏngjong may well have used eunuchs as a way to counterbalance the military. Nevertheless, when his favorite concubine died, Myŏngjong lost all self-control and wept. Soon the king had his daughters attend him, and even sleep with him, to assuage his grief. See *KS* 20:4a–5a, 17a, *KSC* 12:46b–47a, 13:2b; *KS* 20:17b–18a, *KSC* 13:4a–5a.

41. Ch'oe Chinhwan, "Pongsa," pp. 74–75.

42. See Kim, *Muin*, pp. 37–50, for a detailed discussion of Yi Ŭimin's rise to power.

43. *KS* 128:22a–23a; *KSC* 13:30a–b.

44. Kim, *Muin*, pp. 50–57, argues that Ch'oe pursued a moderate stance similar to that taken earlier by Chŏng Chungbu and contends that Ch'oe represented the opposition forming to counter Yi Ŭimin's policies.

45. *KS* 129:1a–2b; *KSC* 13:36a–b.

46. See also Kim Yongsŏn, *Koryŏ ŭmsŏ*, p. 108.

47. *KS* 129:1a–2b; *KSC* 13:36a–38a; *CK* 1:440–445.

48. Especially critical to Ch'oe Ch'unghŏn was support from his nephew, Pak Chinjae, and another relative, No Sŏksung.

49. See Shultz, "Ch'oe Ch'unghŏn," pp. 69 and 76–79, for more detailed discussion.

50. Min Pyŏngha, "Koryŏ musin chipchŏng sidae e taehan ilgo" [A study of the age of the Koryŏ military officers' takeover], *Sanak yŏngu* 6 (1959):27–68.

51. See Shultz, "Ch'oe Ch'unghŏn," p. 71, for a genealogy of the Ch'oe family detailing these links. See also Yi Kyŏnghŭi, "Ch'oe Ch'unghŏn kamun yŏngu" [A study of the family of Ch'oe Ch'unghŏn], *Pusan yŏdae sahak* 5 (December 1987):1–52, for a detailed analysis of Ch'oe family ties.

52. *KS* 129:9b–10a; *KSC* 13:49a–b.

53. None of Ch'oe Ch'unghŏn's direct descendants in the Ch'oe lineage married a crown prince. But Ch'oe Ch'unghŏn's great-granddaughter, who was technically a Kyŏngju Kim, married a prince who became King Wŏnjong (r. 1259–1274). Their son became King Ch'ungyŏl (r. 1274–1308).

54. For Ch'oe Pi see *KS* 100:22a–b and *KSC* 13:40a–b; see also *KS* 129:4a–b.

55. *KS* 20:37a–b; *KSC* 13:43b–44a.

CHAPTER 3: THE CH'OE HOUSE: MILITARY INSTITUTIONS

1. For Council of Generals policy decisions see *KS* 21:21a–b; *KSC* 14:36a–b, 13:29a–b, 14:21b. For Sinjong's death see *KS* 21:17a–18a; *KSC* 14:15b–16b.

2. *KS* 129:31a; *KSC* 15:30b.

3. Kim, in *Muin*, notes that the State Council initially took over many of its functions (p. 115) and then the Kyojŏng Togam assumed the same tasks (p. 78). Naito Shunpo, in "Kōrai jidai no jūbō oyobi seibo ni tsuite" [Concerning the Chungbang and Chŏngbang of the Koryŏ period], in *Inaba hakushi kanreki kinen*

mansenshi ronsō (Seoul, 1938), claims that as the Council of Generals lost power, the Personnel Authority of the Ch'oe House gained influence. In fact the functions of these two agencies were quite different (Chapter 4).

4. U claimed: "Because the front horsemen escort the king, I should select them personally." Later he reviewed them at his residence, where their saddle decorations were far more elaborate than before. See *KS* 129:31b–32a, *KSC* 15:35a; *KS* 22:25a, *KSC* 16:43b.

5. *KS* 81:15a; *KSC* 14:45a. This debilitated state of the dynastic emergency forces was probably caused by Ch'oe Ch'unghŏn siphoning off the talent into his own private forces.

6. *KS* 129:26a; *KSC* 15:20a.

7. As noted earlier, in 1216 he dispatched his son's father-in-law, Chŏng Sukch'ŏm, as commander and sent as deputy commander Cho Ch'ung, a member of the loyal Hoengch'ŏn Cho lineage and a successful examination candidate.

8. *KS* 129:37b, *KSC* 16:8b–9a.The Mongols made six major invasions of Koryŏ between 1231 and 1258 (Chapter 9). For a detailed study of the Mongol invasions see Yun Yonghyŏk, *Koryŏ taemong hangjaengsa yŏngu* [A study of the history of Koryŏ's resistance to the Mongols] (Seoul: Koryŏ University Press, 1991).

9. *KSC* 16:16b.

10. See Shultz, "Ch'oe House," pp. 143–144.

11. *KS* 129:11a–b; *KSC* 13:50b.

12. *KSC* 14:29a–30b.

13. See, for example, *KS* 129:21b, 23a–b; *KSC* 14:33b, 45a–b, 46a–b.

14. *KS* 129:23a–b; *KSC* 14:45a–b, 46a.

15. In 1202, U was watching Ch'oe forces drill; *KS* 129:15b, *KSC* 14:12b–13a. See also *KS* 21:23a; *KSC* 14:22b–23a, 14:24b.

16. *KS* 129:27b–28a; *KSC* 15:20b–21b. Included in this group were Grand General Ch'oe Chunmun, Supreme General Chi Yunsim, and General Yu Sŏngjŏl.

17. *KS* 129:35b–36a; *KSC* 15:46a, 46b. After several Ch'oe units played a game of polo, U gave them rewards and titles. A month later, after reviewing his house troops, he presented them with wine and food.

18. *KS* 129:36b, *KSC* 15:2a; *KS* 129:37b, *KSC* 16:8b–9a; *KS* 129:31a, *KSC* 15:31a–b; *KS* 130:3b–4a, 23:27a–b, *KSC* 16:17a–b.

19. When Tae Chipsŏng, for example, forced people into his service, Ch'oe Ch'unghŏn angrily stopped all activities. Ch'oe Ch'unghŏn was wary lest these troops cause too many disturbances and weaken his authority. See *KS* 129:25b–26a; *KSC* 15:13b–14a.

20. Because the Tobang, other Ch'oe forces, and soldiers labeled retainers *(mungaek)* all performed similar duties, many scholars conclude that they were basically the same organization. See, for example, Yi Kibaek, "Military Tradition," pp. 21–22.

21. *KS* 129:14a; *KSC* 14:8a–b.

22. Kim Tangt'aek, *Muin*, p. 184; Yu Ch'anggyu, "Tobang," *KMC,* p. 121.

23. *KS* 129:20a–b; *KSC* 14:29a–30a. No Yongŭi, who helped rally the Ch'oe forces, was a Tabang member. The Tabang office attended royal needs and acted as a type of escort. See Yi Kibaek, *Yŏkchu,* p. 96.

24. Kim Sanggi, "Koryŏ muin," p. 231. Kim Tangt'aek, in *Muin,* pp. 177–184, shows how the Tobang absorbed many of the functions of the palace army, thus rendering the latter ineffective.

25. Kim Sanggi, *Koryŏ sidaesa,* p. 457; Min Pyŏngha, "Ch'oe ssi chŏnggwŏn ŭi chibae kigu" [The ruling structure of the Ch'oe House government], in *Han-guksa* 7:174. Ikeuchi Hiroshi, in "Kōrai no sambetsushō ni tsuite" [Concerning the Sambyŏlch'o of Koryŏ], *Shigaku zasshi* 37(9) (1926):809–848, offers a slightly different interpretation: he claims that the Mabyŏlch'o became part of the Sinŭigun, an intriguing but unsubstantiated thesis.

26. Ikeuchi, in "Sambetsusho," and Naitō Shunpo, in "Kōrai heisei kanken" [A review of the Koryŏ military system], *Seikyū gakuhō* 15 (1934):1–46, have both studied the Sambyŏlch'o. Kim Sanggi, in "Sambyŏlch'o wa kŭ ŭi nan e tae haya" [Concerning the Sambyŏlch'o and its revolt], *Chindan hakpo* 9 (1939):1–29, has provided the lengthiest study in Korean. Our understanding of the Yabyŏlch'o has been complicated by the development of an earlier dynastic unit called the Special Patrol (Pyŏlch'o); see Shultz, "Ch'oe Rule," pp. 142–144. Kim Sumi points out in "Koryŏ muin chŏnggwŏngi ŭi yabyŏlch'o" [The Yabyŏlch'o of the Koryŏ military government], in *KMC,* that the role of the Yabyŏlch'o changed over the years.

27. *KS* 129:38a–b; *KSC* 16:15a–16a. When U questioned the man on strategy, the Yabyŏlch'o officer failed to respond.

28. Kim Sumi, "Yabyŏlch'o," pp. 159–165.

29. *KS* 122:28a–29a, 129:51b–52a, 103:37a–b; *KSC* 17:1b, 32b.

30. *KS* 103:37a–b; *KSC* 16:16b–17a.

31. *KS* 129:45b, *KSC* 17:1b; *KS* 122:28a–29a, *KSC* 17:32b.

32. *KS* 129:43a, *KSC* 16:40a–b; *KS* 24:33a, *KSC* 17:37b. There are two entries that mention regional Yabyŏlch'o. In 1202, a Kyŏngju Yabyŏlch'o is mentioned; *KS* 57:2b. In 1254, Kyŏngsangdo and Chŏllado each sent eighty Yabyŏlch'o to guard the capital; *KS* 24:15a, *KSC* 17:17b–18a. These seem to be part of a regional military system and are not linked with Ch'oe U's Yabyŏlch'o.

33. *KS* 129:51b–52a; *KSC* 17:28b–29a.

34. *KS* 24:33b, 81:15b. Yi Chehyŏn, in describing the composition of the Sambyŏlch'o nearly a century later in *Yŏgong p'aesŏl* [Scribblings of Old Man Oak] in *Koryŏ myŏnghyŏnjip* (Seoul: Kyŏngin munhwasa, 1972), erroneously asserts that the Sambyŏlch'o was formed out of the Sinŭigun, the Mabyŏlch'o, and the Yabyŏlch'o. Most scholars agree with the *Koryŏsa* version presented here. William Henthorn, in *The Mongol Invasion of Korea* (Leiden: E. J. Brill, 1962), p. 232, suggests that the Sinŭigun night have formed out of the Singigun (Cavalry Corps). Kim Tangt'aek, in *Muin,* p. 198, believes the Sinŭigun might have been formed to resist plans to return the capital from Kanghwa Island to the mainland.

35. See *KS* 24:10b, 24:15a, 23:29b, 26:35a, 27:33b; *KSC* 17:13a, 17:17b–18a, 16:23a. See also Kim Naemi, "Koryŏ muin chŏnggwŏngi ŭi yabyŏlch'o" [The Yabyŏlch'o of the Koryŏ military government], in *KMC,* pp. 131–170. It should

be cautioned that the term "ten thousand" simply indicated a very large force, not necessarily ten thousand men.

36. Kim Sumi, "Yabyŏlch'o," pp. 153–155.

37. *KS* 129:38a–b, *KSC* 16:15a–b; *KS* 103:37a–b, *KSC* 16:16b–17a; *KS* 23:32a, *KSC* 16:25a. Kim Sanggi, in "Sambyŏlch'o," pp. 27–28, offers a slightly different interpretation: he contends that the Sambyŏlch'o was a public unit in contrast to the private Ch'oe Tobang. Institutions evolving at this time should not be judged as either public or private, however, for the Ch'oe House constructed an extralegal organization that superimposed its authority on the established dynastic order.

38. *KS* 129:18a; *KSC* 14:21b. Kim, in *Muin*, pp. 74–76, points out that Ch'oe Ch'unghŏn was suspicious of other men who possessed too many retainers.

39. That the retainer system never developed to the degree found in Japan or Western Europe indicates the sharp differences between these societies. For more discussion see Yi Kibaek, "Military Tradition," p. 22, and Kim Chongguk, "Korai bushin."

40. John W. Hall, "Feudalism in Japan—A Reassessment," in *Studies in the Institutional History of Early Modern Japan*, ed. John W. Hall and Marius B. Jansen (Princeton: Princeton University Press, 1968), p. 33.

41. Peter Duus, *Feudalism in Japan* (New York: Knopf, 1969), p. 50.

42. The retainer received only his lord's support and assistance. There is no evidence of any oaths of allegiance being sealed between lords and retainers. See Yi Kibaek, "Military Tradition," p. 22, and Kim Chongguk, "Korai bushin."

43. Kim Chongguk, "Kōrai bushin," pp. 64–65.

44. *CK* 1:577; Ch'oe Cha, *Pohanjip* [Supplementary jottings in idleness], in *Koryŏ myŏnghyŏnjip* 2:1a.

45. *POH* 2:22a–b; *CK* 1:593.

46. *POH* 3:11b.

CHAPTER 4: CIVIL STRUCTURE AND PERSONNEL: CH'OE CH'UNGHŎN AND CH'OE U

1. See Edward J. Shultz, "Twelfth Century Korea: Merit and Birth," *Journal of Korean Studies* (forthcoming). See Appendix 5.

2. See Hŏ Hŭngshik, *Kwagŏ*, pp. 252–253. The average number of men passing each year rises from 22.5 in Yejong's reign to 28.4 in Sinjong's reign (1197–1204), 27.7 for Hŭijong (1204–1211), and 35.5 for Kangjong's two-year reign (1212–1213). Ch'oe Yong-ho has observed that approximately 80 percent of the men in the central officialdom had passed the state examination during much of Chosŏn; see *The Civil Examinations and the Social Structure in Early Yi Dynasty Korea: 1392–1600* (Seoul: Korea Research Center, 1981).

3. Kim, *Muin*, p. 96, shows that one-quarter of the men in the State Council at this time came from four great civil families: the Kyŏngju Kim, the Hoengch'ŏn Cho, the Chŏngan Im, and the Tongju Ch'oe lineage.

4. For a comparison with Yejong's reign a century earlier see Shultz, "Merit and Birth."

5. Kim, *Muin*, pp. 139–146, details Ch'oe Ch'unghŏn's efforts to show his support for royal authority. See also Chapter 9.

6. *KS* 129:13a; *KSC* 14:5a, 14:10b–11a.

7. On hearing of an assassination attempt in 1209, Ch'oe Ch'unghŏn formed this Directorate General and closed the gates to Kaegyŏng; *KS* 129:18b–19a, *KSC* 14:25a–b. See also *KS* 96:37b–38a; *KSC* 14:35a–b.

8. Yun, who was the grandson of the early twelfth-century leader Yun Kwan, bore a grudge against Chŏng Sukch'ŏm and asked the king for this appointment hoping to get rid of Chŏng Sukch'ŏm. Ch'oe Ch'unghŏn seized Yun Seyu and exiled him; *KS* 96:37b–38a, *KSC* 14:35a–b.

9. *KS* 129:32b; *KSC* 15:38a.

10. For the 1250 incident see *KS* 129:44a, *KSC* 16:39b. A monk asked Tae Chipsŏng to obtain permission from one Pak Pongsi to cut timber in Kangum-hyŏn in Hwanghae. When Pak Pongsi refused, Tae Chipsŏng in anger sent him a Kyojŏng letter; *KS* 129:35a, *KSC* 15:43a.

11. Yun Seyu, an assistant office chief in the Ministry of Rites (*yebu wŏnaerang*), is an exception. It is unclear why he felt he could be a special commissioner while all the other men in this office were the most powerful military figures of the age. Yun's request for this post was refused.

12. Min Pyŏngha, "Ch'oe ssi," p. 149. Kim Sanggi, *Koryŏ sidaesa*, p. 455, offering a similar analysis, suggests that the Directorate General actually replaced the Council of Generals.

13. Kim Tangt'aek, *Muin*, p. 78, questions this interpretation and says that Ch'oe Ch'unghŏn was not concerned with consensus. Ch'oe was indeed a dictator, but he was also concerned with successfully ruling Koryŏ. By resuscitating the traditional consensual approach to decision making, he found an effective means to achieve his goals.

14. See *KS* 129:31b; *KSC* 15:34b. Initially the Directorate General handled personnel responsibilities. As the supreme Ch'oe council the Directorate General controlled selection, but as these institutions matured, the actual process of recommending was relegated to the Personnel Authority.

15. *KS* 75:2b–3a. For a similar entry see *YP* 1:8b–9a. The term "Pijach'i" evolved from the Mongol language and seems to have been attached to the Personnel Authority in its later evolution after the Ch'oe House disappeared. The Administration was a unit given to men with enfeoffments.

16. Kim Tangt'aek, *Muin*, p. 121, asserts that this office, which was closely associated with royal authority, gave added legitimacy to the Personnel Authority. Transmitters in the Security Council oversaw communications between the king and officialdom.

17. *KS* 129:32b. The meaning of "Ch'ebang" and "Sukpang" is unclear, as there is no other mention of them in the histories.

18. John Duncan (pers. comm., August 1998) suggested this idea.

19. *KS* 129:52a, *KSC* 17:29a; *KS* 24:33a, *KSC* 17:37b. Cho Insŏng, in "Ch'oe U chipkwŏnha munhangwan" [Writings under Ch'oe U's rule], *KMC*, pp. 234–249, concluded that Ch'oe U placed men with literary ability in the chamber to oversee personnel matters.

20. *KS* 101:11a; *KSC* 14:26a.

21. *Tong munsŏn* [Selected writings from the East] (Seoul: Taehan kong-nonsa, 1970), 9:650; *KS* 21:30a–b, 101:11a–12a; *KSC* 14:32a; *KS* 60:36a.

22. Yi Illo, *P'ahanjip* [Jottings to break up idleness], *Koryŏ myŏnghyŏnjip* (Seoul: Kyŏngin munhwasa, 1972), 1:6b; *KSC* 12:47b.

23. *KS* 21:4b; *KSC* 12:14b, 13:52a.

24. *KS* 20:17a, 99:23b, 102:1a–3a; *KSC* 13:3a.

25. *KS* 22:18b; *KSC* 15:23a–b.

26. *KS* 129:42a, *KSC* 16:36a–37a, *KS* 101:22b.

27. *KS* 129:28b, *KSC* 15:28b; *KS* 22:21b, 129:30b, *KSC* 15:29a.

28. *KS* 74:6a; *KSC* 16:1b.

29. *KS* 129:32a; *KSC* 15:35b. The *Koryŏsa* reports that in ranking administrators, Ch'oe U placed those who were able in civil and clerical matters first. Those who were able in civil affairs but not in clerical concerns were placed second. Those who excelled in clerical but not civil matters were next, and those who lacked ability in both clerical and civil matters were at the bottom. See *KS* 102:15a; *KSC* 18:8a–b.

30. *KS* 129:31b; *KSC* 15:26b. People felt that since An was the son of a private slave, he was not suited for a position in the Censorate.

31. For Kim Yaksŏn's biography see *KS* 101:21b–22a; for Kim Kyŏngson see *KS* 103:26a–29a.

32. *KS* 103:7a–20a; *KSC* 16:20b–21b.

33. *KS* 129:43a; *KSC* 16:40a–b. For Chu's relation to the Tae family see *KS* 26:14a–b; *KSC* 18:25a–b.

34. *KS* 102:3a–5b.

35. For Ch'oe Chongjun see *KS* 99:9b and *KSC* 16:30b; for Ch'oe In, *KS* 99:4a–5b; for Im Kyŏngsuk, *KS* 73:37a–38a and *POH* 1:7a–b; for Kim Yang-gyŏng, *KS* 102:7a–9a and *KS* 73:35b–36b.

36. Han Yuhan ultimately died in hiding; *KS* 99:42b–43a, *KSC* 14:18a–b.

37. *KS* 102:11a–b.

38. *KS* 102:10b; *PH* 3:9b–10a; *YS* 22:17a–18a.

39. Cho Tongil, *Hanguk munhak t'ongsa* (Seoul: Chisik sanŏpsa, 1989), 2:11–13.

40. *YS, huhu* 1a–3a.

41. *KS* 102:3a–5b.

42. *KS* 129:16b–17a; *KSC* 14:19a. Similar gatherings were held in 1199 (see *POH* 2:17a) and in 1207 (see the introduction to *YS* 9b).

43. Among the major writers of this period were Im Ch'un, author of *Sŏha chip;* Yi Illo, who wrote *P'ahan chip;* Ch'oe Cha, who wrote *Pohan chip;* Kim Ku, who wrote *Chip'ochip;* and Chin Hwa, who wrote *Maehoyugo.*

44. Pak Ch'anghŭi, "Muin chŏnggwŏn haŭi munindŭl" [Civilians under military rule], *Kangchwa* 8 (1991):40–59, discusses the lives of some of these men and their descriptions of the conditions of the period.

45. John B. Duncan, "Confucianism in Late Koryŏ and Early Chosŏn," *Korean Studies* 18 (1994):79–80.

46. Ibid., pp. 87–91. Duncan concludes: "Ch'oe Cha revealed himself to be

not only a self-aware successor to a Koryŏ *komun* Confucian tradition, but also a harbinger of things to come . . . foreshadowing the rise of an anti-Buddhist critique in the late fourteenth century."

47. *KS* 21:20a; *KSC* 14:19a–b.

48. *KSC* 14:5a.

CHAPTER 5: CIVIL STRUCTURE AND PERSONNEL: CH'OE HANG AND CH'OE ŬI

1. Ch'oe U's daughter accused her husband, Kim Yaksŏn, of having relations with Ch'oe U's private women. Her complaints caused Ch'oe U first to exile and then to kill Kim Yaksŏn. See *KS* 101:21b–22a. Ch'oe U ultimately decided not to make Kim Yaksŏn's son Chŏng his heir—perhaps because of his father's disgrace but more likely because of backstairs power struggles between supporters of Ch'oe Hang and backers of Kim Chŏng.

2. *KSC* 16:38a.

3. Chu Suk had been in this Tae clique. Song Kukch'ŏm, Pak Hwŏn, and Yu Ch'ŏnu were members of Ch'oe U's Personnel Authority that Hang isolated from power once he took over.

4. *KS* 129:43b; *KSC* 16:39a.

5. *KS* 129:43b–44a; *KSC* 16:39a–b.

6. Hang gave the king a cart; *KS* 24:5a, *KSC* 17:6a. He also constructed a palace for him; *KSC* 17:7b.

7. See, for example, *KSC* 17:15a–16b.

8. See Min Pyŏngha, "Musin chŏng," pp. 62–63; Hŏ Hŭngsik, *Kwagŏ*, pp. 126–166; and Pak Yongun, *Ŭmsŏje*, pp. 271–272. The examination for the Royal Confucian Academy, although not as prestigious or as rigorous as the *kwagŏ*, nevertheless required a great deal of preparation. Those who passed it could enter the academy and were well prepared for government service.

9. For Ch'oe Yangbaek see *KS* 129:43a, *KSC* 17:34a–36a; for Ch'oe Yong see *KS* 24:20b–21a, 129:52a, *KSC* 17:21a.

10. *KS* 102:12a–b.

11. *KS* 105:1a.

12. For Cho Kyesun see *KS* 103:6b, 129:44b, *KSC* 16:41a–b; for Son Inyŏl see *KS* 24:31b, 129:51b, *KSC* 17:31b; for Yu Nŭng see *KS* 129:53a, *KSC* 17:34a; for Ch'ae Chŏng see *KS* 129:52a, 102:16b–17a.

13. *KS* 129:45a–b; *KSC* 16:44b. At this time the Board of Astronomy became quite daring. Reporting that the moon had crossed the path of several stars, it explained that this phenomenon indicates that an individual has overextended his power and usurped the king. Ch'oe Hang saw this charge as a threat to his position.

14. *KSC* 17:21b. Rulers have often been concerned about the presentation of history. See James B. Palais, "Records and Record Keeping in Nineteeth Century Korea," *Journal of Asian Studies* 30(3) (May 1971):583–591.

15. On being fearful of the popular will see *KSC* 16:40a; on criticism of his policies see *KSC* 17:6a.

16. On opening the granaries see *KS* 129:52a, *KSC* 17:29b; on giving land, cloth, oil, and honey see *KS* 129:52a–b, *KSC* 17:29b; on taking back land see

KSC 17:32a; for the dispatch of tax collectors see *KS* 129:52b–53a, *KSC* 17:33b.

17. For Ch'oe Ŭi's advancement see *KS* 129:51b–53a, *KSC* 17:22b–23a, 28b–29b, 30b, 33b.

18. *KS* 129:53a. *KSC* 17:34a provides a slightly different version, but the meaning is the same.

19. *KSC* 17:32b–33b. The histories bluntly describe Chun as "ugly, but he was good in shooting and liked to give to others to win their hearts. Daily he met with others, drank, and attended to matters."

20. Chŏng Sua, "Kim Chun seryŏk hyŏngsŏng kwa kŭ hyangbae" [Formation of Kim Chun's power and his pros and cons], *KMG*, pp. 286–287, studies the men who joined Kim Chun and concludes that many had first experienced success under Hang's patronage.

21. *KS* 105:1a. Chŏng Sua, "Kim Chun seryŏk," p. 290, concludes: "Kim Chun and Yi Kongju as commanders of the house troops, Yu Kyŏng as the principal person in the Personnel Authority, and Song Kilyu and Pak Songbi as retainers who were generals, rose rapidly in status [under Hang]." Alienated from Ŭi, they had no option but to revolt.

22. For a thorough discussion of the years after the collapse of the Ch'oe House see Chŏng Sua, "Kim Chun seryŏk," and Ch'oe Wŏnyŏng, "Imssi muin chŏnggwŏn ŭi sŏngnip kwa ponggwi" [Rise and fall of the Im family military rule], in *KMG;* see also Kim Tangt'aek, "Im Yŏn chŏnggwŏn kwa Koryŏ ŭi Kaegyŏng hwando" [Im Yŏn's rule and the return to Kaegyŏng], in *Yi Kibaek sŏnsaeng kohŭi kinyŏm, Hanguk sahak nonch'ong* (Seoul: Ilchokak, 1994), 1:783–806. This work has appeared in English in an abridged form as "Im Yon's Regime and Koryo's Return of the Capital to Kaesong," *Korean Social Science Journal* 23 (1997):103–111.

23. One record notes that Im Kyŏngsuk of the Chŏngan Im lineage had "among his successful examinees more than ten persons who reached the highest official rank in a matter of years, among them three former generals and one junior colonel. This was previously unheard of." See *POH* 1:7a–b.

24. Ch'oe Cha, one of Koryŏ's renowned men of letters, in his three-volume anthology *Supplementary Jottings in Idleness (Pohan chip)*, writes about one poetry party in the summer of 1199 when the pomegranates were in bloom; *POH* 2:17a–b. A similar event occurred in 1205; *KSC* 14:19a.

25. These developments are similar to events in Japan at the same time. See John W. Hall, *Government and Local Power in Japan, 500 to 1700* (Princeton: Princeton University Press, 1966), pp. 153–154. Here I have paraphrased Hall because of the unique similarities in institutional development.

26. G. Cameron Hurst III, "The Structure of the Heian Court: Some Thoughts on the Nature of 'Familial Authority' in Heian Japan," in *Medieval Japan: Essays in Institutional History*, ed. John W. Hall and Jeffrey P. Mass (Stanford: Stanford University Press, 1974).

27. Jeffrey P. Mass, *Antiquity and Anachronism in Japanese History* (Stanford: Stanford University Press, 1992), pp. 82–85. On p. 84 Mass describes the *zoshiki* and *bugyōnin* as "stipend retainers not landed vassals. As such they could be manipulated by the lord, who directly controlled their livelihoods."

CHAPTER 6: PEASANTS AND LOWBORNS

1. Scholars at one time believed that lowborns lived in specifically designated localities such as *hyang, so,* or *pugok.* See, for example, Hatada Takashi, "Kōrai jidai no semmin seido 'bukyoku' ni tsuite" [Concerning *pugok* in the lowborn social system of the Koryŏ period], in *Chōsen chūsei shakaishi no kenkyū* [A study of the social history of medieval Korea] (Tokyo: Hōsei daigaku shuppankyoku, 1972), pp. 57–74. See also Kim Yongdŏk, "Hyang, so, pugok ko" [A study of the *hyang, so,* and *pugok*], in *Paek Nakchun paksa hwangap kinyŏm nonmunjip* (Seoul: Sasanggye sa, 1955), pp. 171–246. This thesis has been challenged by Pak Chonggi in *Koryŏ sidae pugok chedo yŏngu* [A study of the *pugok* system of the Koryŏ period] (Seoul: Seoul University Press, 1990), where he has shown that people living in pugok were in fact commoners burdened with additional responsibilities.

2. See John Duncan, *The Koryŏ Origins of the Chosŏn Dynasty: Kings, Aristocrats, and Confucianism* (Seattle: University of Washington Press, 2000) p. 57.

3. For a recent discussion of the Koryŏ regional system see Pak Chonggi, *Pugok,* pp. 77–112, and Ha Hyŏngan, "Chibang ŭi t'ongch'i chojik" [Governing structure of rural Korea], in *Hanguksa,* vol. 13 (Seoul: Tamgudang, 1993).

4. In 1172 the new authorities requested the dispatch of *kammu* to fifty-three districts; *KSC* 12:6a. See also Pak Chonggi, *Pugok,* p. 117, and Duncan, *Koryŏ Origins,* pp. 58–59.

5. Pyŏn T'aesŏp, "Nongmin," p. 230.

6. Hatada Takashi, "Nōmin," *Rekishigaku kenkyū* 2(5) (1934):7–8.

7. *KS* 21:11a–b; *KSC* 14:7b–8a.

8. Pak Chonggi claims that peasant discontent developed out of dissatisfaction with their status as residents of *pugok,* part of a stratified local residence system. See Pak Chonggi, *Pugok,* and Yi Chongsin, "Nongmin hangjaeng," pp. 74–75.

9. Ha Hyŏngang, "Koryŏ chibang chedo ŭi ilyŏngu" [A study of the Koryŏ regional system], *Sahak yŏngu* 14 (November 1962):95.

10. *KSC* 13:30a–b. See also Pyŏn T'aesŏp, "Nongmin," pp. 238–239.

11. *KS* 100:31a–b; *KSC* 14:12a.

12. Kim, *Muin,* p. 168. There was also a pro-Koguryŏ incident in 1217 when a disgruntled soldier rebelled in Sŏgyŏng and tried to rally others to his cause. He failed almost at once, however, and was killed. See *KS* 121:11a; *KSC* 15:8b.

13. *KSC* 13:42b.

14. *KS* 22:5a; *KSC* 14:37a.

15. For example, Uisŏnghyŏn was demoted in Sinjong's reign for suffering a defeat. See No Sasin et al., *Tongguk yŏji sŭngnam* [Geographical survey of Korea] (Seoul: Kojŏn kugyŏk, 1964), 25:13b. Chŏngju, by contrast, was promoted in 1231; *TYS* 52:23a. A look at *TYS* leaves one with the distinct impression that regional designations were enforced and their earlier representations reasserted.

16. Pak Chonggi, *Pugok,* pp. 183–196.

17. *KS* 128:23a; *KSC* 14:2b–3a. Besides following geomancy, Ch'oe Ch'unghŏn may well have wanted to destroy projects associated with Yi Ŭimin.

18. In Proposals 1 and 9, Ch'unghŏn cited various topographical abuses that had caused dynastic problems and warned that they must be corrected. See Chapter 2.

19. *KS* 21:8b–9a; *KSC* 14:5a.

20. *KS* 21:7b; *KSC* 14:4b.

21. When Kyŏngju (Tonggyŏng) was punished in this way, Ch'unghŏn stated: "Tonggyŏng people speak of restoring Silla and send decrees to the *chu* and *kun* plotting rebellions. We cannot but punish them." To some men, this was drastic action because of the area's capital status. But Ch'unghŏn, weary of constant revolt and intrigue, was anxious to end further banditry and peasant disturbances. See *KSC* 14:7a–b.

22. *KSC* 15:34a, 16:30b, 35a.

23. For the first event in 1232 see *KSC* 16:16b–17a. For the second 1232 event see *KS* 130:4a, 23:27a–b, *KSC* 16:19a–b. For the Kyŏngju rebellion see *KS* 103:38b–39a, *KSC* 16:18b–19a. Naju in 1237 revolted, as well, and this uprising was quelled with similar resoluteness; *KS* 103:27b–28b, 16:26a–b.

24. For a detailed survey of this resistance see Yun Yonghyŏk, *Taemong*.

25. The position of local inspector general (*sasimgwan*) was eventually eliminated in 1318. See Hatada, "Kōrai no jishinkan" [The *sasimgwan* of Koryŏ], in *Chōsen*, p. 130. The *hojang* was held accountable to Ch'oe directives and checked closely by centrally dispatched officials.

26. David Brion Davis, *The Problem of Slavery in Western Culture* (Ithaca: Cornell University Press, 1966), p. 32. For a detailed discussion of Koryŏ slavery see Hong Sŭnggi, *Nobi*, and Ellen Salem, "Slavery in Medieval Korea" (Ph.D. dissertation, Columbia University, 1978). See also James B. Palais, "Slavery and Slave Society in the Koryŏ Dynasty," *Journal of Korean Studies* 5 (1984):173–190, for a review of issues on this topic. See also Palais, *Statecraft;* and see James B. Palais, *Views on Korean Social History*, Institute for Modern Korean Studies, Special Lecture Series, No. 2 (Seoul: Yonsei University, 1998).

27. Hatada Takashi, *History of Korea*, p. 39. Hatada in fact sees three classifications—public, official, and private—but official and public are for most purposes nearly identical.

28. Kang Chinch'ŏl, "Land Tenure," p. 62.

29. Yi Chaech'ang, "Sawŏn nobi ko" [A study of temple slaves], in *Hwang Ŭidon sŏnsaeng kohŭi kinyŏm sŏhak nonch'ong* (Seoul: Tongguk University Press, 1960), pp. 251–261.

30. Hatada Takashi, "Kōrai jidai no okeru tochi no chakuchōshi sozoku to dohi no shijo kinbun sōzoku" [Primogeniture inheritance of land and equal inheritance of slaves in the Koryŏ period], *Tōyo bunka* 22 (January 1957); Hatada, *Chōsen*, p. 355.

31. *KS* 129:12a–13a; *KSC* 14:2a–b.

32. See Pyŏn T'aesŏp, "Manjŏknan palsaeng ŭi sahoejŏk soji" [Social foundations of the outbreak of the Manjŏk rebellion], in *Chedosa*, pp. 449–478, for an affirmation of this interpretation.

33. In a private discussion, Professor Pak Chonggi pointed out that as Ch'oe Ch'unghŏn was trying to gain the confidence of the civilian elites, many of

whom held slaves, his strict policy toward slaves was imperative to win their approval.

34. Pyŏn thinks that Ch'oe was trying to maintain the social order, but he does not suggest that this might be a cause for the slave revolts; see "Nongmin," p. 241.

35. Pyŏn offers a similar conclusion; see "Manjok," pp. 471–472.

36. Although other grievances, such as those expressed by the peasants, were undoubtedly present, the changed social, political, and economic conditions confronting the slaves at this time must have been most aggravating to them.

37. See *KS* 128:26a and *KSC* 14:6b–7a for the Chinju revolt and *KS* 129:15b and *KSC* 14:14a for the Kaegyŏng revolt. The slave who revealed the Manjŏk plot was freed and made a commoner. See *KS* 129:12b–13a, *KSC* 14:2a–b.

38. *KS* 81:15a, 103:14a; *KSC* 15:8a.

39. *KS* 129:25b–26a; *KSC* 15:13b–14a.

40. Hong Sŭnggi has studied the slaves affiliated with the Ch'oe House. See his chapter "Ch'oessi muin chŏnggwŏn kwa Ch'oessi ŭi kano" [Ch'oe House military rule and Ch'oe family slaves] in *Nobi*. In "Koryŏ Ch'oessi muin chŏnggwŏn kwa Ch'oessiga ŭi kano" [Koryŏ Ch'oe House military rule and Ch'oe House family slaves], in *KMC*, pp. 177–202, he points out that Ch'oe House slaves were extremely devoted to the Ch'oe leaders. Once this loyalty disappeared, however, slaves became sources of treason because of their proximity to the Ch'oe leaders.

41. *KS* 129:27b–28a; *KSC* 15:20b–21a.

42. Eunuch activities in both Ŭijong's and Myŏngjong's reigns have been discussed in previous chapters. Boys born with certain birth defects became natural candidates to be eunuchs, but often men chose to become eunuchs or eager parents had their sons castrated to become eligible to be eunuchs. See Yi Uch'ŏl, "Hwan'gwan."

43. *KS* 129:9a; *KSC* 13:47a.

44. On artisans see *KSC* 14:4a; on limiting the brothers see *KS* 101:10b, *KSC* 14:14b.

45. The *namban* was the third body in the dynastic administration, along with the *sŏban* (military branch) and *tongban* (civilian branch). At the start of the Koryŏ kingdom the *namban* was filled with prestigious people, but later men with humble social origins could enter. People in the *namban* attended the king and served in regional offices. See Cho Chwaho, "Yŏdae namban ko" [A study of the *namban* of the Koryŏ period], *Tongguk sahak* (1967):1–17, and Yi Pyŏngdo, "Koryŏ namban ko" [A study of the Koryŏ *namban*], *Seoul taehakkyo nonmunjip* 16 (1966):157–168.

46. *KS* 129:17b; *KSC* 14:21a.

47. *KS* 129:31b; *KSC* 15:26b. Each Ch'oe leader had a group of slaves bound to him. See Hong Sŭnggi, "Kano," p. 283.

48. For Yu Sŏk see *KS* 121:3b–4a; for Son Pyŏn see *KS* 102:17b, *KSC* 17:3b; for Yu Ch'ŏnu see *KS* 105:33b. For the eunuch passing first on the examination see *KS* 74:12b.

49. Even though Hang's mother was the daughter of the ranking official Sa

Honggi, she was a concubine to U and consequently of the *ch'ŏnmin* class. Perhaps her mother too was a concubine. See *KS* 129:51b, *KSC* 17:29a, for the reference to the lowborn status of these two women.

50. *KS* 75:24b, 129:53a; *KSC* 17:33b–34a.

51. *KSC* 17:15b–16a.

52. *KS* 103:39b–40a; *KSC* 17:14a. Presumably he burnt the slave registers in his area only.

53. Kim Yongdŏk, in "Hyang, so, pugok ko," contends that generally people of humble origin lived in areas such as *hyang, so,* or *pugok,* but during the military period these designations began to lose their significance as social liberation was occurring amid domestic unrest. Kim's material and the evidence in the histories demonstrate that this terminology was maintained throughout the rules of Ch'oe Ch'unghŏn and U. Only after the Mongol invasions become severe do changes in the *hyang, so,* and *pugok* appear, along with the potential of social mobility for the lowborn. See also Pak Chonggi, *Pugok.*

54. Imanishi Fumio, "Kōraichō ni okeru dohi ni tsuite" [Concerning slaves of the Koryŏ period], in *Kuwahara Hakushi kanreki kinen toyoshi ronso* (Kyoto, 1931), pp. 1160–1161. See also Hung Sŭnggi, *Koryŏ sidae nobi yŏngu,* and Palais, *Statecraft,* pp. 214–217.

55. *KS* 24:5a; *KSC* 17:6b.

56. *KS* 24:9b–10a; *KSC* 17:11b–12a.

57. *KS* 24:33a; *KSC* 17:36b–37a, 18:8a.

CHAPTER 7: BUDDHISM UNDER THE MILITARY

1. Numerous scholars have studied this topic: Min Hyŏngu, "Wŏllamsaji Chingak kuksa pi ŭi ŭmgi e taehan il koch'al" [A study of the tomb inscription to national tutor Chingak at the Wŏllam temple site], *Chindan hakpo* 36 (October 1973):5–38; Kim Tangt'aek "Koryŏ Ch'oessi muin chŏnggwŏn kwa Susŏnsa" [Koryŏ Ch'oe military rule and Susŏn temple], *Yŏksahak yŏngu* 10 (1981), also published in his book *Muin;* Ch'oe Pyŏnghŏn (Byŏng-hŏn), "Significance of the Foundation of Susŏnsa in the History of Koryŏ Buddhism," *Seoul Journal of Korean Studies* 1 (1988):49–68; Ch'ae Sangshik, *Koryŏ hugi pulgyosa yŏngu* [A study of the history of Buddhism in late Koryŏ] (Seoul, 1991); Yu Yŏngsuk, "Ch'oessi musin chŏnggwŏn kwa Chogyejong" [Ch'oe military rule and the Chogye school], *Paeksan hakpo* 33 (1986):157–189; and Kim Kwangsik, *Pulgyo.*

2. Robert E. Buswell Jr., in *The Collected Works of Chinul* (Honolulu: University of Hawai'i Press, 1983), has made a major contribution in English toward explaining the philosophical developments of this period and has given me a solid foundation for my own understanding of the speculations that Buddhism pursues in this period. See also Jae Ryong Shim, "The Philosophical Foundation of Korean Zen Buddhism: The Integration of Sŏn and Kyo by Chinul (1158–1210)" (Ph.D. dissertation, University of Hawai'i, 1979), and Hŏ Hŭngsik, *Koryŏ pulgyosa yŏngu* [A study of Koryŏ Buddhism] (Seoul: Ilchokak, 1986).

3. Hŏ Hŭngsik, *Pulyŏngu,* pp. 145–178.

4. For an examination of Ŭich'ŏn see Ch'oe Pyŏnghŏn, "Ch'ŏnt'aejong ŭi sŏngnip" [Establishment of the Ch'ŏnt'ae school], in *Hangukksa,* vol. 6, and

"Hanguk hwaŏm sasangsae issŏsŏūi Uich'ŏn ŭi wich'i" [The position of Ŭich'ŏn
in Korean Hwaŏm intellectual history], in *Hanguk hwaŏm sasang yŏngu* (Seoul:
Tongguk University Press, 1982), and Cho Myŏnggi, *Koryŏ Taegak kuksa wa ch'ŏn-
t'ae sasang* [Koryŏ national tutor Taegak and Ch'ŏnt'ae thought] (Seoul: Minjung sagwan, 1964).

5. Buswell, *Chinul,* pp. 16–17, discusses Ŭich'ŏn's antipathy toward Sŏn. For
a discussion of this renewed interest in Sŏn see Edward J. Shultz, "Twelfth-Century Koryŏ Politics: The Rise of Han Anin and His Partisans," *Journal of Korean
Studies* 6 (1988–1989):3–39; "Han Aninp'a ŭi tŭngjang kwa yŏkhwal," *Yŏksa
hakpo* 99–100 (December 1983):147–183; and Kim Sangyŏng, "Koryŏ Yejongdae
Sŏnjong ŭi pokhŭng kwa pulgyogye ŭi pyŏnhwa" [The rise of the Sŏn school in
Koryŏ Yejong's reign and changes in Buddhism], *Chŏnggye sahak* 5 (1988):49–
89. Ch'oe Pyŏnghŏn has studied the renewed interest in Sŏn in conjunction
with the study of Taoism during Yejong's reign in "Koryŏ chunggi Yi Chahyŏn
ŭi Sŏn kwa kŏsa pulgyo ŭi sŏnggyŏk" [The Sŏn thought of mid-Koryŏ Yi Chahyŏn and the character of the Buddhism of retired scholars], in *Kim Ch'ŏljun
paksa hwangap kinyŏm sahak nonch'ong* (Seoul: Chisik sanŏpsa, 1983).

6. See Ch'oe, "Susŏnsa," p. 54.

7. See Kim Puch'ŏl's essay in *TMS* 64:27a–30b.

8. *KS* 7:37a, 8:31a; *KSC* 4:62a.

9. *KS* 98:20a; *KSC* 11:37b. Two renowned lineages, the Haeju Ch'oe and the
Inju Yi, were active patrons of Kyo. The son of one Ch'oe Yong, for example,
became a monk at Hongho temple; *CK* 1:363. The son of Yi Kongsu was a monk
at Ch'ongwan temple; *HK* 103.

10. Yu Kyosŏng, "Koryŏ sawŏn kyŏngje ŭi sŏnggyŏk" [The character of the
economy of Koryŏ temples], *Pulgyohak nonmunjip* (1959):608–610. Hyŏnhwa
temple, for example, in addition to its holdings, was granted 1,240 *kyŏl* of land
in 1020; see *KS* 4:34a, *KSC* 3:40b. See also Hatada Takashi, "Kōraichō ni okeru
jiin keizai" [Temple economics in the Koryŏ dynasty], *Shigakku zasshi* 43(5)
(1934):1–37.

11. Yi Chaech'ang, "Sawŏn nobi ko," pp. 608–610, has studied temple slaves.
Yu Kyosŏng, "Hanguk sanggongŏpsa" [Commercial history of Korea], in *Hanguk munhwasa taegye* (Seoul: Korea University Press, 1965), 2B:1038–1044, indicates that in a period of three years temples could collect interest at a rate of
100 percent.

12. More than a hundred monks from Kwibŏp temple invaded the capital's
northern gate. Shortly thereafter, more than two thousand monks from Chungwang, Hongho, Hongwa, and other temples assembled near the capital's eastern gate with the goal of killing General Yi Ŭibang. Yi Ŭibang retaliated and
tried to destroy Chungwang, Hongho, Kwibŏp, Yonghung, Myoji, and Pokhŭng
temples. The military burned or robbed temples and the monks retaliated by
attacking the soldiers. See *KSC* 12:11a–b; *KS* 128:15b–16a.

13. In 1192, Myŏngjong commanded that his son by a concubine become a
monk. The *Koryŏsa chŏlyo* recounts: "Although he was about ten, he dressed in
ceremonial rank and there was no difference between him and the legal sons.
He was called prince and entered the palace at will. It was the practice of the

times for the sons of royal concubines to become monks, select a famous temple, and live there exercising power and collecting bribes." See *KSC* 13:29a.

14. Ch'ae, *Hugi pulgyo*, p. 16.

15. Yejong was a patron of this Sŏn establishment, also known as Yŏnbok temple. Hsu Ch'ing, the twelfth-century visitor from Sung China, claims Poje temple was south of the palace. See Hsu Ch'ing, *Kao-li-tu-ching* [Report on Koryŏ] (Seoul: Asea Munhwasa, 1981), p. 86. For a reference in English see Buswell, *Chinul*, p. 83, n. 106.

16. *KS* 19:19b–20a; *KSC* 12:6b. Earlier in the year he had visited Pongŭn temple, another Sŏn establishment in the capital; *KS* 19:19a. He also made visits to Poje temple a number of other times; see, for example, *KS* 19:21b, *KSC* 12:7b.

17. *KS* 19:24b; *KSC* 12:17a–b.

18. See *KS* 128:8b; *KSC* 12:23b–24a. Chŏng Chungbu had a sumptuous dinner prepared and the king ordered the leading dynastic officials to attend. Coming a year after the Kyo rebellion, perhaps this official in the Censorate harbored ill feelings toward the Sŏn order and wanted to block a royal rapprochement with the sect and the military officialdom.

19. See Shultz, "Han Anin," p. 32.

20. See, for example, the convening of a Hwaŏm meeting at Hongwŏn temple in 1183; *KS* 20:14a, *KSC* 12:56b. Later in the same year the king traveled to Mirŭk temple; *KS* 20:15a, *KSC* 12:60b. In 1185 the king made special prayers to Buddha when a thick fog enveloped the land; *KSC* 13:9b.

21. In 1178, the court sponsored a *toryang*, a special convocation of monks; *KS* 19:37b, *KSC* 12:37a. In an act of piety one month later, the court invited and fed more than thirty thousand monks from around the kingdom; *KS* 19:37b, *KSC* 12:38b. Similar events were repeated periodically throughout the reign; see, for example, *KSC* 12:53a–b and *KSC* 13:3a.

22. In 1176, after losing a skirmish, a regional military officer suggested that monks be enlisted to bolster government forces; *KS* 19:29a, *KSC* 12:25a. In 1178, a monk proposed the establishment of a temporary office to check the growing strife in the kingdom; *KSC* 12:36b.

23. Mangi burned Honggyŏng hall and killed more than ten monks; *KS* 19:32a, *KSC* 12:30a. See *KSC* 12:37b for the attacks in 1178. In 1183, another bandit, Kim Sammi, rebelled and used Unmun temple as his base; Kim Kwangsik, *Pulgyo*, p. 63.

24. In 1177, a monk libeled the king's brother Ch'unghŭi, who after an investigation was not charged; *KS* 19:36a, *KSC* 12:29a. See *KSC* 12:34a for the incident the following year.

25. In 1180, the Council of Generals banished Chongch'am and ten other monks to an offshore island because they had been so closely tied to Chŏng's family; *KS* 128:19a, *KSC* 12:47b–48a.

26. See *KS* 99:23b–24b; *KSC* 13:19a–20a.

27. Kim Kwangsik, *Pulgyo*, p. 63.

28. *KSC* 13:13b.

29. See the royal monk Honggi as an example; *KS* 129:7a, 8b, *KSC* 13:42b, 45a–46a. Sŏn monks did not escape Ch'oe censure: Ch'oe Ch'unghŏn exiled

the Sŏn monk Yŏnsim and several others to southeastern Korea in 1197; *KS* 129:8b, *KSC* 13:45a–46a. See also Ch'oe, "Susŏnsa," p. 53.

30. For the 1202 incident see *KS* 21:14a–b, *KSC* 14:11b–12a. For the 1203 revolt see *KSC* 14:14b. In 1209 several men had assembled some monks to kill Ch'oe Ch'unghŏn and were in the process of enlisting monks at Kwibŏp temple in Kaegyŏng when the plot was discovered and quashed; *KS* 129:18b–19a, *KSC* 14:25a. For the failed assassination attempt in 1211 see *KS* 129:20a–21a, *KSC* 14:29a–b. Finally, in 1217, disgruntled monks took advantage of a Khitan attack and tried once again to kill Ch'oe Ch'unghŏn; see *KS* 129:24a–b, *KSC* 15:1a–2a.

31. See also Kim Chongguk, "Kōrai bushin seiken to soto no tairitsu toso ni kansuru ichi kōsatsu" [An examination of Koryŏ military rule and the resistance of monks], *Chōsen gakuhō* 21–22 (1961):567–589. There is no evidence of any temple affiliated with Sŏn or Ch'ŏnt'ae opposing the Ch'oe order. See Min, "Wŏllamsaji," p. 31.

32. Within days of Ch'oe's coup in 1196, one person reported that Kil In was planning to lead monks from Wangnyun temple in a revolt. Ch'oe Ch'unghŏn later discovered this deception; *KS* 129:2b–4a, *KSC* 13:39b–40a. The next year, Tu Kyŏngsŭng and the monk Yoil of Hŭngwang temple were accused of plotting treason; *KS* 129:7a–b, *KSC* 13:44b–45a.

33. This trip never was carried out because of an anonymous note reporting a plot against Ch'oe Ch'unghŏn; *KS* 129:7a–b, *KSC* 13:44b–45a.

34. *KS* 129:31a; *KSC* 15:31b.

35. See Ch'oe, "Susŏnsa," p. 55. Moreover, Ch'ae, *Hugi pulgyo*, p. 19, notes that Ch'oe U worked with many schools. Kim Kwangsik, *Pulgyo*, pp. 215–217, discusses the Ch'oe House's appeals to the Doctrine school to provide spiritual aid in the fight against the Khitans.

36. Min, "Wŏllamsaji," p. 32.

37. George Sansom, *A History of Japan to 1334* (Stanford: Stanford University Press, 1958), p. 429, notes a similar attraction to Zen among Japanese warriors. This aspect of Sŏn should not be overstressed, however, as the written word was quite important to Sŏn practices. See Robert E. Buswell Jr., *The Zen Monastic Experience* (Princeton: Princeton University Press, 1992).

38. Through established histories of Koryŏ such as the *Koryŏsa*, Confucian scholars have generally criticized these monks. Myoch'ŏng's policies, in particular, did ultimately challenge the survival of the throne. Nevertheless, monarchs to some degree continued to turn to monks as a way to free themselves from the entrenched ruling elites.

39. Kim, *Muin*, p. 236, suggests that Sŏn afforded Ch'oe Ch'unghŏn spiritual relief from the burden of guilt caused by his purges; he also indicates (pp. 239–240) that Ch'oe U looked to Sŏn as a way to bolster his own legitimacy.

40. See notes 1 and 2.

41. See Buswell, *Chinul*, pp. 19–30, for a detailed account in English of Chinul's life. Buswell notes that Susŏn temple, today known as Songgwang temple, was originally called Kilsang temple. This temple was to be named Chŏnghyesa (Samadhi and Prajna Monastery), but since another temple already had the name it was called Susŏn temple. The name of the mountain was changed from Songgwang to Chogye at this time.

42. See Ch'oe "Susŏnsa," p. 54. Chinul is also championed as a transmitter. See An Kyehyŏn, "Chogyejong kwa ogyo yangjong" [The Chogye school and the five schools], in *Hanguksa* 7:312.

43. Ch'oe Ch'unghŏn sent one son to study under Chŏnggak *kuksa;* see *CK* 1:576–577 and Min, "Wŏllamsaji," p. 33. Ch'oe U sent two of his sons, Hang (Manjŏn) and Manjong, to learn from Hyesim (Chingak *kuksa*); see *CK* 1:463–464, *KS* 129:41b.

44. Kim Ku, *Chip'ojip* [Jottings resting on a riverbank], in *Koryŏ myŏnghyŏnjip*, 1:1b. When Ch'oe Hang was a monk, he frequently threatened people and caused a series of complaints about his unruly behavior; see *KS,* 129:42a–b, *KSC* 16:28b–29b.

45. The restoration of Ch'angbok temple occurred in 1211; see *TYS* 25:8b. An Kyehyŏn noted Taean temple's restoration in "Chogyejong," p. 312. Kim, *Muin,* p. 236, shows that Ch'oe Ch'unghŏn's portrait was posthumously placed at Ch'angbok temple, indicating Ch'unghŏn endowed this temple to secure blessings. Kim also records (p. 239) that Ch'oe U donated land to Susŏn temple. Yu, "Chogyejong," p. 187, notes that Ch'oe Hang had work completed on an annex to Poje temple and points out that through four Sŏn temples—Tansok, Ssanggye, Susŏn, and Sŏnwŏn—the Ch'oe leaders were able to support temples in economically important areas.

46. *TMS* 9:577–578 and Min, "Wŏllamsaji," p. 36. This temple, Sŏnwŏn temple, operated as a branch of Susŏn temple in the island capital, demonstrating the especially close links between the Ch'oe authority and Susŏn temple. See Ch'oe, "Susŏnsa," p. 57. For detailed information on the other temples see Kim Kwangsik, *Pulgyo,* pp. 264–324.

47. An, "Chogyejong," p. 314.

48. *CK* 1:576–577 and 593.

49. Min, "Wŏllamsaji," p. 34; *CK* 1:463–464. Equally instructive is the monk Hyowŏn, also known as Chinmyŏng, who passed the Sŏn examination and advanced with the help of Ch'oe U; *CK* 1:593–595.

50. See Buswell, *Chinul,* pp. 26–27; Ch'oe, "Susŏnsa," pp. 52–53; and Ch'ae, *Hugi pulgyo,* pp. 51 and 80. Ch'ae devotes much of his first chapter to studying Paengnyŏn temple. He also thinks the efforts of Chinul and Yose created a new class of patrons of Buddhism characterized by strong regional ties (pp. 27–28). Susŏn temple gradually became associated with the Ch'oe leadership. Paengnyŏng temple retained its links with regional personages. See also Kim Kwangsik, *Pulgyo,* pp. 209–215.

51. Yu, "Chogyejong," pp. 164–165.

52. Buddhist services and festivals, whether Kyo, Sŏn, or Ch'ŏnt'ae, remained at the center of Koryŏ social life. Both the P'algwan and Yŏndŭng ceremonies, with the royal family often playing a key role, were important national holidays enjoyed by all levels of society.

53. Sinjong, for example, visited Wangnyun temple in 1198; *KS* 21:5a, *KSC* 14:1b. Immediately prior to this trip he visited Yŏngt'ong temple and later would visit Myot'ong temple. Kojong visited the same temples in 1252 and 1258; *KS* 24:5a, *KSC* 17:6b, 17:37b. In his sixth year Sinjong visited Poje temple; *KS* 21:15b, *KSC* 14:13b. A cursory review of the *Koryŏsa* reveals that Sinjong visited

at least eleven temples in the capital area in the first three years of his reign; *KS* 21:4a–11b.

54. During the Khitan invasions in the early thirteenth century, a diviner had urged the king to move to this temple to preserve the dynasty; *KS* 22:14b, *KSC* 15:12b.

55. *KS* 22:12b; *KSC* 15:10a–b, 12b. Eight years later, Kangjong's portrait was at Hyŏnhwa temple; *KSC* 15:34b.

56. *KS* 21:22b; *KSC* 14:23a–b.

57. The court had patronized *toryang* throughout the entire dynasty, but these appeals became more urgent during the invasions. See, for example, *KSC* 14:33b; 15:35b, 43b; 16:8a. The Ch'oe leaders called for special prayer meetings to be held annually instead of once every three years; Kim Kwangsik, *Pulgyo,* p. 144.

58. Ch'ae, *Hugi pulgyo,* p. 81, discusses Ch'ŏnt'ae's significance here. Kim Kwangsik, *Muin,* pp. 186 and 199, shows how Ch'oe U marshaled the various sects in his efforts to defeat Koryŏ's northern invaders.

59. Kim Kwangsik, *Muin,* p. 215.

60. Ch'oe, "Susŏnsa," p. 52. Ch'ae, *Hugi pulgyo,* p. 21, notes that the massive effort needed to produce this work brought Sŏn and the Doctrine school closer together. Yu, "Chogyejong," p. 181, notes this result also.

61. See *KSC* 14:44b. One year later when six Khitans entered Kukch'ŏng temple, the monks seized and killed one while the remainder fled; *KS* 22:9b, *KSC* 15:4a–b. Two months later, local soldiers set off together with a monk army to check Khitans; *KS* 22:11a–b, *KSC* 15:7a.

62. The monk Kim Yunhu, who killed the Mongol commander Salita, provides an often repeated tale of courage and humility; *KS* 103:39b, *KSC* 16:18a. The monk Ubon, who helped stabilize local unrest caused by the Mongol invasions, was praised by Ch'oe U for his activities; *KS* 129:37a–b, *KSC* 16:12a.

63. By the end of the Koryŏ dynasty, it is clear that Buddhist temples had grown so large that the new Chosŏn leaders determined to curtail the influence of the Buddhist establishment. T'ongdo temple in 1328 covered some 47,000 paces and included twelve subordinate villages. See Takeda Yukio, "Kōrai jidai ni okeru Tsūdoji no jiryō shihai" [Payments of T'ongdo temple during the Koryŏ period], *Toyoshi kenkyū* 25(1) (1966):71. Ch'oe Hang was originally in charge of a monastery in Chindo, an island off South Chŏlla. By relying on his family's power, he assembled hoodlum monks to infiltrate the local temples and extract property. Other monks, falsely claiming to be disciples, extorted similar fees from the surrounding areas; *KS* 129:41b–42a, *KSC* 16:28b–29b. Yu, "Chogyejong," pp. 161–162, asserts that the Ch'oe House used its ties to temples to exploit the Kyŏngsang area. Yu also shows that Susŏn temple, in particular, grew through donations (pp. 171–173). Tansok temple and Ssangbong temple in the Chŏlla–Kyŏngsang region became additional centers through which the Ch'oe leaders were able to tap the resources of this region.

64. *KS* 110:22b–23a. David McMullen, *State and Scholars in T'ang China* (New York: Cambridge University Press, 1988), pp. 48–49, notes a similar development in Tang China: many Confucian scholars associated with Buddhist and Taoist clerics. I am indebted to John Duncan of UCLA for pointing this out to me.

65. The roots of this development can be traced back at least to Yejong's reign, when scholars were pursuing Sŏn, Taoist, and Confucian speculation simultaneously. See Shultz, "Han Anin," p. 7, as well as Shultz, "Twelfth Century Korea: Merit and Birth," *Journal of Korean Studies* (forthcoming). For a similar analysis see Ch'oe "Susŏnsa," pp. 65–66; Ch'ae, *Hugi pulgyo,* p. 8; and Yi Wŏnmyŏng, "Koryŏ chunggi Puksong sŏngnihak ŭi chŏllae wa sŏngyŏkko" [A study of the introduction and character of Northern Sung Neo-Confucianism in mid-Koryŏ], *Seoul yŏja taehakkyo nonmunjip* 18 (July 1989):79–94.

66. Many of his essays are preserved in *Tongguk Yi sangguk chip (YS);* see, for example, *YS* 25:8b, *CK* 1:460.

67. *KSC* 15:24b–25a.

68. See, for example, Kim Kunyu, who wrote Chinul's biography; *KS* 98:21b–22a. Or see Paek Punhwa, whose family had especially close links with Sŏn clerics; *YS* 36:1a–2b, *CK* 1:473–474.

69. Ch'oe Hang we have already noted. Another Ch'oe family relative, Kim Chŏng, the grandson of Ch'oe U, was initially sent off to a temple on account of misbehavior, but later he was recalled by U; *KS* 101:22a–b, *KSC* 16:31a, 36a–37a. Cho I, who became an interpreter and worked in the Yuan court, was once a monk; *KSC* 18:19b–20a.

70. *CK* 1:460–464. Hyesim had been raised near Susŏn temple and studied under Chinul after his mother's death. Yi Kyubo wrote this inscription. Ch'oe, "Susŏnsa," p. 59, notes that many of the leaders at Susŏn temple came from the Confucian scholar/local functionary class.

71. *PH* 3:18b–19b. See Ch'ae, *Hugi pulgyo,* pp. 83–89, for a detailed discussion of Ch'ŏnin.

72. See Ch'ae, *Hugi pulgyo,* pp. 91–93. Another man who was successful in the state examinations was Yu Chawŏn. Already precocious at five, he was soon encouraged to study by Ch'oe U. As he matured, he gained an interest in Buddhism and became a monk. See *POH* 3:26a.

73. Kim Chidae had passed the examination and served his country for decades, but when he retired he became a monk; *KS* 102:21a–22b. Yun Wi of the famed P'ap'yŏng Yun lineage passed the examination and performed meritorious work for the kingdom, yet he too preferred to live as a monk; *YS* 37:3b–4a.

74. Chinul's most famous works include *Kwŏnsa chonghye kyŏlsamun* [Encouragement to practice], *Kyech'osim haginmun* [Admonition to beginning students], *Susimgyŏl* [Secrets of cultivating the mind], and *Chinsim chiksol* [Straight talk on the true mind]. For an English translation of these works see Buswell, *Chinul.*

75. Hyesim wrote *Sŏnmun yŏmsong chip,* which Buswell, *Chinul,* p. 69, translates as "Collection of Kongan Stories." Hyesim edited many of Chinul's works.

76. This work has been translated into English by Peter H. Lee in *Lives of Eminent Korean Monks: The Haedong Kosŭng chŏn* (Cambridge, Mass.: Harvard University Press, 1969).

77. For an English translation see Lee, *Sourcebook,* pp. 420–421; the original is in *Hanguk pulgyo chŏnsŏ* 6:46c–47b. Ch'oe Hongyun, from the Haeju Ch'oe lineage, had passed the state examination and was a high-ranking civil official under Ch'oe U. Hyesim had once studied under Ch'oe Hongyun; *CK* 1:463.

Robert Buswell, who translated Hyesim's letter, also notes in Lee, *Sourcebook*, p. 411: "Hyesim's essay leads even to a discussion of Taoism, pointing to the intellectual fervor of this age, which allowed scholars and monks to discourse actively across a broad range of ideas." Ch'oe, "Susŏnsa," pp. 63–64, notes Hyesim's efforts at harmonizing Confucianism and Buddhism.

78. See also Ch'ae, *Hugi pulgyo*, p. 83. In quoting from Im Juil, *TMS* 83, he notes how Ch'ŏnin also combined Buddhism and Confucianism and purified the way *(tohaeng kogyŏl)*. See also Hŏ, *Pulyŏngu*, p. 506.

CHAPTER 8: LAND AND OTHER ECONOMIC ISSUES

1. *KS* 20:18b; *KSC* 13:5b–6a, 13:15a. For the expansion of property holdings see Chapter 2. Yi Chunch'ang was slandered for stealing land from a youth in 1183; *KS* 100:25b–26a, *KSC* 12:56a–b.

2. For a thorough discussion of the land system see the studies of James B. Palais and Kang Chinch'ŏl.

3. *KS* 129:5a; *KSC* 13:41a.

4. James B. Palais suggested this interpretation (pers. comm., August 1998).

5. Kang Chinch'ŏl, "Hanguk t'oji chedosa, sang" [History of Korean land systems, part 1], in *Hanguk munhwasa taegye* (Seoul: Korea University Press, 1967), 2B:1342, claims that Ch'oe Ch'unghŏn's reforms were merely a pretense to enable him to gain more power. While this is to some extent true, it should not obscure the fact that by restoring the dynastic institutions and strengthening the bureaucracy, Ch'oe Ch'unghŏn could at the same time build his position.

6. Kang, "T'oji chedosa," pp. 1342–1343.

7. *KSC* 14:19a. Land set aside to pay for various state agencies *(konghaejŏn)* and public land *(kongjŏn)*, as noted earlier, were taxed at 25 percent of the crop yield.

8. *KS* 129:28a–b; *KSC* 15:23b. James B. Palais (pers. comm.) suggests that Ch'oe U may have returned land and people or land and slaves.

9. *KS* 129:34b; *KSC* 15:42b–43a.

10. *KSC* 17:32a.

11. *KS* 129:35a–b; *KSC* 15:46a–b.

12. The court, for example, presented Ch'oe Ch'unghŏn with 100 *kyŏl* of land; *KSC* 14:19a.

13. Kang, "T'oji chedosa," p. 1350; Hatada Takashi, "Kōrai jidai no ōshitsu no shōen: shō/sho" [The estates of the royal house of the Koryŏ period: *chang* and *ch'ŏ*], in *Chōsen*, p. 77. As we shall see, the court did not have *sigŭp* rights at this time. The *ch'ŏ* might have evolved as a possible supplement to its reduced income.

14. *KSC* 17:32a.

15. Kim Chongguk, "Korai bushin," claims this period was characterized by the growth of manors in which the owner controlled all rent, land alienation, and produce rights. As the owner's position and power grew, the tiller lost his tenant rights and became a slave. Little evidence has been uncovered to support Kim's entire thesis.

16. For Ch'oe Ch'unghŏn's *sigŭp* see *KS* 129:16b, *KSC* 14:19b. For Ch'oe U's

see *KS* 129:39b, *KSC* 16:30b–31a. For Ch'oe Hang's see *KS* 129:50b, *KSC* 17:23b. See also Ha Hyŏngang, "Koryŏ sigŭp ko" [A study of the Koryŏ *sigŭp*], p. 137.

17. *KS* 129:50b; *KSC* 17:23b.

18. *KS* 129:17a–b; *KSC* 14:20b. In this case Ch'oe Ch'unghŏn politely refused the title *"hu"* and took the less prestigious title *"kong."* Six years later he changed the name of his administration to Chingang.

19. For Ch'oe U see *KS* 129:39a, *KSC* 16:21b–22a. For Ch'oe Hang see *KS* 129:47b–48a, *KSC* 17:4b, 7a–b.

20. *CK* 1:442. Ha Hyŏngang and Kim Chongguk disagree over the length of Ch'oe Ch'unghŏn's stay in the Kyŏngsang area: Ha believes that Ch'oe Ch'unghŏn did not necessarily have a close tie to Chinju before he received his *sigŭp* there; Kim claims that Ch'oe Ch'unghŏn spent nearly ten years in the area. See Ha, "Sigŭp," pp. 132–133. Given that Ch'oe Ch'unghŏn's mother came from Chinju and that children and even grandchildren were often raised in the mother's house, it is most likely that Ch'oe Ch'unghŏn spent at least part of his youth in the Chinju area. For marriage and family ties see Deuchler, *Transformation,* p. 66.

21. Yi Kyŏnghŭi, "Ch'oe ka," p. 11.

22. Ha, "Sigŭp," shows that generally the larger figure was a formal yet fictitious size; the latter numbers, in this case three hundred households, are more reflective, he says, of the actual size of the *sigŭp.*

23. For Ch'oe Ch'unghŏn's *sigŭp* see *KS* 129:16b, *KSC* 14:19b. For Ch'oe U's see *KSC* 16:30b–31a. For Ch'oe Hang's see *KS* 129:49b–50b, *KSC* 17:23b.

24. *KS* 129:40a; *KSC* 16:31b–32a; Ha, "Sigŭp," p. 129.

25. *KS* 129:44a–b; *KSC* 16:39b.

26. Yun Hoe et al., *Sejong sillok chiriji* [Gazetteer of the veritable records of Sejong] (Seoul: Sejong saŏphoe, 1973), 150:27b–28a.

27. Ha, "Sigŭp," p. 134; Kang, "T'ojichedosa," p. 1356.

28. *KS* 130:15a; Ha, "Sigŭp," p. 138.

29. *KSC* 16:28b–29a. See also Chapter 7, note 63. One *sŏk* equals about five bushels. Manjŏn was Ch'oe Hang.

30. For a detailed discussion of these ties see Kim Kwangsik, *Pulgyo,* pp. 237–347.

31. *KS* 22:6a; *KSC* 14:38a. The negative tone of this entry may well reflect the anticommercial bias of the fifteenth-century compilers of the dynastic records.

32. For the 1205 incident see *KS* 21:20a, *KSC* 14:19b. For the 1231 passage see *KS* 129:36b.

33. For Ch'oe U's endeavor see *KS* 129:34b–35a, *KSC* 15:43b. For the 1244 event see *KS* 23:37a–b, *KSC* 16:32b–33a. For accounts of the Japanese pirate raids at this time see Benjamin Harrison Hazard Jr., "Japanese Marauders and Medieval Korea" (Masters thesis, University of California at Berkeley, 1958).

34. *KS* 130:8b–9a; *KSC* 17:15a–b.

35. For the reduction of the corvée see *KS* 22:27a. For the 1202 incident see *KSC* 14:10b.

36. *KS* 129:5a–b, *KSC* 13:41a–b; *KS* 22:14a, *KSC* 15:12a. An accepted assumption by many scholars of Koryŏ—see, for example, the writings of Kang Chin-

ch'ŏl—was that the expansion of estates, especially after the rise of the military, bankrupted the state. But as this evidence demonstrates, even in the Ch'oe period, despite the proliferation of large private landholdings, the state and the Ch'oe House were able to collect revenues and use the tax system to forward their policies.

37. *KS* 80:27a; *KSC* 16:22b.

38. *KSC* 17:33b, *KS* 24:21b; *KSC* 17:21b, *KS* 23:29b–30a; *KSC* 16:35a, 17:24a–b.

39. *KS* 21:22a–b; *KSC* 14:23a.

40. *KS* 103:8b, 129:22a–b; *KSC* 14:40b–41a.

41. *KSC* 17:30b.

42. *KSC* 17:32a. The reader is reminded that this division occurred one year before the collapse of the Ch'oe House.

43. In addition to Chinju, the *Koryŏsa* specifically mentions that the Ch'oe House had estates in Imp'i (near modern Iri) in Chŏlla; see *KS* 104:39b–40a. For a map showing Ch'oe holdings see Yun Yonghyŏk, *Taemong*, p. 222.

44. *KSC* 17:45a, 43a.

45. *KS* 129:55b.

46. Kang Chinch'ŏl, "Land Tenure," p. 62.

CHAPTER 9: THE CH'OE DILEMMA

1. *KS* 129:7b; *KSC* 13:45a.

2. *KS* 129:2a; *KSC* 13:37a.

3. Chapter 2 showed how Ch'oe Ch'unghŏn fought with his brother Ch'ungsu to protect the sanctity of the court. See *KS* 129:9b–12a.

4. For Myŏngjong's mourning see *KS* 64:6b, *KSC* 14:13a. For Sinjong see *KS* 64:7a, 21:17a–18a, *KSC* 14:15b–16b.

5. To kings he favored, Ch'oe Ch'unghŏn generally accorded a position of importance in royal tombs. Sinjong was enshrined in the third right altar in the royal shrine (*KSC* 14:20a–b), for example, and later Kangjong received similar treatment, causing the removal of the eleventh-century monarch Munjong (*KSC* 14:35a). Hŭijong and Myŏngjong received no such honors. See also Kim Tangt'aek, *Muin*, p. 152.

6. *KS* 24:23b; *KSC* 17:23a.

7. *KS* 100:28a; *KSC* 15:2a–b.

8. *KS* 129:26a; *KSC* 15:19b.

9. *KS* 88:34b. Little else is known about this person; his lineage origin is unclear.

10. *KS* 129:19b; *KSC* 14:27b–28a. For the 1232 gift see *KS* 129:38a, *KSC* 16:15a.

11. *KS* 129:52b; *KSC* 17:29b.

12. Kim Tangt'aek, *Muin*, p. 155.

13. *KS* 129:18a–b; *KSC* 14:21b–22a.

14. *KS* 129:32b–33b; *KSC* 15:38a–39b.

15. For Sinjong's pardons see *KSC* 13:51b. For gifts to the aged and so forth

see *KS* 21:22b–23a, 68:10b–11a, *KSC* 14:23b. For the dispatch of palace attendants see *KS* 22:33b, *KSC* 15:42a–b.

16. For Hŭijong's demand see *KS* 21:22b, *KSC* 14:23a–b. For the quotations see *KS* 20:38b–39b, *KSC* 13:46a–47a, 14:8b.

17. Confucian ideology accepted an absolute monarch who in practice was often the arbitrator of disputing groups. There was a stress on personal relationships that envisioned the king as the father of the household. The government was responsible for the welfare of its people, and example rather than law was considered the most effective means of persuasion. It was a Confucian dictum that government offices should go to men of merit and ability. This Confucian scheme was based on the authority of the classics. For further discussion see Edward A. Kracke, *Civil Service in Early Sung China* (Cambridge, Mass.: Harvard University Press, 1953), pp. 21–24.

18. See Kang, "Ruling Class," especially chap. 5 on the current of thought.

19. *KS* 129:7b–9a; *KSC* 13:45a–46a. Other than possible ties with Ch'oe Ch'ungsu through his concubine, the identity of Marquis Chin remains unclear. Kim Tangt'aek, *Muin*, p. 149, contends that the question of Myŏngjong's successor caused the split between Choe Ch'unghŏn and Ch'ungsu, inasmuch as Ch'ungsu favored Marquis Chin but Ch'unghŏn's candidate won.

20. See Michael C. Rogers, "Sukchong of Koryŏ: His Accession and His Relations with Liao," *T'oung Pao* 47(1–2) (1959):30–42; and "Koryŏ's Military Dictatorship and Its Relations with Chin," *T'oung Pao* 47(1–2) (1959):43–62. Ch'oe Ch'unghŏn at this time followed the same procedures Chŏng Chungbu used to explain Ŭijong's abdication.

21. See Rogers, "Military Dictatorship," p. 55. Rogers says that Ch'oe Ch'unghŏn "had evidently decided to hasten the process of obtaining Chin's recognition of his puppet T'ak (Sinjong) by eliminating Ho (Myŏngjong) altogether from the scene." Myŏngjong's alleged earlier death might help explain why Ch'oe Ch'unghŏn sought to bury this king with the rites of a queen. By spending less time on the funeral, he would attract less attention, leaving Chin unaware of the fabrication.

22. Rogers, "Military Dictatorship," p. 60, states that the Chin history "notes that Wang Yŏng (Hŭijong) died in the eighth month of 1212 to be succeeded by his son. It thereby administers the coup de grâce to the *Koryŏsa* account; for it actually was Wang O who died on the ninth day of that month (August 26) and was succeeded by his son Ch'ŏl (Kojong). Wang Yŏng lived in exile until 1237. The conclusion is inescapable that the Koreans had no alternative but to retain the name of Wang Yŏng in their report of the king's death; so far as Chin was concerned, he was still the reigning king."

23. See *KS* 99:32a–33b, 19:14a–b; *KSC* 12:2a–3b, 22b–23a. Rogers presents this scenario in "Military Dictatorship," pp. 46–52.

24. See Chapter 2, and see *KS* 100:9a–b, *KSC* 12:21b–22a, 23a–b. See also Rogers, "Military Dictatorship," pp. 50–52. As Rogers notes, the Chin emperor had already acknowledged the accession of Myŏngjong and therefore chose to disregard Cho Wich'ong's appeal.

25. Kwangjong is a good example of a king who ruled and reigned. See, for example, Hugh H. W. Kang, "Institutional Borrowing: The Case of the Chinese Civil Service Examination System in Early Koryŏ," *Journal of Asian Studies* 34(1) (1974):109–125.

26. Yun, *Taemong*, pp. 40–41.

27. Ibid., pp. 163–170.

28. In 1235, for example, royal garments were circulated between Kaegyŏng and Namgyŏng (modern Seoul) as a way to fight the Mongols spiritually; *KSC* 16:22a–b. In 1243, Koryŏ leaders dispatched special commissioners to prepare defenses on mountain fortresses; *KSC* 16:31b.

29. For tax exemptions see Chapter 8 and *KSC* 16:35a, 39b, and 17:21b. On the state treasury being empty see *KSC* 17:14b, 15a–b. And for the state granaries offering food see *KSC* 17:29b, 30a.

30. For Ch'oe Hang's opposition to meeting the Mongols see *KS* 129:49a–b, *KSC* 17:7b–8b. On deferring to the king see *KS* 24:9b–10a, *KSC* 17:11b–12a. The Mongols saw through the facade; see *KSC* 17:19a. And for Ch'oe Hang's calling for resistance see *KS* 130:32a–b, *KSC* 17:26a–b. After the Ch'oe House disappeared, the court blamed it for preventing good relations with the Mongols.

BIBLIOGRAPHY

An Kyehyŏn. "Chogyejong kwa ogyo yangjong" [The Chogye school and the five sects and two schools]. In *Hanguksa*, vol. 7. Seoul: T'amgudang, 1973.

———. "Koryŏ sidae ŭi muin chŏngch'i e taehayŏ" [Concerning the military government of the Koryŏ period]. *Haegun* 46 (1956).

———. "P'algwanhoe ko" [A study of the Assembly of Eight Prohibitions]. *Tongguk sahak* 4 (1966):31–54.

———. "Yŏdae sŭnggwan ko" [A study of monk offices in the Koryŏ period]. *Tongguk sahak* 5 (1967):95–105.

Aoyama Koryū. "Kōraichō Kosōchō oyobi Gensōchō no wakō" [Pirate raids in the Koryŏ dynasty from Kojong to Wŏnjong's reign]. *Shigaku zasshi* 38 (4) (1927):384–395.

Buswell, Robert E. Jr. *The Collected Works of Chinul.* Honolulu: University of Hawai'i Press, 1983.

———. *The Zen Monastic Experience.* Princeton: Princeton University Press, 1992.

Ch'ae Sangshik. *Koryŏ hugi pulgyosa yŏngu* [A study of the history of Buddhism in late Koryŏ]. Seoul: Ilchogak, 1991.

Chang Wŏngyu. "Chogyejong ŭi sŏngnip kwa palchŏn e taehan koch'al" [A study of the establishment and growth of the Chogye school]. *Pulgyo hakpo* 1 (1963):311–351.

Chi Myŏnggwan. "Manjŏk kwa Hong Kyŏngnae minjungsa ŭi kyŏngnang" [People's history of Manjŏk and Hong Kyŏngnae]. *Tongsŏ ch'unch'u* 1 (4) (1967): 189–197.

Cho Chwaho. "Yŏdae namban ko" [A study of the *namban* of the Koryŏ period]. *Tongguk sahak* (1967):1–17.

Cho Insŏng. "Ch'oe U chipkwŏnha munhangwan" [Writings under Ch'oe rule]. In *Koryŏ muin chŏnggwŏn yŏngu*, ed. Hong Sŭnggi. Seoul: Sŏgang University Press, 1995.

Cho Kyut'ae. "Ch'oe muin chŏnggwŏn kwa kyojŏng togam ch'eje" [Ch'oe military rule and the Kyojŏng Togam]. In *Koryŏ muin chŏnggwŏn yŏngu*, ed. Hong Sŭnggi. Seoul: Sŏgang University Press, 1995.

Cho Myŏnggi. *Koryŏ Taegak kuksa wa ch'ŏnt'ae sasang* [Koryŏ national tutor Taegak and Ch'ŏnt'ae thought]. Seoul: Minjung sagwan, 1964.

Cho Tongil. *Hanguk munhak t'ongsa* [History of Korean literature]. Vol. 2. Seoul: Chisik sanŏpsa, 1989.

Ch'oe Cha. *Pohan chip* [Supplementary jottings in idleness]. *Koryŏ myŏnghyŏnjip.* Seoul: Kyŏngin munhwasa, 1972.

Ch'oe Chinhwan. "Ch'oe Ch'unghŏn ŭi pongsa sipcho" [Ch'oe Ch'unghŏn's ten injunctions]. In *Koryŏ muin chŏnggwŏn yŏngu,* ed. Hong Sŭnggi. Seoul: Sŏgang University Press, 1995.

Ch'oe Pyŏnghŏn (Byŏng-Hŏn). "Ch'ŏnt'aejong ŭi sŏngnip" [Establishment of the Ch'ŏnt'ae school]. In *Hanguksa,* vol. 6. Seoul: T'amgudang, 1975.

―――. "Hanguk hwaŏm sasangsae issŏsŏŭi Ŭich'ŏn ŭi wich'i" [The position of Ŭich'ŏn in Korea's Hwaŏm intellectual history]. In *Hanguk hwaŏm sasang yŏngu.* Seoul: Tongguk University Press, 1982.

―――. "Koryŏ chunggi Yi Chahyŏn ŭi Sŏn kwa kŏsa pulgyo ŭi sŏnggyŏk" [The Sŏn thought of mid-Koryŏ Yi Chahyŏn and the character of Buddhism of retired scholars]. In *Kim Ch'ŏljun paksa hwangap kinyŏm sahak nonch'ong.* Seoul: Chisik sanŏpsa, 1983.

―――. "Significance of the Foundation of Susŏnsa in the History of Koryŏ Buddhism." *Seoul Journal of Korean Studies* 1 (1988):49–68.

Ch'oe Wŏnyŏng. "Imssi muin chŏnggwŏn ŭi sŏngnip kwa ponggwi" [Rise and fall of the Im family military rule]. In *Koryŏ muin chŏnggwŏn yŏngu,* ed. Hong Sŭnggi. Seoul: Sŏgang University Press, 1995.

Chong Inji et al. *Koryŏsa* [History of Koryŏ]. Yŏnse edition. Seoul: Kyŏngin munhwasa, 1972.

Chŏng Sua. "Kim Chun seryŏk hyŏngsŏng kwa kŭ hyangbae" [Formation of Kim Chun's power and his pros and cons]. In *Koryŏ muin chŏnggwŏn yŏngu,* ed. Hong Sŭnggi. Seoul: Sŏgang University Press, 1995.

Chōsen kinseki sōran [Compilation of Korean epigraphy]. Vols. 1 and 2. Seoul: Governor General's Office, 1933.

Chosŏn wangjo sillok [Veritable records of the kings of the Chosŏn dynasty]. Kuksa p'yŏnch'an wiwŏnhoe edition. Seoul, 1955–1958.

Chŭngbo munhŏn pigo [Revised reference compilation of documents on Korea]. Seoul: Tongguk munhwasa, 1964.

Davis, David Brion. *The Problem of Slavery in Western Culture.* Ithaca: Cornell University Press, 1966.

Deuchler, Martina. *The Confucian Transformation of Korea: A Study of Society and Ideology.* Cambridge, Mass.: Council on East Asian Studies, Harvard University, 1992.

Duncan, John B. "Confucianism in Late Koryŏ and Early Chosŏn." *Korean Studies* 18 (1994):76–102.

―――. "Formation of the Central Aristocracy in Early Koryŏ." *Korean Studies* 12 (1988):39–61.

―――. *The Koryŏ Origins of the Chosŏn Dynasty: Kings, Aristocrats, and Confucianism.* Seattle: University of Washington Press, 2000.

Duus, Peter. *Feudalism in Japan.* New York: Knopf, 1969.

Fujita Ryōsaku. "Ri Shien to sono kakei" [Yi Chayŏn and his family]. *Seikyū gakusō* 13 (August 1933):1–37; 15 (February 1934):109–135.

Ha Hyŏngang. "Chibang ŭi t'ongchi chojik" [Governing structure of rural Korea]. In *Hanguksa*, vol. 13. Seoul: T'amgudang, 1993.

————. "Koryŏ chibang chedo ŭi ilyŏngu" [A study of the Koryŏ regional system]. *Sahak yŏngu* 14 (1962):67–103.

————. "Koryŏ Hyŏnjong ŭi chŏngpyŏn" [Political change in Koryŏ Hyŏnjong's reign]. *Sahak yŏngu* 20 (1968):193–208.

————. "Koryŏ sigŭp ko" [A study of the Koryŏ *sigŭp*]. *Yŏksa hakpo* 26 (January 1965):107–139.

————. "Koryŏ Ŭijongdae ŭi sŏngyŏk" [The character of Koryŏ king Ŭijong's reign]. *Tongbang hakchi* 26 (1981):1–29.

————. "Musin chŏngbyŏnun wae irŏnannun ka?" [Why did the military officers revolt?]. *Hanguksa simin kangchwa* 8 (1991):1–20.

Hall, John W. "Feudalism in Japan—A Reassessment." In *Studies in the Institutional History of Early Modern Japan*, ed. John W. Hall and Marius B. Jansen. Princeton: Princeton University Press, 1968.

————. *Government and Local Power in Japan, 500 to 1700*. Princeton: Princeton University Press, 1966.

Hatada Takashi. *Chōsen chūsei shakaishi no kenkyū* [A study of medieval Korean social history]. Tokyo: Hōsei daigaku shuppankyoku, 1972.

————. *History of Korea*. Translated by Warren W. Smith and Benjamin H. Hazard. Santa Barbara: ABC Clio, 1969.

————. "Kōraichō ni okeru jiin keizai" [Temple economics in the Koryŏ dynasty]. *Shigaku zasshi* 43 (5) (1934):1–37.

————. "Kōrai jidai ni okeru tochi no chakuchōshi sōzoku to nuhi no shijo kinbun sōzoku" [Primogeniture land inheritance and the equal inheritance of slaves in the Koryŏ period]. *Tōyo bunka* 22 (January 1957) and *Chōsen chūsei shakaishi no kenkyū*, pp. 325–361.

————. "Kōrai jidai no ōshitsu no shōen: shō/sho" [Estates of the royal house of the Koryŏ period: *chang* and *ch'ŏ*]. *Chōsen chūsei shakaishi no kenkyū*, pp. 75–104.

————. "Kōrai jidai no semmin seido 'bukyoku ni tsuite'" [Concerning *pugok* in the lowborn social system of the Koryŏ period]. *Chōsen chūsei shakaishi no kenkyū*, pp. 57–74.

————. "Kōrai no jishinken" [The *sasimgwan* of Koryŏ]. *Chōsen chūsei shakaishi no kenkyū*, pp. 105–139.

————. "Kōrai no Meisō Shinsō jidai ni okeru nōmin ikki" [Peasant revolts in the age of Koryŏ kings Myŏngjong and Sinjong]. *Rekishigaku kenkyū* 2 (4) (August 1934):2–15; 2 (5) (September 1934):2–14.

Hazard, Benjamin Harrison Jr. "Japanese Marauders and Medieval Korea." Masters thesis, University of California at Berkeley, 1958.

Henthorn, William. *The Mongol Invasion of Korea*. Leiden: E. J. Brill, 1962.

Hŏ Hŭngsik. *Koryŏ kwagŏ chedosa yŏngu* [A study of the institutional history of the Koryŏ state civil service examination]. Seoul: Ilchokak, 1981.

————. *Koryŏ pulgyosa yŏngu* [A study of the history of Korean Buddhism]. Seoul: Ilchokak, 1986.

Hong Sŭnggi. "Koryŏ Ch'oessi muin chŏnggwŏn kwa Ch'oessi ŭi kano" [Koryŏ

Ch'oe House military rule and the Ch'oe House slaves]. In *Koryŏ muin chŏng-gwŏn yŏngu*, ed. Hong Sŭnggi. Seoul: Sŏgang University Press, 1995.

———. *Koryŏ sidae nobi yŏngu* [A study of slavery in the Koryŏ period]. Seoul: Hanguk yŏngu ch'ongsŏ, 1981. Revised as *Koryŏ kwijok sahoe wa nobi* [Aristocratic society of Koryŏ and slavery]. Seoul: Ilchokak, 1983.

Hsu Ch'ing. *Kao-li tu-ching* [Report on Koryŏ]. Seoul: Asea Munhwasa, 1981.

Hurst, G. Cameron. "The Structure of the Heian Court: Some Thoughts on the Nature of 'Familial Authority' in Heian Japan." In *Medieval Japan: Essays in Institutional History*, ed. John W. Hall and Jeffrey P. Mass. Stanford: Stanford University Press, 1974.

Ikeuchi Hiroshi. "Kōrai no sambetsushō ni tsuite" [Concerning the Sambyŏl-ch'o of Koryŏ]. *Shigaku zasshi* 37 (9) (1926):809–848.

Imanishi Fumio. "Kōraichō ni okeru nuhi ni tsuite" [Concerning the slaves of the Koryŏ dynasty]. In *Kuwahara Hakushi kanreki kinen toyoshi ronso*. Kyoto, 1931.

Iryŏn. *Samguk yusa* [Memorabilia of the Three Kingdoms]. Ch'oe Namsŏn edition. Seoul: Minjung sogwan, 1946.

Kang Chinch'ŏl. "Hanguk t'oji chedosa, sang" [History of Korean land systems, part 1]. In *Hanguk munhwasa taegye*, vol. 2B. Seoul: Korea University Press, 1965.

———. "Koryŏ ch'ogi ŭi kuninjŏn" [Soldier's land of the early Koryŏ period]. *Sungmyŏng yŏjadae nonmunjip* 3 (1963):131–183.

———. "Koryŏ chŏngi ŭi kongjŏn/sajŏn kwa kŭ ŭi ch'aryul sujo e taehaeyŏ" [*Kongjŏn* and *sajŏn* in early Koryŏ and the different rates of *cho* on them]. *Yŏksa hakpo* 29 (December 1965):1–49.

Kang, Hugh H. W. "The Development of the Korean Ruling Class from Late Silla to Early Koryŏ." Ph.D. dissertation, University of Washington, 1964.

———. "Institutional Borrowing: The Case of the Chinese Civil Service Examination System in Early Koryŏ." *Journal of Asian Studies* 34 (1) (1974):109–125.

Kim Chongguk. "Kōrai bushin seiken to sōto no tairitsu tōsō ni kansuru ichi kōsatsu" [An examination of Koryŏ military rule and the resistance of monks]. *Chōsen gakuhō* 21–22 (1961):567–589.

———. "Kōrai bushin seiken no tokushitsu ni kansuru ichi kōsatsu" [An examination of the special characteristics of Koryŏ military rule]. *Chōsen gakuhō* 17 (October 1960):51–80.

Kim Chongsŏ et al. *Koryŏsa chŏryo* [Essentials of Koryŏ history]. Tokyo: Gaku-shūin, 1960.

Kim Ku. *Chip'o chip* [Jottings while resting on a riverbank]. *Koryŏ myŏnghyŏnjip*. Scoul: Kyŏngin munhwasa, 1972.

Kim Kwangsik. *Koryŏ muin chŏnggwŏn kwa pulgyogye* [Koryŏ military rule and Buddhism]. Seoul: Minjoksa, 1995.

Kim Nakchin. "Kyŏllyonggun kwa musin nan" [The Kyŏllyong army and the military officers revolt]. In *Koryŏ muin chŏngkwŏn yŏngu*, ed. Hong Sŭnggi. Seoul: Sŏgang University Press, 1995.

Kim Pusik et al. *Samguk sagi* [History of the Three Kingdoms]. Chŏngdŏk edition. Seoul: Koten Kankokai, 1931.

Kim Sanggi. "Koryŏ muin chŏngch'i kigu ko" [An examination of the structure of the Koryŏ military government]. *Tongbang munhwa kyoryusa nongo.* Seoul: Uryu munhwasa, 1948.

———. *Koryŏ sidaesa* [History of the Koryŏ period]. Seoul: Tongguk munhwasa, 1961.

———. "Sambyŏlch'o wa kŭ ŭi nan e tae haya" [Concerning the Sambyŏlch'o and its revolt]. *Chindan hakpo* 9 (1939):1–29.

Kim Sangyŏng. "Koryŏ Yejongdae Sŏnjong ŭi pokhŭng kwa pulgyogye ŭi pyŏnhwa" [The rise of the Sŏn school in Koryŏ Yejong's reign and changes in Buddhism]. *Chŏnggye sahak* 5 (1988):49–89.

Kim Sŏngjun. "Koryŏ chŏngbang ko" [A study of the Koryŏ Chŏngbang]. *Sahak yŏngu* 13 (June 1962):153–160.

Kim Sumi. "Koryŏ muin chŏnggwŏngi ŭi yabyŏlch'o" [The Yabyŏlch'o of the Koryŏ military government]. In *Koryŏ muin chŏnggwŏn yŏngu,* ed. Hong Sŭnggi. Seoul: Sŏgang University Press, 1995.

Kim Tangt'aek. "Chŏng Chungbu, Yi Ŭimin, Ch'oe Ch'unghŏn." *Hanguksa simin kangchwa* 8 (1) (1991):21–39.

———. "Im Yŏn chŏnggwŏn kwa Koryŏ ŭi Kaegyŏng hwando" [Im Yŏn's rule and the return to Kaegyŏng]. In *Hanguk sahak nonch'ong: Yi Kibaek sŏnsaeng kohŭi kinyŏm.* Seoul: Ilchokak, 1994.

———. "Im Yŏn's Regime and Koryŏ's Return of the Capital to Kaesŏng." *Korean Social Science Journal* 23 (1997):103–111.

———. "Koryŏ Ch'oessi muin chŏnggwŏn kwa Susŏnsa" [Koryŏ Ch'oe military rule and Susŏn temple]. *Yŏksahak yŏngu* 10 (1981). Also published in *Koryŏ muin chŏnggwŏn yŏngu.* Seoul: Saemunsa, 1987.

———. "Koryŏ muin chipkwŏn ch'ogi millan ŭi sŏnggyŏk" [The character of popular revolts at the start of Koryŏ military rule]. *Kuksagwan nonch'ong* 20 (1990):119–139.

———. *Koryŏ muin chŏnggwŏn yŏngu* [A study of Koryŏ military rule]. Seoul: Saemunsa, 1987.

———. *Koryŏ muin chŏnggwŏn yŏngu* [A study of Koryŏ military rule]. Seoul: Kukha charyowŏn, 1999.

———. "Koryŏ Ŭijongdae ŭi chŏngch'ijŏk ŭi sanghwang kwa musinran" [The political circumstances of Koryŏ Ŭijong's period and the military officers' revolt]. *Chindan hakpo* 75 (June 1993): 35–55.

———. "Sangjŏng kogŭm yemun ŭi p'yŏnch'an sigi wa kŭ ŭido" [The period of publication and the goals of the Sangjŏng Kogŭm Yemun]. *Honam munhwa yŏngu* 21 (1992):1–12.

Kim Tudam. "Koryŏ musin chipchŏng sidea e kwanhan sogo" [A brief study of Koryŏ military rule]. *Pusan taehakkyo mullidae hakpo* 6 (1968):14–20.

Kim Ŭigyu. "Koryŏ muin chŏnggwŏngi munsa ŭi chŏngch'ijŏk hwaldong" [Political activities of scholars during the period of Koryŏ military rule]. In *Han Ugŭn paksa chongnyŏn kinyŏm sahak nonch'ong.* Seoul: Chisiksangŏpsa, 1981.

Kim Yongdŏk. "Hyang, so, pugok ko" [A study of the *hyang, so,* and *pugok*]. In *Paek Nakchun paksa hwangap kinyŏm nonmunjip.* Seoul: Sasanggyesa, 1955.

Kim Yongsŏn. *Koryŏ ŭmsŏ chedo yŏngu* [A study of the Koryŏ protective appoint-ment system]. Seoul: Ilchokak, 1991.

Kim Yungon. "Koryŏ kwijok sahoe ŭi che mosun" [Contradictions of Koryŏ aris-tocratic society]. In *Hanguksa*, vol. 7. Seoul: T'amgudang, 1973.

Koryŏsa [History of Koryŏ]. Yŏnse edition. Seoul: Kyŏngin munhwasa, 1972.

Koryŏsa chŏryo [Essentials of Koryŏ history]. Hosa Bunko edition. Tokyo: Gaku-shūin, 1969.

Koryŏ musin chŏnggwŏn [Koryŏ military rule]. *Hanguksa*, vol. 18. Seoul: T'amgu-dang, 1973.

Kracke, Edward A. *Civil Service in Early Sung China.* Cambridge, Mass.: Harvard University Press, 1953.

Lee, Peter H. *Lives of Eminent Korean Monks: The Haedong Kosŭng chŏn.* Cam-bridge, Mass.: Harvard University Press, 1969.

———. ed. *Sourcebook of Korean Civilization.* Vol. 1. New York: Columbia Univer-sity Press, 1993.

Mass, Jeffrey. *Antiquity and Anachronism in Japanese History.* Stanford: Stanford University Press, 1992.

McMullen, David. *State and Scholars in T'ang China.* New York: Cambridge Uni-versity Press, 1988.

Min Hyŏngu. "Wŏllamsaji chingak kuksabi ŭi ungi e taehan ilgoch'al" [A study of the tomb inscription to national tutor Chingak at the Wŏllam temple site]. *Chindan hakpo* 36 (October 1973):7–38.

Min Pyŏngha. "Ch'oe ssi chŏnggwŏn ŭi chibae kigo" [The ruling structure of the Ch'oe House government]. In *Hanguksa*, vol. 7. Seoul: T'amgudang, 1973.

———. "Koryŏ musin chipchŏng sidae e taehan ilgo" [A study of the age of the Koryŏ military officers' takeover]. *Sahak yŏngu* 6 (1959):27–68.

———. *Koryŏ musin chŏnggwŏn yŏngu* [A study of Koryŏ military officers' rule]. Seoul: Sŏnggyungwan University Press, 1990.

Naitō Shunpo. "Kōrai heisei kanken" [A review of the Koryŏ military system]. *Seikyū gakuhō* 15 (1934):1–46.

———. "Kōrai jidai no jūbō oyobi seibo ni tsuite" [Concerning the Chungbang and Chŏngbang of the Koryŏ period]. In *Inaba hakushi kanreki kinen mansen-shi ronsō.* Seoul, 1938.

No Sasin et al. *Tongguk yŏji sŭngnam* [Geographical survey of Korea]. Kojŏn kugyŏk edition. Seoul, 1964.

Pak Ch'anghŭi. "Ch'oe Ch'unghŏn sogo" [A short study of Ch'oe Ch'unghŏn]. *Sahakchi* 3 (1969):105–115.

———. "Muin chŏnggwŏn haŭi munindŭl" [Civilians under military rule]. *Han-guksa simin kangchwa* 8 (1) (1991):40–59.

———. "Musin chŏnggwŏn sidae ŭi munin" [Civilians in the period of military rule]. In *Hanguksa*, vol. 7. Seoul: T'amgudang, 1973.

Pak Chonggi. *Koryŏ sidae pugok chedo yŏngu* [A study of the *pugok* system of the Koryŏ period]. Seoul: Seoul University Press, 1990.

Pak Hanju, ed. *Mansŏng taedongbo* [Genealogical records]. Seoul: Hangmungak, 1972.

Pak Yongun (Park Yongwoon). "Koryŏjo ŭi taegan chedo" [The censorial institutions of the Koryŏ dynasty]. *Yŏksa hakpo* 52 (December 1971):1–51.

———. *Koryŏ sidae taegan chedo yŏngu* [A study of the censorial institutions of the Koryŏ period]. Seoul: Ilchisa, 1980.

———. *Koryŏ sidae ŭmsŏje wa kwagŏje yŏngu* [A study of the Koryŏ protective appointment system and the state civil service examination system]. Seoul: Ilchisa, 1990.

Palais, James B. *Confucian Statecraft and Korean Institutions: Yu Hyŏngwŏn and the Late Chosŏn Dynasty.* Seattle: University of Washington Press, 1996.

———. "Land Tenure in Korea: Tenth to Twelfth Century." *Journal of Korean Studies* 4 (1982–1983):75–205.

———. "Records and Record Keeping in Nineteenth-Century Korea." *Journal of Asian Studies* 30 (3) (May 1971):583–591.

———. "A Search for Korean Uniqueness." *Harvard Journal of Asian Studies* 55 (2) (1995):409–425.

———. "Slavery and Slave Society in the Koryŏ Dynasty." *Journal of Korean Studies* 5 (1984):173–190.

———. *Views on Social History.* Institute for Modern Korean Studies, Special Lecture Series, No. 2. Seoul: Yonsei University, 1998.

Pyŏn T'aesŏp. "Chungang ŭi chŏngch'i chojik" [Central political structure]. In *Hanguksa*, vol. 13. Seoul: Tamgudang, 1993.

———. *Koryŏ chŏngch'i chedosa yŏngu* [A study of Koryŏ political institutional history]. Seoul: Ilchokak, 1971.

———. "Manjŏk nan palsaeng ŭi sahoejŏk soji" [Social foundation of the outbreak of the Manjŏk rebellion]. In *Koryŏ chŏngch'i chedosa yŏngu.* Seoul: Ilchokak, 1971.

———. "Musin nan kwa Ch'oe ssi chŏnggwŏn ŭi sŏngnip" [The military revolt and the establishment of Ch'oe House rule]. In *Hanguksa*, vol. 7. Seoul: T'amgudang, 1973.

———. "Nongmin-ch'ŏnmin ŭi ran" [Revolts by peasants and lowborns]. In *Hanguksa*, vol. 7. Seoul: T'amgudang, 1973.

Rogers, Michael C. "Koryŏ's Military Dictatorship and Its Relations with Chin." *T'oung Pao* 47 (1–2) (1959):43–62.

———. "National Consciousness in Medieval Korea: The Impact of Liao and Chin on Koryŏ." In *China Among Equals: The Middle Kingdom and Its Neighbors, 10th to 14th Centuries,* ed. Morris Rossabi. Berkeley: University of California Press, 1983.

———. "P'yŏnnyŏn t'ongnok: The Foundation Legend of the Koryŏ State." *Journal of Korean Studies* 4 (1982–1983):3–72.

———. "Sukchong of Koryŏ: His Accession and His Relations with Liao." *T'oung Pao* 47 (1–2) (1959):30–42.

Rutt, Richard, ed. *James Scarth Gale and His History of the Korean People.* Seoul: Taewon, 1972.

Salem, Ellen. "Slavery in Medieval Korea." Ph.D. dissertation, Columbia University, 1978.

Sansom, George. *A History of Japan to 1334*. Stanford: Stanford University Press, 1958.

Shim Jae Ryong. "The Philosophical Foundation of Korean Zen Buddhism: The Integration of Sŏn and Kyo by Chinul (1158–1210)." Ph.D. dissertation, University of Hawai'i, 1979.

Shultz, Edward J. "Ch'oe Ch'unghŏn: His Rise to Power." *Korean Studies* 8 (1984):58–82.

———. "Institutional Developments in Korea Under the Ch'oe House: 1196–1258." Ph.D. dissertation, University of Hawai'i, 1976.

———. "Military Revolt in Koryŏ: The 1170 Coup d'Etat." *Korean Studies* 3 (1979):19–48.

———. "Twelfth Century Korea: Merit and Birth." *Journal of Korean Studies* (forthcoming).

———. "Twelfth-Century Koryŏ Politics: The Rise of Han Anin and His Partisans." *Journal of Korean Studies* 6 (1983).

———. "Han Aninp'a ŭi tŭngjang kwa yŏkhwal." *Yŏksa hapo* 99–100 (December 1983):147–183.

Sŏ Kŏjŏng. *Tongguk t'onggam* [Comprehensive mirror of the Eastern Kingdom]. 6 vols. Seoul: Chōsen kenkyukai, 1915.

Sudō Yoshiyuki. "Kōraichō ni okeru sanshi to sono chii" [The Samsa and its position in the Koryŏ dynasty]. *Chōsen gakuhō* 77 (October 1975):39–90.

Suematsu Yasukazu. "Kōrai heibashi kō" [An examination of the Koryŏ *pyŏngmasa*]. *Toyo gakuhō* 39 (1) (1956):1–43.

Takeda Yukio. "Kōrai jidai ni okeru Tsūdoji no jiryō shihai' [Payments to T'ongdo temple during the Koryŏ period]. *Toyoshi kenkyū* 25 (1) (June 1966):70–91.

Tong munsŏn [Selected writings from the East]. Seoul: Taehan kongnonsa, 1970.

Weems, Clarence N., ed. *Hulbert's History of Korea*. New York: Hillary House, 1962.

Yi Chaech'ang. "Sawŏn nobi ko" [A study of temple slaves]. In *Hwang Ŭidon sŏnsaeng kohŭi kinyŏm sōhak nonch'ong*. Seoul: Tongguk University Press, 1960.

Yi Chehyŏn. *Yŏgong p'aesŏl* [Scribblings of Old Man Oak]. In *Koryŏ myŏnghyŏnjip*. Seoul: Kyŏngin munhwasa, 1972.

Yi Chŏngsin. *Koryŏ musin chŏnggwŏngi nongmin-ch'ŏnmin hangjaeng yŏngu* [A study of peasant-lowborn resistance during Koryŏ military rule]. Seoul: Koryŏ University Press, 1991.

Yi Hongjik, ed. *Kuksa taesajŏn* [Great dictionary of national history]. Seoul: Paekmansa, 1974.

Yi Illo. *P'ahan chip* [Jottings to break up idleness]. *Koryŏ myŏnghyŏnjip*. Seoul: Kyŏngin munhwasa, 1972.

Yi Kibaek (Kibaik Lee). "Korea: The Military Tradition." In *The Traditional Culture and Society of Korea: Thought and Institutions*, ed. Hugh H. W. Kang. Honolulu: Center for Korean Studies, 1975.

———. *Koryŏ pyŏngjesa yŏngu* [A study of the history of Koryŏ military institutions]. Seoul: Ilchokak, 1968.

———. *Koryŏsa pyŏngji: Yŏkchu* 1 [Translation of the military treatise section of the *Koryŏsa*]. Seoul: Kyŏngin munhwasa, 1969.

——. *Kuksa sillon* [New history of Korea]. Seoul: Taesŏngsa, 1961.

Yi Kyŏnghŭi. "Ch'oe Ch'unghŏn kamun yŏngu" [A study of the family of Ch'oe Ch'unghŏn]. *Pusan yŏdae sahak* 5 (December 1987):1–52.

Yi Kyubo. *Tongguk Yi sangguk chip* [Collected works of Minister Yi of Korea]. *Koryŏ myŏnghyŏnjip*. Seoul: Kyŏngin munhwasa, 1972.

Yi Nanyŏng. *Hanguk kŭmsŏngmun ch'ubo* [Additions to Korean epigraphy]. Seoul: Chungang University Press, 1968.

Yi Pyŏngdo. *Hanguksa: Chungsep'yŏn* [Korean history: Middle ages]. Seoul: Uryu munhwasa, 1961.

——. "Koryŏ namban ko" [A study of the Koryŏ *namban*]. *Seoul taehakkyo nonmunjip* 16 (1966):157–168.

——. *Koryŏ sidae ŭi yŏngu* [A study of the Koryŏ period]. Seoul: Uryu munhwasa, 1954.

Yi Sanghun. "Koryŏ chunggi hyangni chedo ŭi p'yŏnhwae taehan ilgoch'al" [A study of the changes in the local functionary system during mid-Koryŏ]. In *Koryŏ muin chŏnggwŏn yŏngu*, ed. Hong Sŭnggi. Seoul: Sŏgang University Press, 1995.

Yi Uch'ŏl. "Koryŏ sidae ŭi hwangwan e taehayŏ" [Eunuchs of the Koryŏ period]. *Sahak yŏngu*, 1 (1958):11–44.

Yi Usŏng. "Koryŏ chunggi ŭi minjok sŏsasi" [National epic poetry from mid-Koryŏ]. *Sŏnggyundae nonminjip* 7 (1963):84–117.

——. "Koryŏjo ŭi 'i' e taehayŏ" [Concerning the clerks of the Koryŏ dynasty]. *Yŏksa hakpo* 14 (April 1961):25–44.

Yi Wŏnmyŏng. "Koryŏ chunggi Puksong sŏngnihak ŭi chŏnnae wa sŏngyŏkko" [A study of the introduction and character of Northern Song Neo-Confucianism in mid-Koryŏ]. *Seoul yŏja taehakkyo nonmunjip* 18 (July 1989):79–94.

Yŏksa wa hyŏnsil [History and reality]. Vol. 11 (1994).

Yu Kyosŏng. "Hanguk sanggongŏpsa" [Commercial history of Korea]. In *Hanguk munhwasa taegye*, vol. 2B. Seoul: Korea University Press, 1967.

——. "Koryŏ sawŏn kyŏngje ŭi sŏnggyŏk" [Character of the economy of Koryŏ temples]. *Pulgyohak nonmunjip* (1959):605–626.

Yu Yŏngsuk. "Ch'oessi musin chŏnggwŏn kwa Chogyejong" [Ch'oe military rule and the Chogye school]. *Paeksan hakpo* 33 (1986):157–189.

Yun Hoe et al. *Sejong sillok chiriji* [Gazetteer of the veritable records of Sejong]. Seoul: Sejong saŏphoe, 1973.

Yun Yonghyŏk. *Koryŏ taemonghangjaengsa yŏngu* [A study of the history of Koryŏ resistance to the Mongols]. Seoul: Koryŏ University Press, 1991.

Yun Yonggyun. "Kōrai Kisōchō ni okeru Tei Chūfu ran no soin to sono eikyō" [The cause of Chŏng Chungbu's revolt in Koryŏ, Ŭijong's reign, and its influence]. *Seikyū gakusō* 2 (November 1930):91–106.

INDEX

About the Author

EDWARD J. SHULTZ, who completed his Ph.D. in history at the University of Hawai'i, is director of the Center for Korean Studies at the University of Hawai'i at Mānoa and professor of history at the University of Hawai'i–West O'ahu. He translated, with Edward Wagner, Ki-baik Lee's *New History of Korea*. His major area of research is Koryŏ history.